COGNITIVE BEHAVIOR THERAPY

Research and Application

COGNITIVE BEHAVIOR THERAPY

Research and Application

Edited by
John P. Foreyt
Baylor College of Medicine
Houston, Texas

and
Diana P. Rathjen
Rice University
Houston, Texas

PLENUM PRESS • NEW YORK AND LONDON

Library of Congress Cataloging in Publication Data

Main entry under title:

Cognitive behavior therapy.

Includes bibliographies and index.
1. Cognitive therapy. I. Foreyt, John Paul. II. Rathjen, Diana P.
RC489.C63C63   616.8'914   78-15948
ISBN 0-306-31145-3

© 1978 Plenum Press, New York
A Division of Plenum Publishing Corporation
227 West 17th Street, New York, N.Y. 10011

Printed in the United States of America

Contributors

Aaron T. Beck, M.D., Department of Psychiatry, University of Pennsylvania, Philadelphia, Pennsylvania

John G. Bruhn, Ph.D., Community Affairs and Special Programs, University of Texas, Medical Branch, Galveston, Texas

David D. Burns, M.D., Department of Psychiatry, University of Pennsylvania, Philadelphia, Pennsylvania

Roy Cameron, Ph.D., Department of Psychology, University of Saskatchewan, Saskatoon, Saskatchewan, Canada

Patrick H. Doyle, Ph.D., Department of Psychology, University of Houston, Clear Lake City, Texas

John P. Foreyt, Ph.D., Departments of Medicine and Psychiatry, Baylor College of Medicine, Houston, Texas

W. Doyle Gentry, Ph.D., Department of Psychiatry, Duke University Medical Center, Durham, North Carolina

Alice Hiniker, Ph.D., Texas Research Institute of Mental Sciences, Houston, Texas

Raymond W. Novaco, Ph.D., Program of Social Ecology, University of California, Irvine, California

v

Diana P. Rathjen, Ph.D., Department of Psychology, Rice University, Houston, Texas

Eric D. Rathjen, Ph.D., Mental Health—Mental Retardation Authority, Harris County, Houston, Texas

Jeffrey C. Steger, Ph.D., Department of Rehabilitation Medicine, University of Washington School of Medicine, Seattle, Washington

Dennis C. Turk, Ph.D., Department of Psychology, Yale University, New Haven, Connecticut

G. Terence Wilson, Ph.D., Graduate School of Applied and Professional Psychology, Rutgers University, New Brunswick, New Jersey

Foreword

The recent development of cognitive theories and therapies within the ranks of behavior therapy has to be classified as one of the more intriguing developments in contemporary clinical psychology. After all, "behaviorists" have long been stereotyped as cold, hard-headed environmentalists who have been anything but subtle in their attacks on mentalism. To those who have accepted such a stereotype, a "cognitive behavior therapist" might sound like a self-contradictory creature, one steeped in two separate and incompatible psychological traditions. How can one be both "cognitive" and "behavioral"? This is only one of the issues addressed in the present volume, which represents a valuable contribution toward both theoretical and empirical refinements in the area. Here one can read how the behavioristic emphases on assessment and experimentation can be fruitfully integrated with therapeutic procedures designed to alter patterns of human distress. Many of those procedures involve specific focus on a client's thoughts and fantasies.

This book represents a strong and timely overview of an exciting new area, and its contributors include some of the most energetic researchers in the field. A theme of cautious optimism is blended with a commitment to empirical scrutiny, and there is an admirable recognition of the important difference between inferred therapeutic *process* and operationally specified therapeutic *procedure*. It is therefore a volume that should appeal to both researcher and practitioner, and it is a valuable resource for exploring some of the newer applications of cognitive behavioral techniques.

There are those within behavioral and nonbehavioral camps who will be dismayed by the appearance of a volume such as the present one. They are, however (I think), in the minority relative to the number of professionals who will be intrigued by these strange bedfellows and eager to explore their theoretical and pragmatic viability. A recent survey of American clinical psychologists suggests that cognitive behavioral approaches are now more popular than client-centered therapy, and that the recent increase in ideological eclecticism may partially reflect the increasing permeability between former polarities. The behavior therapist is now relying on assessment and treatment strategies that acknowledge the importance of cognitive processes in human adaptation. Likewise, the nonbehavioral counselor seems to be more frequently borrowing from traditionally behavioral methods. In integrating their relative skills and special interests, it is my hope that we may soon be able to abandon the unfortunate polarities and isolationism that have dominated clinical psychology and psychiatry.

The present volume is, I think, a valuable step toward demonstrating the compatability and rich therapeutic promise of combining intrapersonal, environmental, and scientific concerns. It does not promise miracles and is, in fact, commendable in its critical self-scrutiny. With modeling such as that offered in this book, we may hope to see continuing refinements of our understanding as well as revisions of our treatment strategies. *Cognitive Behavior Therapy: Research and Application* represents a welcome addition to the literature.

MICHAEL J. MAHONEY

Pennsylvania State University

Preface

Commenting on the first 50 years of behaviorism, Skinner (1964), in the early 1960s, noted:

> No entity or process which has any useful explanatory force is to be rejected on the ground that it is subjective or mental. The data which have made it important must, however, be studied and formulated in effective ways. The assignment is well within the scope of an experimental analysis of behavior, which thus offers a promising alternative to a commitment to pure description on the one hand and an appeal to mentalistic theories on the other. (Skinner, B. F. Behaviorism at fifty. In T.W. Wann (Ed.), *Behaviorism and phenomenology: Contrasting bases for modern psychology.* Chicago: The University of Chicago Press, 1964, p. 96.)

In the intervening years, psychologists applying behavioral principles to clinical problems have attempted to provide the data Skinner suggests. In particular, the work of Albert Ellis, Aaron Beck, and Albert Bandura has steadily kept alive a cognitive framework introduced by the early social psychologists such as Julian Rotter and George Kelly.

The renewed interest in a merger or at least dialogue between the proponents of a cognitive and a behavioral perspective in understanding human behavior is an exciting recent development in the field of psychology. In addition to the intellectual stimulation provided by such a rapprochement, practical implications for clinical treatment may also be forthcoming.

This book is an effort to explore current answers to the question, What is the role of cognitive factors in clinical treatment? Each of the authors presents a unique perspective revealing no overall consensus but rather a diverse collection of thought-provoking possibilities.

The idea for this volume originated at the Sixth Annual Symposium of the Houston Behavior Therapy Association (HBTA), Houston, Texas. We are deeply indebted to each of the authors for their outstanding contributions. We are also grateful to the co-sponsors of the symposium: University of Houston, Rice University, Baylor College of Medicine, and Spring Branch Academy, Houston, Texas. Each year HBTA presents a topic of significance to behavior therapists and others concerned with behavioral issues. Our symposium is successful only because of the hard work of many people, including HBTA members Drs. Pat Doyle, Richard Jones, Ed Keuer, Paul Mader, Sander Martin, Ben Williams, and in particular, Martha Frede and Larry Brandt who co-chaired the conference. Thanks also to Mr. Bill Kortas for his hard work and Ms. Susi LeBaron for her never-ending task of typing the manuscript. To all of them, our deepest gratitude.

JOHN P. FOREYT
DIANA P. RATHJEN

Houston , Texas

Contents

Introduction

The present book provides several perspectives to the question, What is the role of cognitive factors in clinical treatment? In the first chapter, Wilson traces the growth of interest in cognitive variables within the behavior therapy field and identifies the major conceptual models: *applied behavior analysis*, with its emphasis on overt behavior; the *neobehavioristic mediational S-R model*, applying classical conditioning and counterconditioning principles to the treatment of abnormal behavior; *social learning theory*, in which cognitive mediational processes, in addition to classical and operant conditioning, play an important role in the development of learning; and *cognitive behavior therapy*, or what Wilson terms the "cognitive connection." Included in the areas of cognitive behavior therapy, according to the author, are the rational psychotherapies, coping-skills therapies, and problem-solving therapies.

Wilson perceptively cautions cognitive therapists against an exclusive focus on thinking to the point that behavior is overlooked and the patients are left immersed in introspection, much as Tolman's rats were said to have been at the choice point in the maze.

Another cogent criticism presented by Wilson is the distinction between theoretical process and treatment procedure. Although cognitive mechanisms are increasingly used to explain the acquisition of abnormal behavior, the question is whether cognitive treatment methods are more effective than their behavioral counterparts in facilitating therapeutic change. His view of the current evidence

1

suggests that the behaviorally based treatments are more effective in producing change in psychological functioning than verbal, imaginal, or even vicarious procedures.

Wilson argues that cognitive research and application is best viewed as an extension of Bandura's social-learning theory, which seems to best integrate the three regulatory systems of antecedent, consequent, and mediational influences into a comprehensive testable framework. He states that although cognitive behavior techniques show some promise they do not yet give indication for a shift in paradigm. He concludes that the term "behavior therapy" is probably the least troublesome of all because, in the final analysis, any effects of therapy must be evaluated by direct behavioral measures. He writes, "Parsimony and present usage suggest that there might be little to be gained by the use of a new label."

Rathjen, Rathjen, and Hiniker, in our second chapter, use a structural learning model as the basis for an overview of cognitive factors in social-skills training. In particular, they examine the implications of this model for defining behavioral tasks and treatment objectives, cognitive competencies underlying successful performance, cognitive characteristics of the subject population, methods of assessment, and treatment techniques. They suggest that the role of cognitive variables is most important in specifying the underlying rules that govern effective social performance and explain that these rules can be taught through a variety of techniques, both behavioral and cognitive.

In the third chapter, Steger presents a comprehensive overview of both the behavioral and cognitive approaches to sexual disorders and sexual deviations. He describes, in detail, guided imagining, cognitive rehearsal, covert reinforcement, thought-stopping, covert assertion, covert sensitization, and implosive therapy. His summary of the outcome research suggests that the *in vivo* behavioral techniques are already so successful for certain problems (e.g., premature ejaculation and primary orgasmic dysfunction) that the addition of cognitive techniques would only serve to perhaps speed up the process.

With respect to other dysfunctions, however, he suggests that the cognitive approaches may be particularly useful (e.g., when the sexual dysfunction is moderated by anxiety, fear, self-doubt, or relationship concerns). He feels that the cognitive techniques can be useful in the treatment of erectile failure, ejaculatory incompetence, and secondary orgasmic dysfunction.

Burns and Beck, in our fourth chapter, provide an overview of a cognitive-behavior modification treatment program for mood disorders that has received some impressive empirical validation. In an interesting contrast to the ideas presented in Wilson's chapter, they suggest that the patient's thoughts themselves appear to be the focus of cognitive treatment. Phenomenology, assessment, treatment, and evaluation are covered in a presentation liberally sprinkled with case illustrations. They present a step-by-step outline, beginning with the use of the Beck Depression Inventory to confirm the presence of the disorder, through each of the cognitive techniques that may be helpful to reduce its intensity.

In the fifth chapter, Novaco reviews the relevant literature on stress and aggression to develop a functional analysis of the role of anger in human behavior. Using a stress-inoculation model, he develops a comprehensive cognitive treatment of anger control that instructs the client in all phases of anger, from initial provocation to self-reinforcement for a conflict well handled, and presents effectiveness data from naturalistic studies (law-enforcement officers). His detailed therapist manual (see Appendix) provides explicit instructions for the implementation of the methods with individual clients.

Gentry, in the following and sixth chapter, reviews the small but growing number of studies that have utilized cognitive behavior therapy in the treatment of somatic disorders, including asthma, ulcers, tension, migraine headaches, and epilepsy. He discusses studies employing systematic desensitization, thought-stopping, positive imagery, and classical conditioning with a wide variety of somatic disorders. A particularly interesting application of cognitive techniques in the medical field, which Gentry points out, would be their use in enhancing compliance with a medical regimen, a topic expanded upon by Cameron in the ninth chapter.

Gentry points out that most of the work in this area has followed an operant approach, which stresses the relationship between behavior (B) and the environmental events that precede (antecedents-A) and follow (consequences-C) it. Gentry suggests an alternative model (CAB), in which the relationship between cognitions (C), affect (A), and behavior (B) are applied to physical disorders.

In our seventh chapter, Doyle and Bruhn present a novel specific example and application of a type of covert sensitization, countersensitization, as a way of reducing excessive performance standards. They suggest that the use of physical disorders as the aversive component in the countersensitization paradigm may be especially helpful with psychosomatic problems.

Turk, in the next and eighth chapter, has provided an overview that underscores the complex nature of the phenomenon of pain. He goes on to review a number of cognitive behavioral approaches to the treatment of anxiety-based dysfunctions and cognitive coping strategies designed to enhance pain tolerance. Both laboratory-analogue and clinical pain examples are included in his discussion of specific and multidimensional strategies for pain management. The technique of stress inoculation has received particular attention as a method that has been empirically demonstrated to effectively increase pain tolerance.

The important issues of therapeutic compliance and resistance from a cognitive viewpoint are discussed by Cameron in the ninth chapter. He poses two key questions: What cognitions regarding the therapeutic process would facilitate therapeutic change? and What can we do to ensure that our clients' cognitions about the therapeutic process are positive rather than negative? In addressing these questions, Cameron considers every stage of the treatment process and offers many helpful suggestions from his clinical experience with two usually resistant populations, psychosomatic and pain patients. This chapter will be particularly helpful for the therapist who will implement some of the strategies outlined in the preceding chapters.

Taken as a whole, the chapters in this book demonstrate clearly the growing interest in the application of cognitive behavior therapy techniques to a wide variety of disorders. All the authors emphasize that changes in patient cognitions are of crucial importance in determining therapeutic outcome; however, the most effective methods to change cognitions seem to be a combination of the more established behavioral and the more recently developed cognitive intervention strategies. Future research is needed to provide an empirical basis for determining the maximally effective combination of techniques.

1

Cognitive Behavior Therapy

PARADIGM SHIFT OR PASSING PHASE?

G. TERENCE WILSON

Psychology, it has recently been said, has "gone cognitive" (Dember, 1974). Moreover, judging from an examination of the theoretical and clinical literature, behavior therapy has followed suit (Bandura, 1974; Mahoney, 1974). The attention devoted to cognitive variables in behavior therapy has grown steadily in the 1970s (Franks and Wilson, 1973–77), and several recent developments have tended to make formal this trend toward a cognitive mediational model of the modification of behavior. These have included pertinent publications (e.g., Beck, 1976; Meichenbaum, 1976), the appearance of the journal *Cognitive Therapy and Research*, and an inaugural convention on "cognitive behavior therapy" in New York City in 1976.

Any attempt to provide an overview of cognitive behavior therapy, of its conceptual bases, empirical foundations, and clinical applications, is predicated upon an understanding of the nature of behavior therapy. Immediately a problem is encountered. Simply stated, there is no clearly agreed upon or commonly accepted definition of behavior therapy. Behavior therapy means different things to different people, a reality captured in Franks's (1969) concinnous

G. TERENCE WILSON • Graduate School of Applied and Professional Psychology, Rutgers University, New Brunswick, New Jersey 08903.

comment that "there is both diversity and complexity of meaning to the words 'behavior therapist.' " Behavior therapy is not, nor was it ever, a monolithic structure (Wilson, 1978).

Behavior Therapy in the 1970s: Current Conceptual Models

Behavior therapy in the 1970s is marked by a catholicity of views, diverse procedures, and free-wheeling debate. A careful look at the contemporary scene, however, reveals several distinctive emphases or developments with reasonably consistent conceptual bases.

Applied Behavior Analysis. Applied behavior analysis can be defined as the applications of the experimental analysis of behavior problems of social importance (Baer, Wolf, and Risley, 1968). Exemplified by the *Journal of Applied Behavior Analysis* (JABA), it is philosophically consistent with Skinner's (1953, 1971) doctrine of radical behaviorism and is based on the principles and procedures of operant conditioning. Overt behavior alone is accepted as the proper subject of scientific investigation. Although Skinner (1953) has stated that the study of subjective events should not be dismissed *a priori* simply because they are private events, operant conditioners and applied behavior analysts have consistently eschewed the analysis and modification of private events. Cognitive processes are rejected as improper targets of experimental study or relegated to the status of epiphenomenal events that are merely the by-products of physical actions in the body and/or the external environment; they exert no causal effect on a person's behavior or subjective state. Aside from genetic influences, the Skinnerian view that infuses applied behavior analysis is that human behavior is controlled exclusively by environmental forces that are ultimately beyond personal control. As Skinner (1971) bluntly put it, "a person does not act upon the world, the world acts upon him" (p. 211).

Three other characteristic features of applied behavior analysis might be mentioned. The first is that with its insistence on the study of the individual organism it has contributed a distinctive methodology to the study of behavior. Repeated measurement of a single subject under highly controlled conditions and the rejection of statistical comparisons between groups of subjects have been cardinal tenets of applied behavior analysis. The second characteristic is the reliance on the principles of reinforcement and punishment as the primary learning influences on behavior. The third characteristic of applied behavior analysis is that it has been extended to what, with some oversimplification, may be termed individuals with limited or impaired cognitive capacities. Young children, retarded persons, and institutionalized psychotic patients have been the primary focus of operant behavior modification. Moreover, although there are exceptions (Kazdin, 1978), the majority of the problems tackled in applied behavior analysis have involved less complex behaviors in situations in which considerable external control can be brought to bear on the behavior (e.g., in the home, classroom, or institution).

There are several modification programs that depart from some of the foregoing characteristics yet are clearly related to applied behavior analysis. A prominent example is Azrin's (1977) approach. While espousing the operant model and repudiating cognitive concepts, Azrin's clinical research has been distinguished by the use of group outcome designs, by the recognition of the insufficiency of reinforcement principles in devising effective treatment methods, by the pragmatic and eclectic use of what he has called "emergent principles" of behavior therapy, and by the diversity and severity of problems that have been successfully modified.

The Neobehavioristic Mediational S-R Model. The approach has been defined as the application of the principles of conditioning, especially classical conditioning and counterconditioning, to the treatment of abnormal behavior. It derives from the pioneering contributions of Eysenck (1960, 1964), Rachman (1963), and Wolpe (1958), who sought to base theory and practice in behavior therapy on the learning theories of such figures as Pavlov, Guthrie, Hull, Mowrer, and Miller. This has always been a liberalized S-R approach in which intervening variables and hypothetical constructs play a prominent part. The two-factor theory of avoidance learning (Mowrer, 1947, 1960) is a classic example. According to this mediational theory, escape–avoidance behavior was assumed to be acquired and maintained on the basis of the reduction of a classically conditioned fear response to the aversive stimulus.

The construct of fear or anxiety has been central to this conceptualization of behavior therapy because the concern with neurotic disorders has always been its major therapeutic thrust. For example, the treatment techniques of systematic desensitization and flooding that are most closely associated with this model are both directed toward the extinction of the underlying anxiety that is assumed to maintain phobic disorders. Imaginal and to a lesser extent verbal mediational processes are inherent in the techniques that derive from this view. In systematic desensitization, for instance, clients are instructed to imagine the phobic stimulus and the treatment typically proceeds according to their self-report of emotional experience. Imaginal representation of the stimulus object or event is frequently used in aversive counterconditioning, while in a technique such as covert sensitization the client is instructed to visualize the stimulus, the response, and its consequences. Other covert conditioning procedures include covert reinforcement, covert extinction, and coverant control. The latter, the creation of Homme (1965), refers to the alteration of maladaptive thoughts by reinforcing alternative cognitions. The rationale behind all these methods is that covert processes follow the same laws of learning that govern overt behaviors.

The neobehavioristic nature of this approach dictates that unobservable constructs such as the imaginal representation of an anxiety-eliciting event are anchored to antecedent and consequent operational referents. Thus, psychophysiological studies have shown that symbolic representation of a feared stimulus produces autonomic arousal similar to that evoked by the stimulus itself. Moreover, these arousal responses have been shown to covary systematically with the introduction and repeated representation of hierarchy items during systematic desensitization in a manner consistent with conditioning concepts (Lang, Melamed, and Hart, 1970).

It is important to note that although frequent use is made of symbolic processes such as imagery in behavioral techniques of the genre, covert activities in the typical Wolpean view of behavior therapy have always been strictly defined in terms of S and R (or more accurately, a chain of s and r reactions).[1] Cognitive formula-

---

[1] Similarly, Staats (1970) has retained the S-R framework for describing his A-R-D theory of human motivation that includes an analysis of processes that are very much part of current cognitive behavior therapy.

tions of these mediational constructs have found little favor in this approach. Wolpe (1958), for example, relegated the significance of cognitive interventions in therapy to the provision of background materials and the correction of clients' misconceptions. This emphasis on conditioning as opposed to cognitions as the conceptual basis of behavior therapy is not surprising in view of the early reliance on principles from the animal conditioning laboratory.

Social-Learning Theory. The social-learning conceptualization of behavior therapy is a comprehensive approach to human functioning in which both deviant and prosocial behaviors are assumed to be developed and maintained on the basis of three distinct regulatory systems (Bandura, 1969,[2] 1974, 1977a). Some response patterns are primarily under the control of external stimulus events and are affected largely by classical conditioning processes. The influence of external reinforcement, the main focus of operant conditioning, constitutes a second form of control. The third and most important system of regulatory influence operates through cognitive mediational processes.

In terms of a social-learning analysis, the influence of environmental events on the acquisition and regulation of behavior is largely determined by cognitive processes. The latter determine what environmental influences are attended to, how they are perceived, and whether they might affect future action. Modeling, one of the best known and most widely used social learning methods, provides an excellent example of cognitive learning. In operant conditioning, in order for learning to occur, a response must be performed and followed by reinforcement. However, complex human behavior would never be acquired unless learning occurred through observation alone without the need for direct reinforcement of specific behaviors.

A second distinguishing feature of social-learning theory is that psychological functioning involves a reciprocal interaction between a person's behavior and the environment.

> Environments have causes, as do behaviors. It is true that behavior is regulated by its contingencies, but the contingencies are partly of a person's own making. By their actions, people play an active role in producing the reinforcing contingencies that impinge upon them . . . be-

[2] Behavior therapy can be operationally defined as everything that falls between the covers of Bandura's (1969) book.

havior partly creates the environment, and the environment influences the behavior in a reciprocal fashion. To the oft-repeated dictum "change contingencies and you change behavior," should be added the reciprocal side "change behavior and you change the contingencies." (Bandura, 1977a, p. 203)

In this conceptual scheme a person is neither driven by internal forces nor a passive reactor to external pressure. Rather, a person is both the agent as well as the object of environmental influence.

A third characteristic of social-learning theory is that by recognizing that cognitions have causal influence and emphasizing the reciprocal determinism of behavior, it highlights the human capacity of self-directed behavior change. Operant-conditioning accounts of behavioral self-control ultimately reduce to analyses of situational, environmental control, and fundamentally deny the notion of *self-control* (Rachlin, 1974). In addition to the acquisition and maintenance of behavior, activation and persistence of behavior is based mainly on cognitive mechanisms. The importance assigned to cognitive processes that explain how learning experiences have lasting effects and serve to activate future actions enables social-learning theory to explain the intuitively obvious and experimentally demonstrable fact that humans initiate behavior that at least in part shapes their own destinies (Thoresen and Mahoney, 1974). The analysis of self-control sharply focuses the different conceptual bases of the strict operant-conditioning approach and social-learning theory. This is illustrated in several lively interchanges between Bandura (1976) and Catania (1975); Goldiamond (1976) and Mahoney (1976); and Mahoney (1977a) and Rachlin (1977).

A fourth feature of the social-learning view of behavior therapy that is pertinent to the present paper is the theoretically consistent integration of the different sources of influence governing behavior that it provides. This is illustrated in Bandura's (1977b) conceptual analysis of the modification of phobic behavior. The key assumption in this analysis is that psychological treatment methods produce changes in the cognitive concept of self-efficacy. Expectations of self-efficacy are said to determine the activation and maintenance behavioral strategies for coping with anxiety-eliciting situations. Self-efficacy expectations are modified by different sources of psychological influence, including performance-based feedback (e.g., participant modeling), vicarious information (e.g., symbolic modeling), physiological changes (e.g., systematic desensitization), and verbal persuasion (e.g., traditional psychotherapy). Of major importance are the findings that directly produced behavior change is the most effective means of altering the cognitive mechanisms (self-efficacy expectations) that mediate subsequent performance.

Cognitive (Behavior) Therapy. The most recent discernible development within behavior therapy is the emergence of what can be loosely described as the "cognitive connection." The referents include Ellis's (1962) rational-emotive therapy, the review by Mahoney and Arnkoff (1978) of the cognitive therapies, Meichenbaum's (1977) text on *Cognitive Behavior Modification,* and Beck's (1976) book on *Cognitive Therapy.*[3] It is difficult to categorize the admixture of diverse and often inchoate principles and procedures encompassed by the term "cognitive behavior therapy" (the term "behavior" is often omitted). Acknowledging the many differences among proponents of this approach, Mahoney and Arnkoff (1978) have nonetheless distilled the following commonalities: (a) "that humans develop adaptive and maladaptive behavior and affective patterns via cognitive processes (e.g., selective attention, symbolic coding, etc.); (b) these cognitive *processes* are functionally activated by *procedures* which are generally isomorphic with those of the human learning laboratory; and (c) the resultant task of the therapist is that of a diagnostician–educator who assesses maladaptive cognitive processes and subsequently arranges learning experiences which will alter cognitions and, in turn, the behavior-affect patterns with which they correlate."

Mahoney and Arnkoff (1978) identify three major forms of cognitive therapies: rational psychotherapies, coping-skills therapies, and problem-solving therapies. The oldest and most prominent of

[3] Lazarus's (1976) multimodal therapy clearly fits this development. However, his views might be considered a fifth distinctive position within a broad understanding of behavior therapy. Abandoning his pioneering neobehaviorist/Wolpean position, Lazarus (1971) was one of the first to emphasize the important role of cognitive factors and apply primarily cognitive techniques. His current position combines this emphasis (cognition and imagery are two of the modalities of the BASIC ID) with a pragmatic eclecticism with respect to treatment methods. However, Franks and Wilson (1974) have criticized multimodal therapy for failing to set forth explicit criteria for the choice of different techniques and its apparent reliance on intuition and subjective judgment rather than on well-defined conceptual bases.

the rational psychotherapies unquestionably is Albert Ellis's (1962) rational emotive therapy (RET). The details of this approach are well-known and require little elaboration here. Suffice it to say that, according to Ellis, the road to hell is paved not with good intentions but with irrational assumptions. Irrational interpretations of objective reality are said to be the fundamental cause of emotional disorders. Ellis (1970) has identified 12 such irrational ideas or self-statements. An example of this dirty dozen is the belief that "it is a dire necessity for an adult to be loved by everyone for everything he does." Other examples are that "it is easier to avoid than to face life difficulties," and that "one has no control over one's emotions and that one cannot help feeling certain things." The task of therapy is to assist the client to recognize self-defeating irrational ideas and replace them with more constructive rational thoughts. Careful analysis of the therapeutic method indicates that it consists of the following steps:

a. Verbal persuasion aimed at convincing the client of the philosophical tenets of RET.
b. Identification of irrational thoughts through client self-monitoring and the therapist's feedback.
c. The therapist directly challenges irrational ideas and models rational reinterpretations of disturbing events.
d. Repeated cognitive rehearsal aimed at substituting rational self-statements for previously irrational interpretation.
e. Behavioral tasks ("shame exercises") designed to develop rational reactions where there were once irrational, distress-producing assumptions.

A second variation of rational psychotherapy is self-instructional training (SIT) (Meichenbaum, 1973). The rationale for this approach derives from two main sources: (1) Ellis's (1962) RET and its emphasis on irrational self-talk as the cause of emotional disturbance; and (2) the developmental sequence according to which children develop internal speech and verbal-symbolic control over their behavior (Luria, 1961). In terms of this latter analysis children's behavior is first regulated by the instructions of other people; subsequently they acquire control over their own behavior through the

use of overt self-instructions that they ultimately internalize as covert self-instructions.

SIT involves the following steps:

a. Training the client to identify and become aware of maladaptive thoughts (self-statements).
b. The therapist models appropriate behavior while verbaliz-
   ing effective action strategies; these verbalizations include
   an appraisal of task requirements, self-instructions that
   guide graded performance, self-statements that stress personal adequacy and counteract worry over failure, and covert self-reinforcement for successful performance.
c. The client then performs the target behavior first while ver-
   balizing aloud the appropriate self-instructions and then by
   covertly rehearsing them. Therapist feedback during this
   phase assists in ensuring that constructive problem-solving
   self-talk replaces previously anxiety-inducing cognitions associated with that behavior.

The results of several studies have shown that self-instructional
training can produce significant changes in cognitive and behavioral functioning in clients with test and speech anxieties, in impulsive children, and instutionalized schizophrenics (Meichenbaum,
1974; Meichenbaum and Cameron, 1973). Moreover, incorporating
self-instructions in techniques such as systematic desensitization
and modeling appear to increase their efficacy.

The third variation of rational psychotherapy is Beck's (1976)
cognitive therapy. As in RET and SIT, the ultimate goal of cognitive
therapy is the development of rational, adaptive thought patterns.
Cognitive therapy progresses through the following phases:

a. Clients become aware of their thoughts.
b. They learn to identify inaccurate or distorted thoughts.
c. These inaccurate thoughts are replaced by accurate, more
   objective cognitions.
d. Therapist feedback and reinforcement is a necessary part of
   this process.

The specific procedures used to accomplish these therapeutic objectives are both behavioral and cognitive in nature. The former in-

clude the prescription of an explicit activity schedule, graded tasks aimed at providing success experiences, and various homework assignments. The latter include techniques such as "distancing" and "decentering." Distancing is the process of regarding thought objectively. Decentering is the ability to separate oneself from the occurrence and impact of external events.

The second major form of cognitive therapy identified by Mahoney and Arnkoff (1978) is what they term "coping-skills therapy." Coping-skills therapies are not categorized without difficulty since they tend to represent a different use of existing methods rather than distinctive technical innovations. They also overlap considerably with other approaches such as SIT. Examples include covert modeling[4] (Kazdin, 1974), modified systematic desensitization (Goldfried, 1971), anxiety-management training (Suinn and Richardson, 1971) and stress inoculation (Meichenbaum, 1973). The critical dimension that characterizes the diverse methods subsumed under this rubric is that of the individual *coping* with distress-producing events.

According to Mahoney and Arnkoff (1978), problem-solving therapies represent the third major form of cognitive therapy. As in the case of the coping-skills therapies, this category subsumes a heterogeneous collection of principles and procedures that overlap considerably with other cognitive and noncognitive approaches. The relevant literature is sparse (e.g., D'Zurilla and Goldfried, 1971; Mahoney, 1977b; Spivack, Platt, and Shure, 1976), with few formal clinical applications and little empirical confirmation.

The Cognitive Therapies: A Paradigm Shift?

The view taken here is that cognitive (behavior) therapy as described above is not a recent conceptual development of paradigmatic significance. The major shift in behavior therapy from a simplistic S-R psychology dominated by animal conditioning models to

---

[4] Cautela (1971) first conceptualized this as a conditioning method. As Kazdin (1974) has noted, however, covert modeling involves the same mechanisms that underlie symbolic modeling or vicarious learning. Bandura (1977a) has shown that it is more accurate to construe this form of learning in informational or cognitive rather than in conditioning terms.

a more cognitive framework was formally ushered in by Bandura's (1969) influential book. During the late 1960s several developments had emphasized the limiting nature of a strict conditioning approach and resulted in increased attention given to cognitive mechanisms. Examples of the more important sources of this expansion of behavioral assessment and modification along cognitive–social learning lines include the contributions of Davison (1969), Kanfer and Phillips (1970), Lang (1969), Lazarus (1971), Mischel (1968), and Peterson (1968).[5] Bandura (1969) not only emphasized the primary importance of cognitive mediational processes in the regulation of behavior as discussed earlier in this paper, but also presented theoretical interpretations of the mechanisms of both classical conditioning and reinforcement contingencies in more cognitive terms. In this interpretation classical conditioning is no longer viewed as an automatic reflexive process; rather, conditioned responses are seen as self-activated on the basis of learned expectations. Similarly, reinforcement is not an automatic strengthener of behavior but a source of information and incentive that regulates behavior.

In short, it is argued that the recent cognitive research and therapy conducted by Beck (1976), Mahoney (1977b), and Meichenbaum (1977) are best seen as important extensions and clinically relevant applications consistent with an existing conceptual model and empirical base. In this connection it is instructive to re-examine the three points Mahoney and Arnkoff (1978) hold to be the defining features of the contemporary cognitive therapies. It is clear that they are also fundamental characteristics of social-learning theory.

Important consequences attach to viewing the cognitive therapies that were described briefly above within the social-learning framework. The conceptual models of behavior therapy in the 1970s can each be said to place primary emphasis on one dimension of psychological functioning to the relative neglect of the others. Thus, applied behavior analysis is preoccupied with overt behavior; Wolpe's counterconditioning approach emphasizes autonomic or emotional habits; and the cognitive therapists, of course, focus on the causal role of maladaptive thought patterns. One of the advan-

---

[5] Views of abnormal behavior that emphasized cognitive factors and the role of self-verbalizations preceded the 1960s. Kelly's (1955) personal construct system and Rotter's (1954) expectancy learning theory are two prominent examples.

tages of social-learning theory is that it integrates these three regulatory systems of antecedant, consequent, and mediational influence in a comprehensive yet testable framework.

A basic tenet of social-learning theory is that while cognitive mechanisms are increasingly used to explain the acquisition and regulation of abnormal behavior, the most powerful methods of behavior change are increasingly shown to be those that are performance-based. It would be difficult to exaggerate the importance of this distinction between treatment *procedure* and theoretical *process;* its relevance to the cognitive therapies is particularly great. Beck (1976) and Mahoney and Arnkoff (1978) state that behavioral procedures are employed to alter cognitive processes in what they call cognitive therapy. This crucial distinction is far from evident in Ellis's (1962) RET, however. In his formulation most abnormal behavior is viewed as nothing but a question of irrational, disordered cognitions. Moreover, the treatment methods emphasized most heavily in RET are cognitive: verbal persuasion, rational argument, and logical reasoning.[6] The question is whether behavioral treatment methods are more effective than their cognitive counterparts in facilitating therapeutic change.

The evidence seems clear. Behaviorally based treatment methods are significantly more effective in producing change on multiple subjective and objective measures of psychological functioning than methods that rely on verbal, imaginal, or even vicarious procedures (Bandura, 1977b). Participant modeling is a performance-based method that has been shown to be significantly more effective in eliminating phobic behavior than either symbolic modeling or imaginal systematic desensitization (Bandura, Blanchard, and Ritter, 1969; Blanchard, 1970). Similarly, Rachman and Hodgson (in press) have pointed to the superiority of performance-based treatment over imaginal and vicarious methods in the modification of obsessive-compulsive disorders. Other studies have shown the superiority of performance-based treatment over imaginal desensitization (Crowe, Marks, Agras, and Leitenberg, 1972; Sherman,

---

[6] As noted, the practice of RET involves behavioral tasks although they are not usually accorded much prominence. The success of RET is as plausibly attributed to these behavioral tasks as to philosophical shifts purportedly produced by logical examination of personal belief systems.

1972) and imaginal flooding (Emmelkamp and Wessels, 1975; Sterns and Marks, 1973). Finally, Kockott, Dittmar, and Nesselt (1975) and Mathews, Bancroft, Whitehead, Hackmann, Julier, Bancroft, Gath, and Shaw (1976) reported that sexual dysfunction was most effectively treated by a Masters and Johnson-type program that relied on directed practice *in vivo* as opposed to imaginal systematic desensitization.

The preceding studies demonstrated the greater efficacy of a performance-based treatment method over *imaginal* techniques such as systematic desensitization, flooding, symbolic, and covert modeling. There is no *a priori* reason to expect that cognitive methods such as RET that rely on covert verbal operations should be any more effective than those that involve mental imagery. This is borne out by the available evidence. SIT was no more effective than imaginal systematic desensitization in the treatment of either public-speaking anxiety (Meichenbaum, Gilmore, and Fedoravicius, 1971) or under-assertive clients (Thorpe, 1975). On the basis of a *post hoc* analysis of their data Meichenbaum *et al.* (1971) indicated that systematic desensitization was significantly more effective with those clients who showed specific, well-focused fear of speaking in public, whereas SIT was more effective in those cases where anxiety was more generalized and abstract. Meichenbaum (1973) noted the distinction that has been made between information-coding systems based on imagery and verbal processes respectively (Bower, 1970; Nebes, 1974), and suggested that techniques mediated by these different operations should have differential treatment effects across different target behaviors. As support of this proposition, Meichenbaum (1973) reported that a stress-inoculation technique produced greater generalization of improvement than imaginal systematic desensitization. However, since self-instructional training is only one component of the stress-inoculation procedure it is difficult to interpret the results. Beyond this the available evidence provides little support for such a notion (Goren, 1975).

In other studies neither D'Zurilla, Wilson, and Nelson (1973) nor Wein, Nelson, and Odom (1975) found cognitive restructuring, a technique designed to teach clients to relabel anxiety-eliciting thoughts in a more rational manner, to be superior to systematic desensitization in the treatment of fears of small animals. Lastly, in a well-controlled comparative outcome study of interpersonal anxiety, DiLoreto (1971) found that systematic desensitization resulted in significantly greater improvement on clients' self-rating and objective behavioral ratings of interpersonal anxiety than RET at posttreatment and at a three-month follow-up. RET was superior in terms of subjects' estimates of their interpersonal activity in the natural environment. Systematic desensitization was equally effective with both introverted and extroverted subjects, whereas RET differed from the attention-placebo control treatment only with respect to introverts. In the absence of additional evidence it is impossible to know whether this sort of person variable is a useful predictor of the outcome of cognitive therapies like RET.

There is little doubt that coping is a critical factor in effective therapy. However, the cognitive coping-skills therapies identified by Mahoney and Arnkoff (1978) may be weaker forms of coping-skill training. For example, participant modeling, an explicitly behavioral form of coping therapy, has been demonstrated to have greater efficacy than covert modeling in the reduction of phobic behavior (Thase and Moss, 1976). The concept of coping entails an active cognitive appraisal of events initiated by the person that transcends pristine S-R conditioning theory. However, the differences between conventional conditioning theory and a cognitive self-regulatory formulation of behavior change methods were elaborated by Bandura (1969). The implications of this distinction for clinical practice were illustrated in the following analysis of aversive counterconditioning:

> If the major purpose of aversion experiences is to provide clients with a means of exercising control over harmful behavior, then clients should play an active role in practicing self-control techniques in the presence of progressively stronger evocative stimuli, rather than serving merely as passive recipients of stimulus pairings. Thus, for example, in the treatment of alcoholism, after persons have been taught how to self-induce nauseous feelings, they should be exposed for increasingly longer periods to social and stress situations that involve high instigation to drinking behavior. (p. 552)

Problem-solving therapy is included by Mahoney and Arnkoff (1978) as one of the new cognitive therapies. The rationale offered is that in behavior therapy the therapist is said to assume primary responsibility for assessment and modification of the client's difficulties. The cognitive therapist is said to teach the client problem-solving skills for devising effective solutions for the specific presenting problem as well as more general difficulties that might be encountered. Although not always labeled as such, it is not difficult to view a great deal of conventional behavior therapy as directed toward this very purpose. A method such as behavior rehearsal, for example, is often used to develop specific responses. Implicitly or explicitly it is also used to equip the client with more general trans-situational skills that are used to cope with a variety of different problem situations. Furthermore, problem-solving is not a recent form of treatment. An excellent example of the comprehensive use of behavioral training in problem-solving is Fairweather's (1964) treatment program for institutionalized patients.

Another advantage of social-learning theory is that the concern with cognitive mediating processes is deliberately tied to overt action. This interdependency between cognitions and behavior underscores the fact that whereas cognitive mechanisms may underlie behavior change, they are not the treatment targets *per se*. Mahoney and Arnkoff (1978) are careful to emphasize this point, but it is not always obvious in the descriptions of the new cognitive therapies. It is frequently stated that alteration of faulty attitudes seems to be *the* goal of treatment. Unless the reciprocal determinism between specific cognitions and behaviors is explicitly built into treatment programs, we run the risk of leaving the patient immersed in introspective analyses of his or her thought patterns, just as Tolman's rats were said to have been buried in thought at the choice-point in the rodent's role of problem-solving, maze learning.

COGNITIVE (BEHAVIOR) THERAPY: A PASSING PHASE?

The relatively recent focus on cognitive mechanisms in therapeutic behavior change that has transcended narrower notions based upon simple classical and operant conditioning principles may not be a paradigm shift but neither is it likely to be a passing fad. On the contrary, it appears to be well-grounded in contemporary experimental psychology (Brewer, 1974). Contrary to the radical behavioristic view, cognitions exert causal influence on behavior (Mahoney, 1974). For instance, the effect of external events on behavior is largely mediated by cognitive processes. Bandura (1974) has marshaled evidence showing that the dictum that behavior is a function of its environmental consequences "fares better for antici- pated than for actual consequences" (p. 166). The overriding impor- tance of the cognitive representation of contingencies in the regula- tion of behavior is convincingly demonstrated by Moore, Mischel, and Zeiss (1976). Their findings show that the manner in which children cognitively represent rewards is a significantly more potent determinant of self-control behavior than the actual reward stimu- lus the child is physically exposed to. It is not the objective reality of *what* the child looks at but *how* the child perceives the reward that governs behavior.

Consider the following clinical illustration. Mrs. H. was a se- vere agoraphobic who showed some initial improvement as a result of treatment with participant modeling. However, a point was soon reached beyond which no further progress was made. Observation of her behavior during a behavioral assignment to approach a feared situation then revealed that Mrs. H. was sustaining her par- ticipation in activities she had previously avoided by telling herself that "it would soon be over," "a few more minutes and then I can retire to safety," and statements to that effect. In short, although she had shown some behavioral change she had not ceased repre- senting the situation as dangerous, as a place she could (and should) soon withdraw from. Although her repeated exposure to the fear-producing situation satisfied the operations that define the procedure of extinction, her subjective representation of these con- ditions seemed to negate the usual effects of the procedure. Com- plementing these graded behavioral tasks with SIT directed at mod- ifying her view of the situation was associated with marked improvement.

Two points can be made in connection with this clinical ex- ample. The first is that it is almost certain that the use of RET alone without the guided behavioral practice would have been largely ineffective. Beck (1976) himself has observed that what he calls the client's subjective "estimate of the probabilities of harm" shifts as a function of exposure to the feared situation. Under protective cir- cumstances removed from the threatening situation (e.g., the therapist's office), the client can agree that the probability of harm in approaching the feared situation is minimal. However, the closer the client comes to making actual contact with the feared situation, the greater the estimates of threat and the more pronounced the unrealistic anxiety. In the case of Mrs. H., it was necessary to elicit this irrational reaction by *in vivo* exposure so that the threat she perceived could be neutralized. Lang (1977) has proposed that basic to the emotional response of fear is a fear image consisting of propositional response structures. This prototype image is activated by various stimulus sources that match the propositional structures. It follows from this model that verbal instructions and pictorial representations may be as effective as *in vivo* stimuli in matching the prototype and evoking fear. However, the evidence thus far suggests that direct behavioral activation of the fear response is the most reliable means of induction.

The second point concerns a long-standing theoretical puzzle in behavior therapies. It has been pointed out that the maintenance of phobic reactions despite often frequent nonreinforced exposure to the feared situation poses a dilemma for learning theory (Eysenck, 1976; Seligman, 1971). After all, nonreinforced exposure to the conditioned stimulus (CS) defines the extinction procedure. Of course, it can be argued that systematic and repeated exposure rather than haphazard encounters is necessary for extinction to occur, but this view looks suspiciously like a convenient rationalization in at least some instances. Borkovec (1975) has proposed an important theoretical explanation of this apparent exception to the extinction rule.

In short, Borkovec suggests a cognitive extension of Mowrer's classic two-factor theory in which he asserts that physical exposure to the external CS is not sufficient to ensure extinction. Rather, *functional exposure* to the CS may be the critical ingredient, and this can be negated or interfered with by cognitive avoidance responses. This position is supported by data from Borkovec's (1972, 1974) avoidance response control condition. In this condition snake phobic subjects were imploded until they signaled anxiety, at which point they visualized an avoidance response they might have typically made in the actual situation. In marked contrast to both the desensitization and implosion therapy treatments in this study, the avoidance control condition resulted in neither improvement on the behavioral avoidance test nor reductions in heart rate during the therapy sessions.

One of the interesting implications of this view is that cognitive escape/avoidance with or without behavioral escape may result in the development of avoidance behaviors that would otherwise rapidly extinguish in the face of nonreinforced exposure. How neurotic fear/avoidance responses are acquired in the first place remains to be adequately explained, and Borkovec's hypothesis offers a promising lead. Another implication of immediate clinical relevance is that treatment will only be effective to the extent that cognitive avoidance responses are prevented.

Cognitive influences play a pervasive role in the regulation of behavior and attempts to modify it. Recently, both Lazarus (1975) and Meichenbaum (1976) have described how cognitive processes may affect biofeedback training. Particularly intriguing is Meichenbaum's (1976) suggestion that the current status of biofeedback research is analogous to the verbal conditioning literature prior to the demonstration that it is not an automatic conditioning process but a function of subjects' awareness of the behavior to be changed. Hoon, Wincze, and Hoon (1977), for example, found that biofeedback was ineffective when subjects had no knowledge of the target response.

Reactions and Ripostes. The growing emphasis on cognitive mediational processes in behavior therapy has not gone unchallenged. Wolpe (1976) has branded as malcontents those who espouse something labeled "cognitive exclusivism." A malcontent is defined as a "critic of (behavior therapy) whose criticisms stem from misunderstandings of one or more of its basic premises" (p. 109). Cognitive exclusivism is not defined, but it is identified by its protagonists, Ellis and Meichenbaum. According to Wolpe, cognitive therapy is a subclass of behavior therapy that cannot modify autonomic habits that are elicited directly by external stimuli.

In short, this defense of a simple S-R theory neither does justice to the contributions of the cognitive therapies nor comes to grips with recent developments in social-learning theory. Lang (1977) has described his information-processing analysis of fear as an elaboration of Wolpe's (1958) position. However, while it is consistent with Wolpe's emphasis on the use of imagery to modify an associated psychophysiological state of fear, the cognitive conceptual framework of information processing represents a fundamental departure from the reciprocal inhibition hypothesis and the peripheralistic S-R model on which it is based.

Eysenck (1976), another prime mover in the development of behavior therapy, has acknowledged the importance of cognitive factors in conditioning and its clinical applications. The suggestion is that Pavlov's second-signaling system might accommodate the cognitive extensions of conditioning principles.[7] However, this simply restates the problem as it exists since the second-signaling system is a loose construct that is itself in need of explanation.

Eysenck (1976) suggests that the conditioning and cognitive theories will have few differential experimental consequences. That this is not necessarily so is demonstrated by Bandura's (1976b) findings that the social-learning analysis of self-efficacy is a significantly better predictor of behavior change than traditional conditioning theory. In one study severely phobic subjects were treated with systematic desensitization until they completed the stimulus hierarchy, i.e., they showed no anxiety to imaginal representation of the most aversive scenes. In addition to measures of behavioral avoidance, subjects' self-efficacy expectations were assessed before treatment, after treatment but prior to the posttest, and following the posttest. Although all subjects had been equally desensitized, the reductions in avoidance behavior that they showed were typically variable. Subjects' self-efficacy expectations, however, were accurate predictors of subsequent performance on 89% of the behavioral tasks. Similar results were obtained in analyses of the effects of participant and symbolic modeling methods. These results support the cognitive theory that treatment-induced reduction of physiological arousal changes behavior by increasing efficacy expectations rather than by extinguishing a conditioned autonomic drive as postulated by reciprocal inhibition or the two-factor theory of avoidance learning.

Operant conditioning disdains all dalliance with mediational processes, cognitive or otherwise. *Post hoc* operant formulations of

---

[7] The average date of publication of the very narrow range of studies Eysenck (1976) cites as evidence for cognitive factors is 1964.

various social learning procedures such as modeling and self-rein-forcement (Catania, 1975) in which cognitive operations are trans-lated into behavioral terms have been put forward. In fact, the elas-tic use of operant concepts such as stimulus control and a law of effect based not on immediate response consequences but on an aggregate effect over time allows explanation of almost any beha-vior-change method. The important point is that these explanations have been *post hoc*. To take but one example, the demonstrably suc-cessful use of vicarious observation methods, including covert, symbolic, and live modeling, derived not from operant condition-ing, but social-learning theory. The fact that some Procrustean ma-neuver may be engaged in to accommodate these methods within an operant framework is less important than the failure of this con-ceptual scheme to generate such techniques. The significance of social-learning concepts rests in their heuristic function, their util-ity in generating more effective treatment methods for a wider range of problems. To the extent that this purpose is achieved, the resort to theoretical constructs will be amply rewarded.

The Clinical Efficacy of the Cognitive Therapies

It is sobering to reflect upon Mahoney and Arnkoff's (1978) ob-servation that the recent enthusiasm for RET cannot be a function of its empirical support. There is really no more reason for uncritically accepting RET today than there was for rejecting or ignoring it in the 1960s.

The comparison between treatment methods based on verbal and imaginal operations respectively was summarized above. In sum, there is no compelling evidence that cognitive therapies that rely upon specific verbal mediational mechanisms are more effec-tive than systematic desensitization using visual imagery. At least one major outcome study found that desensitization was more broadly effective than RET (DiLoreto, 1971). Moreover, treatments based on direct behavioral intervention appear to be reliably more effective than methods using imaginal or vicarious modes of induc-tion (Bandura, 1977b).

Smith and Glass (1977), in what they term a meta-analysis of the results of 375 clinical outcome studies, found that of 10 types of therapy evaluated (including psychodynamic, Gestalt, and client-centered therapies), RET was second only to systematic desensitization in efficacy. However, no regard was paid to the quality of the individual studies entering into this misleading analysis. Among others, this problem makes a global survey of outcome research of this kind uninterpretable (cf. Kazdin and Wilson, 1978).

Beck's (1976) cognitive therapy—in effect a combination of behavioral and cognitive methods—has received the most persuasive empirical support. An impressive outcome study comparing cognitive therapy to tricyclic antidepressant medication in the treatment of severely depressed patients showed the clear-cut superiority of the former (Rush, Beck, Kovacs, and Hollon, 1977). Beyond these data several studies have provided encouraging results. However, the preliminary nature of these findings requires emphasis.

A TERMINOLOGICAL NOTE

The difficulties associated with the term "behavior therapy" have been noted. Does "cognitive behavior therapy" or simply "cognitive therapy" provide a superior alternative? Ideally, therapy brand names would become unnecessary to the degree that there is consensus on experimentally validated applications and outcomes. That is a distant goal, and in the meantime those who seek to ground their thinking and practice in the findings of experimental psychology will want some way of distinguishing their endeavors from the ever-increasing array of therapists who ignore the scientific discipline of psychology.

Given the unavoidability of using some label, behavior therapy may be the least troublesome. If nothing else, the term "behavior" is consistent with the fact that behavioral methods are the most effective in altering psychological functioning. It serves as a reminder that in the ultimate analysis the effects of therapy must be evaluated, at least in part, by direct behavioral measures. The term "cognitive therapy" fails to emphasize these points. The focus on behavior as the object of change in its own right and the legitimacy of the direct modification of behavior have been hard won. It would be unfortunate to fail to stress the overriding importance of the behavior *per se* even though cognitive variables might currently provide the most convincing explanatory mechanisms for behavioral techniques. The hybrid term "cognitive behavior therapy" merely prompts the question why the affective or autonomic system is excluded.

The term "behavior therapy" does identify a common core among all present behavioral approaches, a commitment to measurement, methodology, concepts, and procedures derivable from experimental psychology. The importance of cognitive processes is increasingly part of the general understanding of behavior therapy. Parsimony and present usage suggest that there might be little to be gained by the use of a new label.

ACKNOWLEDGMENTS

This paper was written while the author was a Fellow at the Center for Advanced Study in the Behavioral Sciences at Stanford, California. While the views expressed here are my own, I wish to acknowledge the influence of numerous discussions with Stewart Agras, Nathan Azrin, Alex George, Alan Kazdin, Walter Mischel, and Jack Rachman.

REFERENCES

Azrin, N.H. A strategy for applied research: Learning based but outcome oriented. *American Psychologist*, 1977, *32*, 140–149.
Baer, D., Wolf, M., and Risley, T. Some current dimensions of applied behavior analysis. *Journal of Applied Behavior Analysis*, 1968, *1*, 91–97.
Bandura, A. *Principles of behavior modification*. New York: Holt, Rinehart and Winston, 1969.
Bandura, A. Behavior theory and models of man. *American Psychologist*, 1974, *29*, 859–869.
Bandura, A. Self-reinforcement: Theoretical and methodological considerations. *Behaviorism*, 1976, *4*, 135–155.
Bandura, A. *Social learning theory*. Englewood Cliffs, N.J.: Prentice-Hall, 1977a.
Bandura, A. Self-efficacy: Towards a unifying theory of behavior change. *Psychological Review*, 1977b, *84*, 191–215.
Bandura, A., Blanchard, E.B., and Ritter, B. Relative efficacy of desensitization and modelling approaches for inducing behavioral, affective, and attitudinal changes. *Journal of Personality and Social Psychology*, 1969, *13*, No. 3, 173–199.
Beck, A.T. *Cognitive therapy and the emotional disorders*. New York: International Universities Press, 1976.
Blanchard, E.B. The generalization of vicarious extinction effects. *Behaviour Research and Therapy*, 1970, *8*, 323–330.

Borkovec, T.D. Effects of expectancy on the outcome of systematic desensitization and implosive treatments for analogue anxiety. *Behavior Therapy*, 1972, *3*, 29–40.

Borkovec, T.D. Heart-rate process during systematic desensitization and implosive therapy for analogue anxiety. *Behavior Therapy*, 1974, *5*, 636–641.

Borkovec, T.D. Cognitive Extensions of Two-Factor Theory. Paper presented at the 9th Annual Meeting of the Association for Advancement of Behavior Therapy. San Francisco, December, 1975.

Bower, G.H. Analysis of mnemonic device. *American Scientist*, 1970, *58*, 496–510.

Brewer, W.F. There is no convincing evidence for operant or classical conditioning in adult humans. In W.B. Weimer and D.S. Palermo (Eds.), *Cognition and the symbolic processes*. Hillsdale, N.J.: Lawrence Erlbaum Associates, 1974, 1–42.

Catania, A.C. The myth of self-reinforcement. *Behaviorism*, 1975, *3*, 192–199.

Cautela, J.R. Covert conditioning. In A. Jacobs and L.B. Sachs (Eds.), *The psychology of private events: Perspectives on covert response systems*. New York: Academic Press, 1971.

Crowe, M.J., Marks, I.M., Agras, W.S., and Leitenberg, H. Time-limited desensitization, implosion and shaping of phobic patients: A cross-over study. *Behaviour Research and Therapy*, 1972, *10*, 319–328.

Davidson, G.C. Behavior modification techniques in institutional settings. In C.M. Franks (Ed.), *Behavior therapy: Appraisal and status*. New York: McGraw-Hill, 1969, 220–278.

Dember, W.N. Motivation and the cognitive revolution. *American Psychologist*, 1974, *29*, 161–168.

DiLoreto, A. *Comparative psychotherapy*. New York: Aldine-Atherton, 1971.

D'Zurilla, T.J., and Goldfried, M.R. Problem solving and behavior modification. *Journal of Abnormal Psychology*, 1971, *78*, 107–126.

D'Zurilla, T., Wilson, G.T., and Nelson, R. A preliminary study of the effectiveness of graduated prolonged exposure in the treatment of irrational fear. *Behavior Therapy*, 1973, *4*, 672–685.

Ellis, A. *Reason and emotion in psychotherapy*. New York: Stuart, 1962.

Ellis, A. *The essence of rational psychotherapy: A comprehensive approach to treatment*. New York: Institute for Rational Living, 1970.

Emmelkamp, P.M.G., and Wessels, H. Flooding in imagination vs. flooding in vivo; a comparison with agoraphobics. *Behaviour Research and Therapy*, 1975, *13*, 7–15.

Eysenck, H.J. *Behaviour therapy and the neuroses*. Oxford: Pergamon Press, 1960.

Eysenck, H.J. *Experiments in behavior therapy*. Oxford: Pergamon Press, 1964.

Eysenck, H.J. Behaviour therapy—dogma or applied science? In P. Feldman and A. Broadhurst (Eds.), *The experimental bases of behaviour therapy*. New York: Wiley, 1976.

Fairweather, G.W. *Social psychology in treating mental illness: An experimental approach*. New York: Wiley, 1964.

Franks, C.M. Behavior therapy and its Pavlovian origins. In C.M. Franks (Ed.), *Behavior therapy: Current status and appraisal*. New York: McGraw-Hill, 1969, 1–26.

Franks, C.M., and Wilson, G.T. *Annual review of behavior therapy: Theory and practice* (Vol. I). New York: Brunner/Mazel, 1973.

Franks, C.M., and Wilson, G.T. *Annual review of behavior therapy: Theory and practice* (Vol. II). New York: Brunner/Mazel, 1974.

Franks, C.M., and Wilson, G.T. *Annual review of behavior therapy: Theory and practice* (Vol. III). New York: Brunner/Mazel, 1975.

Franks, C.M., and Wilson, G.T. *Annual review of behavior therapy: Theory and practice* (Vol. IV). New York: Brunner/Mazel, 1976.

Goldfried, M.R. Systematic desensitization as training in self-control. *Journal of Consulting and Clinical Psychology*, 1971, *37*, 228–234.

Goldfried, M.R., and Davison, G.L. *Clinical behavior therapy*. New York: Holt, Rinehart and Winston, 1976.

Goldiamond, I. Self-reinforcement as an explanatory fiction. *Journal of Applied Behavior Analysis*, 1976, *9*, 509–514.

Goren, E. A comparison of systematic desensitization and self-instruction in the treatment of phobias. Unpublished Masters Thesis, Rutgers University, 1975.

Homme, L.E. Perspectives in psychology: XXIV. Control of coverants, the operants of the mind. *Psychological Record*, 1965, *15*, 501–511.

Hoon, P.W., Wincze, J.P., and Hoon, E.F. The effects of biofeedback and cognitive mediation upon vaginal blood volume. *Behavior Therapy*, 1977, *8*, 694–702.

Kanfer, F.H., and Phillips, J.S. *Learning foundations of behavior therapy*. New York: Wiley, 1970.

Kazdin, A.E. Effects of covert modeling and modeling reinforcement on assertive behavior. *Journal of Abnormal Psychology*, 1974, *83*, 240–252.

Kazdin, A.E. The application of operant techniques in treatment, rehabilitation, and education. In S.L. Garfield and A.E. Bergin (Eds.), *Handbook of psychotherapy and behavior change* (2nd ed.) New York: Wiley, 1978.

Kazdin, A.E., and Wilson, G.T. *Evaluation of behavior therapy: Issues, evidence, and research strategies*. Cambridge, Mass.: Ballinger, 1978.

Kelly, G.A. *The psychology of personal constructs*. New York: Norton, 1955.

Kockott, G., Dittmar, F., and Nusselt, L. Systematic desensitization of erectile impotence: A controlled study. *Archives of Sexual Behavior*, 1975, *4*, 493–500.

Lang, P.J. The mechanics of desensitization and the laboratory study of human fear. In C.M. Franks (Ed.), *Assessment and status of the behavior therapies*. New York: McGraw-Hill, 1969.

Lang, P.J. Imagery in therapy: An information processing analysis of fear. *Behavior Therapy*, 1977, *8*, 862–886.

Lang, P.J., Melamed, B.G., and Hart, J.H. A psychophysiological analysis of fear modification using an automated desensitization procedure. *Journal of Abnormal Psychology*, 1970, *76*, 220–234.

Lazarus, A.A. *Behavior therapy and beyond*. New York: McGraw-Hill, 1971.

Lazarus, A.A. *Multimodal behavior therapy*. New York: Springer, 1976.

Lazarus, R.S. A cognitively oriented psychologist looks at biofeedback. *American Psychologist*, 1975, *30*, 553–561.

Luria, A. *The role of speech in the regulation of normal and abnormal behavior*. New York: Liveright, 1961.

Mahoney, M.J. *Cognition and behavior modification*. Cambridge, Mass.: Ballinger, 1974.

Mahoney, M.J. On terminal terminology. *Journal of Applied Behavior Analysis*, 1976, *9*, 515–517.

Mahoney, M.J. On the continuing resistance to thoughtful therapy. *Behavior Therapy*, 1977a, *8*, 673–677.

Mahoney, M.J. Personal science: A cognitive learning therapy. In A. Ellis and R. Grieger (Eds.), *Handbook of rational psychotherapy*. New York: Springer, 1977b.

Mahoney, M.J., and Arnkoff, D. Cognitive and self-control therapies. In S.L. Garfield and A.E. Bergin (Eds.), *Handbook of psychotherapy and behavior change* (2nd ed.). New York: Wiley, 1978.

Mathews, A., Bancroft, J., Whitehead, A., Hackmann, A., Julier, D., Bancroft, J., Gath, D., and Shaw, P. The behavioral treatment of sexual inadequacy: A comparative study. *Behaviour Research and Therapy*, 1976, *14*, 427–436.

Meichenbaum, D. Cognitive factors in behavior modification: Modifying what clients say to themselves. In C.M. Franks and G.T. Wilson (Eds.), *Annual review of behavior therapy: Theory and practice* (Vol. I). New York: Brunner/Mazel, 1973, 416–431.

Meichenbaum, D. *Cognitive behavior modification.* Morristown, N.J.: General Learning Press, 1974.

Meichenbaum, D. Cognitive factors in biofeedback therapy. *Biofeedback and Self-Regulation*, 1976, *1*, 201–215.

Meichenbaum, D. *Cognitive behavior modification.* New York, Plenum, 1977.

Meichenbaum, D., and Cameron, R. Training schizophrenics to talk to themselves: A means of developing attentional controls. *Behavior Therapy*, 1973, *4*, 515–534.

Meichenbaum, D., Gilmore, J., and Fedoravicius, A. Group insight vs. group desensitization in treating speech anxiety. *Journal of Consulting and Clinical Psychology*, 1971, *36*, 410–421.

Mischel, W. *Personality and assessment.* New York: Wiley, 1968.

Moore, B., Mischel, W., and Zeiss, A. Comparative effects of the reward stimulus and its cognitive representation in voluntary delay. *Journal of Personality and Social Psychology*, 1976, *34*, 419–424.

Mowrer, O.H. On the dual nature of learning—A reinterpretation of "conditioning" and "problem solving." *Harvard Educational Review*, 1947, *17*, 102–148.

Mowrer, O.H. *Learning theory and the symbolic processes.* New York: Wiley, 1960.

Nebes, R.D. Hemispheric specialization in commissurolomized man. *Psychological Bulletin*, 1974, *81*, 1–14.

Peterson, D.R. *The clinical study of social behavior.* New York: Appleton-Century-Crofts, 1968.

Rachlin, H. *Self control.* Behaviorism, 1974, *2*, 94–107.

Rachlin, H. Reinforcing and punishing thoughts. *Behavior Therapy*, 1977, *8*, 659–665.

Rachman, S. Introduction to behaviour therapy. *Behaviour Research and Therapy*, 1963, *1*, 3–15.

Rachman, S., and Hodgson, R. *Obessions and compulsions.* Englewood Cliffs, N.J.: Prentice-Hall, in press.

Rotter, J.B. *Social learning and clinical psychology.* Englewood Cliffs, N.J.: Prentice-Hall, 1954.

Rush, A.J., Beck, A.T., Kovacs, M., and Hollon, S. Comparative efficacy of cognitive therapy and pharmacotherapy in the treatment of depressed out-patients. *Cognitive Therapy and Research*, 1977, *1*, 17–37.

Seligman, M.E.P. Phobias and preparedness. *Behavior Therapy*, 1971, *2*, 307–320.

Sherman, A.R. Real-life exposure as a primary therapeutic factor in the desensitization treatment of fear. *Journal of Abnormal Psychology*, 1972, *79*, 19–28.

Skinner, B.F. *Science and human behavior.* New York: Macmillan, 1953.

Skinner, B.F. *Beyond freedom and dignity.* New York: Alfred A. Knopf, 1971.

Smith, M.L., and Glass, G.V. Meta-analysis of psychotherapy outcome studies. *American Psychologist*, 1977, *32*, 752–760.

Spivack, G., Platt, J.J., and Shure, M.D. *The problem-solving approach to adjustment*. San Francisco: Jossey-Bass, 1976.

Staats, A.W. Social behaviorism, human motivation, and the conditioning therapies. In B. Maher (Ed.), *Progress in experimental personality research*. New York: Academic Press, 1970.

Stern, R., and Marks, I. Brief and prolonged flooding. *Archives of General Psychiatry*, 1973, *28*, 170–276.

Suinn, R.M., and Richardson, F. Anxiety management training: A nonspecific behavior therapy program for anxiety control. *Behavior Therapy*, 1971, *2*, 498–510.

Thase, M.E., and Moss, M.K. The relative efficacy of covert modeling procedures and guided participant modeling on the reduction of avoidance behavior. *Journal of Behavior Therapy and Experimental Psychiatry*, 1976, *7*, 7–12.

Thoresen, C.E., and Mahoney, M.J. *Behavioral self-control*. New York: Holt, Rinehart and Winston, 1974.

Thorpe, G.L. Desensitization, behavior rehearsal, self-instructional training and placebo effects on assertive-refusal behavior. *European Journal of Behavioural Analysis and Modification*, 1975, *1*, 30–44.

Wein, K.S., Nelson, R.O., and Odom, J.V. The relative contributions of reattribution and verbal extinction to the effectiveness of cognitive restructuring. *Behavior Therapy*, 1975, *6*, 459–474.

Wilson, G.T. On the much discussed nature of the term "behavior therapy." *Behavior Therapy*, 1978, *9*, 89–98.

Wolpe, J. *Psychotherapy by reciprocal inhibition*. Stanford, Stanford University Press, 1958.

Wolpe, J. Behavior therapy and its malcontents—II. Multimodal eclecticism, cognitive exclusivism and "exposure" empiricism. *Journal of Behavior Therapy and Experimental Psychiatry*, 1976, *7*, 109–116.

2

A Cognitive Analysis of Social Performance

IMPLICATIONS FOR ASSESSMENT AND TREATMENT

DIANA P. RATHJEN, ERIC D. RATHJEN, AND ALICE HINIKER

A COGNITIVE AND BEHAVIORAL DEFINITION OF SOCIAL COMPETENCE

The importance of cognitive factors in social interaction has long been recognized and studied by both social psychologists and more traditionally oriented clinicians, sometimes to the point of overlooking behavioral factors. Until recently, cognitive factors have been minimized in behavior therapy, perhaps as an over-reaction to more traditional clinical approaches. However, with the emergence of cognitive behavior therapy, cognitive factors have been embraced with an enthusiasm that often outstrips empirical evidence for their importance. Cognitive behavioral techniques are being developed at a rapid rate for a wide variety of interpersonal problems (e.g., anger, interpersonal anxiety, social withdrawal, self-deprecation). In fact, there is some danger that in "going cognitive," behavior therapy may lose its uniqueness and the advantages it derives from placing an emphasis on observable behavior.

DIANA P. RATHJEN • Department of Psychology, Rice University, Houston, Texas 77001. **ERIC D. RATHJEN** • Mental Health—Mental Retardation Authority, Harris County, Houston, Texas 77001. **ALICE HINIKER** • Texas Research Institute of Mental Sciences, Houston, Texas 77001.

The authors feel that it is both possible and desirable to integrate the empirical work on social cognition and the newly devised cognitive techniques of behavior therapy while maintaining a firm grounding in observable behavior. One model that we feel will allow us to achieve such a successful integration is a theory of structural learning proposed by Joseph M. Scandura (1977). He states that his theory "provides a unifying theoretical framework within which to view the concerns of the teacher or competence researcher, the cognitive scientist and the individual differences specialist" (1977, p. 34), to which we add the cognitive behavior therapist. Briefly, structural-learning theory is a model of instruction in which the major variables of importance are subsumed under the headings of "content domain," "methods of analysis," "underlying competencies" or "knowledge," "performance testing," and "processing characteristics" of the learner (see Fig. 1). The theory is a relativistic one since what people know and what they are able to do are always judged relative to a predetermined content domain and subject population. *Content domains* are defined as sets of potentially observable stimulus situations (input) and corresponding responses (outputs) that happen to be of interest. Content domains relevant to social interaction could be defined by type of relationship, e.g., marital, child–parent, therapeutic, or sexual. Interpersonal domains could also be defined in terms of skills such as conversational skills, initiation and approach behavior, assertive behavior, negotiation skills, impression management, social influence, development of intimacy, communication, and coping with interpersonal stress. As the examples indicate, the content domains are not mutually exclusive; certain skills, such as communication, may be common to several types of relationships.

In the context of social interaction the two components of a content domain could be defined as follows: (1) the *stimulus* is a relevant interpersonal situation or problem, e.g., getting to know another person; and (2) the *response* is the observable behavior, including motor, verbal, physiological, and affective dimensions, e.g., walking toward the person, mumbling hello, sweating profusely and feeling anxious, or, in the case of a desirable response, approaching a person, saying hello, having a low heart rate, and feeling calm.

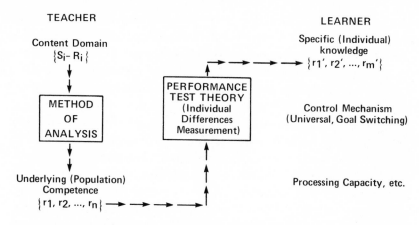

Figure 1. Structural-learning theory as proposed by Scandura. Copyright 1977 by the American Psychological Association. Reprinted by permission.

A strictly behavioral approach usually restricts itself to consideration of the content domain (i.e., identifying the problem situations and appropriate responses or behavioral objectives). A structural-learning model includes two additional variables: underlying rules of competence, and processing characteristics of the subject population. In Scandura's terms, rules of competence are the processes that, collectively, make it possible to solve problems in a content domain. For example, in the problem cited above, getting to know another person could be solved by a series of rules that (1) identify whether the other person is approachable (is she busy or free to talk?); (2) specify introductory remarks (greetings and small talk); (3) suggest appropriate motor and nonverbal behavior (conversational distance and pleasant expression); and (4) rules for producing facilitory affective responses, i.e., positive self-statements. Taken together, a set of rules for a content domain is called the *competence account*. It is in the competence accounts that cognitive factors most clearly come into play. An application of the concept of competence account to social interaction will allow us to identify the way cognitive variables could most usefully be assessed and incorporated into intervention plans.

An adequate competence account involves the specification of three sets of variables: the *behavioral objectives* making up the content domain, the *"knowledge"* or *set of rules* underlying competent performance, and the *processing characteristics* of the subject population of interest. Behavioral objectives tell what the learner is expected to be able to do after learning, e.g., initiate a conversation and ask for a date. Knowledge refers to an underlying rule (cognition/procedure/algorithm/relational net/construct) that reflects the potential for the behavior specified in the behavioral objective. In the above example, relevant rules might tell how to discriminate an approachable woman from an unapproachable one, how to communicate interest, how to proceed if rejected, etc. Processing characteristics fall into two classes: (1) universal characteristics (i.e., working memory), and (2) individual knowledge that is judged relative to the competence in question. An example of a universal characteristic could be visual ability (in teaching social skills to blind persons, the rules for use of nonverbal feedback, for example, would be limited to auditory rather than visual cues). Individual knowledge could refer to cues that can be used to determine approachability of a potential date (verbal and nonverbal signs of interest on her part, her age, attractiveness, etc.).

The strength of traditional behavioral approaches has been in their specification of behavioral objectives. However, as Scandura cogently points out, "specifying behavioral objectives does not tell what the learner must learn or what the teacher must teach" (1977, p. 37). For example, the behavioral objective, "arrange an encounter or date with a woman," does not specify what the nondating individual needs to learn. Breaking the objective down into smaller units of behavior does not necessarily solve the problem. McFall (1976) mentions a hypothetical program attempting to use increased eye contact as one subgoal in a program to increase dating frequency. Research (Patterson, 1976) has indicated that the appropriateness of eye contact varies with the situational context; incessant staring can be as interpersonally ineffective as avoidance of eye contact. Clients in the program needed to learn a rule specifying when increases in eye contact can be used to facilitate an encounter. Another example involves the frequently noted lack of generalization in assertiveness training (Rich and Schroeder, 1976). One possible explanation is that people have learned specific behaviors that are effective for certain situations but have not learned how to generate similar but novel responses to new situations that may be covered by a similar rule. Hersen and Bellak (1976) cite the example of V.A. patients who learned protective and assertive responses in a training group but who did not employ similar responses in a different context to demand payment promised to them by the experimenters for their participation in the program. Appropriate discrimination and generalization almost invariably involve application of an underlying rule.

Specifying the knowledge or underlying competence of the target population is important for several other reasons: (a) given any class of social tasks, e.g., behavioral objectives, if there is one rule that will generate a solution, there are likely many other rules that will do the same thing; (b) in practice there is often more than one reliable rule for generating behavior associated with a behavioral objective. The feasibility of using any particular rule depends on the characteristics of the population in question. For example, a rule specifying which person to approach for a date might be qualified by the physical attractiveness of the person using the rule; a rule suggesting how close to stand to a conversational partner would depend on the personal space rules of the particular culture involved.

For any given social task or problem, then, there are theoretically many possible rules that will generate a solution. In practice, however, the number of alternatives actually used by competent members of a subject population may be small in number. Scandura gives the example of subtraction: German children use the equal additions method while American children use borrowing. In the area of social competence, an example might be the expression of liking either by body language and spatial distance, or through compliments and invitations, etc., or getting to know a person by using the rule, "express interest," or the rule, "be a good listener." To use another cultural example, appreciation for a Turkish meal may be expressed with a nonverbal burp whereas a verbal rule for appreciation is more typical in American homes. In sum, the rule sets that may account for a given content domain or interpersonal task are restricted by practical limitations imposed by the subject population such as abilities, attractiveness, age, social class, and cultural norms.

It is important to note at this point that knowledge of the subject matter or the ability to recognize competent responses is not equivalent to specifying the underlying relevant rules. An interesting example involves the use of personal space and body language. The recent amount of empirical research and popularized books and articles have sensitized many individuals to the rules involved. Prior to the interest in the area it was common for an individual to feel uncomfortable in the presence of another person, particularly someone from another culture, without being able to "put one's finger" on what was wrong, or, in other words, without being able to specify the inappropriate rule being used (e.g., expressing interest by moving physically close). A similar example is available in the literature on dating. Untrained female undergraduates were able to discriminate between low- and high-frequency male daters in terms of global-skill ratings but were unable to distinguish between the two groups on any more specific criteria, e.g., they could not specify what rules were leading to skillful responses.

Any viable theory of social-performance assessment will take into account the rules underlying behavioral competence. Such a method making use of rules makes it possible to identify not only what individuals can and cannot do, but also what the learner knows of the relevant rules involved. As in all good behavioral assessment, implications for treatment follow directly: assume the paths that the learner already knows and concentrate on those that he or she does not. Direct assessment of knowledge of the rules may be a far more efficient technique than assessment of all behaviors implied by the rule once the relationship between the rules and the behavior implied by knowledge of the rule has been firmly empirically established (e.g., if knowledge of the rules has been shown to discriminate reliably between those who can display the adaptive target behaviors and those who cannot). If a person knows the rules for appropriate self-disclosure, it may not be necessary to assess each specific behavioral component such as asking questions, giving information, asking follow-up questions, etc.

Maladaptive or incorrect responses can also be expressed in rules. For example, Jourard (1964) suggests that unskilled persons self-disclose to strangers whereas skilled persons restrict disclosure to friends. Scandura gives the example of the poor math student who tries to apply the division rule to all numbers while the knowledgeable student's division rule applies to the numbers but excludes zero. Both students would get most of the division problems correct; however, when the poor student tried to divide by zero he would make errors. Again, we can see that assessment based on rules may be more efficient than assessing performance on numerous individual tasks.

A second point that is relevant for assessment concerns the existence of what Scandura terms "higher order rules." The phrase *higher order* refers to the use to which the rules are put and not a property of the rule *per se*. An example is the conversion rule of the form A→B, B→C, which can be expressed in terms of A→C. If a person who knows the higher-order conversion rule of translating A→C, it is not necessary to assess the lower-order ones. An example from math would include the rule for converting yards to feet (multiply by 3) and the rule for converting feet to inches (multiply by 12). Children who know the conversion rule could succeed at a task involving the conversion of yards to inches while children not using that rule would fail. An analogy might be made with the development of intimacy. There may be a rule for converting strangers into friends (greetings and small talk) and a rule for converting friends into intimates (self-disclosure). A socially skilled person would be able to combine the two rules to eventually develop an intimate relationship with a stranger. However, an unskilled person who did not have a rule for combining the skills might attempt to apply the friend rule to strangers and destroy the relationship with inappropriate self-disclosure.

An understanding of the underlying rules has implications for teaching competence as well. Although rules can often be specified verbally and with precision, it is possible to specify them nonverbally (i.e., through modeling, imagery, or proprioceptive feedback, as in contact desensitization). Further, the language used to represent rules may vary in precision according to the subject population. Generally, the more sophisticated or knowledgeable the population, the less detailed the rules need to be. Rules for social-skills training for psychiatric patients may need to be more specific than those for college students. The ability to specify the rules is not the same as the ability to teach them effectively. The most efficient teaching method may involve direct instruction in rules, experiental methods, Socratic techniques, inductive or deductive reasoning, modeling, vicarious learning, etc.

In summary, a structural-learning model suggests that in order to be effective, an instructional program for competence must answer the following questions:

1. What are the relevant tasks making up the content domain?
2. What behavior defines competent and incompetent solutions for the population in question?
3. What is the subject population and what are its relevant processing characteristics?
4. What "knowledge" or underlying rules lead to competent and incompetent performance?
5. How is individual "knowledge" assessed?
6. How is the necessary knowledge taught and learned?

In order to use this model to outline an instructional method for social competence, we will briefly review the way that researchers and clinicians working in the field of interpersonal relationships have attempted to answer these questions. Our discussion will begin with an overview of the methods psychologists have used to define the tasks involved in social competence and to identify the specific behaviors that are considered competent solutions for interpersonal problems (questions one and two).

We will then review the relevant processing characteristics that are typical of clinical populations and the methods psychologists have used to determine the underlying rules of competence that make up effective social performance (questions three and four). Finally, we will review the answers psychologists have provided regarding assessment and treatment (questions five and six).

1. and 2. *What tasks are to be mastered for social competence and what behaviors constitute the competent and incompetent solutions for these tasks?*

Social interaction includes the full range of human tasks involved in relating to one or more other people. Following Scandura's model, social competence or adequate social performance is broken down into specific behavioral objectives. Basic researchers studying normal social interaction have identified an array of responses that could become behavioral objectives in a program to improve interpersonal relations. Responses investigated have included affect (satisfaction, low anxiety, positive self-concept), response from others (liking, compliance, attitude change), and mutual responses (trust, intimacy, cooperation, conflict resolution).

McFall (1976) recently reviewed the techniques used by clinicians and psychopathologists to define behavioral social competence. He categorized the techniques into four basic types: fiat, consensus, known-groups approach, and the experimental method.

When competence is defined by fiat, certain behaviors are identified as desirable because one person in authority suggests that they are (e.g., a parent feels a child should be more outgoing; a therapist suggests a person should be more assertive). This method has the obvious disadvantage of being idiosyncratic; the behavior selected may be considered desirable by the authority figure but may be punished by others in the client's environment. The fiat method is useful primarily when the judge is a person the client interacts with frequently, e.g., a parent, spouse, or teacher, and if the client learns to discriminate among individuals.

Competence as defined by consensus involves the judgments of several raters, which are scored and intercorrelated or averaged. This technique is an improvement over fiat, as it substitutes the opinion of several individuals for the opinion of one person and thus may correspond more closely with appropriate norms in the natural environment. However, this advantage is less likely if the judges are not drawn from the client's environment (clinicians) than if they are (peers). As McFall notes, this method defines competence by a majority vote but does not insure validity; the opinion of several judges is not necessarily any more valid than that of one judge. In fact, consensus may reflect commonly held biases, ignorance, or perhaps cultural stereotypes.

The third method used to define the range of appropriate responses or behavioral objectives is the known-groups approach. This method involves selection of two groups known to differ in overall adequacy of their responses to a situation, such as daters and nondaters or members of distressed and nondistressed marriages. The two groups are presented with a similar stimulus and their situational performance is measured. Any specific behavior or response that differentiates between the two groups is then taken as an essential component or manifestation of the general skill on which the two groups were originally sorted. The basic problem with this method is the "error of assumed essence," i.e., the logical error of assuming that the criterion that served as the original basis for sorting the individuals reflects the essential difference and that all subsequently observed differences are necessarily related to this assumed essence (McFall, 1976). The method overlooks the fact that the groups may differ on some unconsidered factor that may account for the observed differences. A second problem with this method that has often been recognized, but perhaps more often ignored, is the tendency to treat performance samples as though they were indices of underlying personality traits. For example, "assertiveness" is sometimes treated as a personality characteristic when evidence indicates that the degree of assertiveness expressed by an individual will vary with the situation (Rich and Schroeder, 1976). One value of the known-groups approach is as a source of hypotheses to be examined in future research.

The most scientifically rigorous way to define situation-specific competence is through the use of the experimental method. This technique involves deriving definitions of competence from various sources (interviews, hunches, etc.) and subjecting them to an empirical test, e.g., seeing which behavior comes closest to achieving the client's goal. Although specific guidelines for the use of this method have been set forth (Goldfried and D'Zurilla, 1969; Mager and Pipe, 1970), few researchers have used it (e.g., Goldsmith and McFall, 1975, with psychiatric patients; Freedman, 1974, with juvenile delinquents).

3. and 4. *What is the subject population and what are its relevant processing characteristics? What underlying rules lead to competent and incompetent performance?*

Once the content domain, including tasks and behavioral objectives, has been adequately identified, the next step is to develop a method of analysis for identifying the underlying rules of competence and the processing characteristics of the target population. It is at this point that we feel the cognitive behavioral approach can be most usefully applied. The literature that appears most relevant in this context has been recently reviewed by Mahoney (1974; 1977) and Meichenbaum (1976). Based on this literature, we have identified several different possible methods that could be used to specify underlying rules and processing characteristics.

One approach that Meichenbaum labels "semantic" includes Ellis's work on rational-emotive therapy (1961) and Beck's cognitive analysis of various emotional disorders (1970). This approach would lead to derivation of the underlying rules on a rational or logical basis; e.g., it implies that negative affect and maladaptive behavior are a result of faulty beliefs or irrational thinking styles, and that facilitory affect and adaptive behavior are a result of rational belief systems and thinking styles. The task then becomes one of specifying the irrational beliefs and thinking styles that are interfering with performance and the rational beliefs, and the rational beliefs and thinking styles that could facilitate desired affect and performance. Ellis has compiled a set of 12 core irrational ideas common to this culture that he believes encompass most of the irrational beliefs clients present. This list has been frequently reprinted in texts (Rimm and Masters, 1974; Goldfried and Davison, 1976) although the rational counterbeliefs have rarely been given equal prominence (Mahoney, 1974, p. 171). The first three irrational beliefs, as summarized by Ellis in 1970, are listed below.

Irrational Ideas That Cause and Sustain Emotional Disturbance

Rational therapy holds that certain core irrational ideas, which have been clinically observed, are at the root of most emotional disturbance. They are:

1. *The idea that it is a dire necessity for an adult to be loved by everyone for everything he does*—instead of his concentrating on his own self-respect, on winning approval for practical purposes, and on loving rather than being loved.

2. *The idea that certain acts are awful or wicked, and that people who perform such acts should be severely punished*—instead of the idea that certain acts are inappropriate or antisocial, and that people who perform such acts are *behaving* stupidly, ignorantly, or neurotically and would be better helped to change.

3. *The idea that it is horrible when things are not the way one would like them to be*—instead of the idea that it is too bad, that one would better try to change or control conditions so that they become more satisfactory, and, if that is not possible, one had better temporarily accept their existence.

A detailed discussion of the kinds of rational counterbeliefs that can be substituted is presented in a recent manual on asser-

tiveness training (Lange and Jakubowski, 1976). The following are
examples of the counterbeliefs they suggest for the first three irrational ideas:

> *Some general rational alternatives to irrational idea number one
> concerning personal rejection are:*
> 1. I would *like* to be approved of by every significant person, but I
> do not *need* such approval.
> 2. If I am not approved of by someone I would like to have like me,
> I can attempt to determine what it is that person does not like *about the
> way I behave* and decide whether I want to change it.
> 3. If I decide that this rejection is not based on any inappropriate
> behavior on my part, I can find others I can enjoy being with.
> 4. I can determine what I want to do rather than adapting or react-
> ing to what I think others want.
> *Consequently, general rational messages to counteract the second irra-
> tional idea concerning social competence could be:*
> 1. I would like to be perfect or best at this task but I do not *need* to
> be.
> 2. I'm still successful when I do things imperfectly.
> 3. What I do doesn't have to be perfect in order to be good.
> 4. I may be happier if I am successful, but success does not deter-
> mine my worth as a person, unless I let it.
> 5. I will be happier if I attempt to achieve at a realistic level rather
> than a perfect level.
> 6. I still want to achieve and to be successful and if I am, I will
> likely be happier. If I am not successful, I will likely be unhappy but not
> depressed and miserable.
> 7. It is impossible for anyone to be perfectly competent, achiev-
> ing, etc.
> 8. Above all, if I *demand* that I be perfect, I will always be pushing
> or worrying when I'll slip; instead, if I do what I want and what I enjoy
> as well as I can, I'll feel happier and perform better.
> *Rational substitutes for idea three concerning fairness might be:* This
> person has really treated me badly and I don't like the situation or that
> person's behavior. What can I do to change either? If I can't change ei-
> ther, it is frustrating but not dreadful and awful. I can begin to make
> plans for making my life as desirable and enjoyable as I can.

Beck's analysis implies that socially competent people may be
distinguished from socially incompetent people by their processing
characteristics. He focuses on the stylistic qualities of cognitions;
that is, maladaptive behavior is assumed to result from a distortion
in thought processes. Common distortions include:

> 1. Arbitrary inference—the drawing of a conclusion when evidence
> is lacking or is actually contrary to the conclusion
> 2. Magnification—exaggeration of the meaning of an event

3. Cognitive deficiency—disregard for an important aspect of a life situation

4. Overgeneralization—taking a single incident, such as a failure, as a sign of total personal incompetence, and in this way generating a fallacious rule

5. Other distortions, such as dichotomous reasoning, catastrophizing, etc. (Bellack and Hersen, 1976, p. 144)

An example of the way that patients use incorrect rules or primary assumptions and faulty logic that leads to negative affect is given in Table 1 below, reprinted from Beck (1976). The successful client learns to draw conclusions from adequate evidence, put things in perspective, attend to all relevant aspects of a social situation, generalize from multiple rather than single instances, and to make attributions along a continuum rather than dichotomously.

Additional maladaptive cognitive processes that have been identified using this same general approach are summarized by Mahoney (1974). One category of factors he considers important is that involving attention and perception. The dysfunctions he lists (with our social examples) include (1) selective inattention to performance-relevant stimuli, i.e., a person fails to use environmental cues (example: people who do not use nonverbal feedback from others, disproportionate attention to negative feedback relative to positive feedback); (2) misperception of environmental cues, i.e., environmental information is noted but incorrectly labeled (examples in social interaction include "mind reading," projection, egocentrism, etc.); (3) maladaptive focusing, i.e. an individual attends to stimuli that are irrelevant or deleterious to performance (example: assertive behavior is sometimes inhibited by characteristics of the stimulus person such as age, sex, status, etc.); (4) maladaptive self-arousal refers to the generation of private stimuli that are irrelevant or detrimental to performance such as depression, anger, anxiety. This last process is similar to maladaptive focusing except that the distracting cues are internal rather than external. Examples include a wide variety of avoidance behaviors generated by negative affect: low-frequency dating, reduced marital contact, and poor sexual performance. The deficits listed above imply that certain processing characteristics crucial to adequate social performance include the ability to adequately attend to and perceive an array of both external and internal cues.

TABLE I. EXAMPLE OF THE WAY PATIENTS USE INCORRECT RULES OR PRIMARY ASSUMPTIONS AND FAULTY LOGIC THAT LEADS TO NEGATIVE AFFECT [a]

Primary assumption	If I'm nice (suffer for others, appear bright and beautiful), bad things (death of spouse, stopped-up sink) won't happen to me.		
Secondary assumption	I should be nice (or bad things will happen).	It is my fault when bad things happen (because I wasn't nice).	Life is unfair (because I'm nice and bad things happen).
Automatic thoughts	People will think I'm stupid.	I caused my son's birth defect.	Why don't I have a husband?
	People will think I'm fat.	I ruined my children's life by moving.	God tricked me.
	I hurt when I see others suffer.	I lost my son.	It's not fair.
	If I look gross, people will notice.	I must be doing something wrong.	Why me?
	Therapist probably thinks I'm stupid	I shouldn't have bought a house.	Why do my children act bad?
	___ will think something wrong with children.	I never have good times.	They shouldn't yell at my daughter.
		What have I done?	
Affect	Anxiety	Sadness Depression	Anger

a From Beck, 1976, with permission.

The second group of cognitive dysfunctions that Mahoney discusses refer to relational processes, e.g., after a stimulus has been attended to and encoded, a person may process the information in a way that leads to maladaptive behavior. The dysfunctions he discussed under the heading "relational processes" correspond closely to what we have described as "rules of competence." These include (1) classification errors, in which a stimulus is translated incorrectly (a person may interpret a gruff tone of voice as a negative reaction to her assertion instead of a bad mood on the speaker's part; a person may fail to discriminate situations in which his rights have been violated). Dichotomous thinking, mentioned above in the discussion of Beck's analysis, is one example of a classification error, the tendency to see things in binary rather than continuous fashion; for example, aggressive versus passive behavior, masculine versus feminine behavior, a good or bad marriage, etc. Faulty comparative processes are the second possible dysfunction. Research indicates that people tend to use other people as standards of comparison for their behavior, particularly with respect to opinions and social abilities for which there are no objective standards available. Predictions from social-comparison theory tested on normal college students revealed that most people have a tendency to see themselves a little bit better than other people or are motivated to change either their performance or their comparison group (Festinger, 1957). Comparison processes that have been related to maladaptive behavior include the use of unusually high standards as is characteristic of depressed patients, the use of different standards for self and others, characteristic of high socially anxious individuals, and emphasis on previous past performance resulting in fear of any future evaluation that may fall short.

A third dysfunction concerns retentional deficiencies that lead to maladaptive performance. A person may forget certain necessary steps in a social interaction sequence, perhaps because he is anxious or lacks practice. Inferential errors constitute the fourth dysfunction. These include faulty reasoning of the type described by Ellis as well as incorrect conclusions drawn from others' responses; (others' compliance in response to aggression may be mistakenly labeled as respect) and incorrect anticipation of consequences (assuming the assertive behavior will cause others to dislike the assertive person, etc.).

A final area in which cognitive dysfunctions can inhibit performance is in the use of experiential feedback. Research in vicarious
learning and attribution theory have revealed numerous rules people can use to interpret feedback (see Bandura, 1977; Jones, Kanouse, Kelly, Nisbett, Valins, and Weiner, 1972). Three sources of
feedback can be identified: overt feedback from others in the environment through rewards or information; feedback acquired vi-
cariously by watching others perform; and self-generated feedback
involving internal cues. "Incorrect" rules, e.g., those that lead to
maladaptive performance, can be specified for the use of each type
of feedback. Dysfunctions include attribution of success to external
causes rather than internal (task difficulty rather than effort), attribution of failure to stable (ability) rather than unstable causes
(effort), and the errors mentioned earlier with respect to overgeneralization from one poor performance and exclusive focus
on the negative aspects of the information.

The set of processing dysfunctions outlined by Mahoney
suggests that rules for competent social interaction include careful
classification of information about social situations and others' responses, appropriate use of comparative processes, memory for all
sequences of a behavior, correct inferences about the implications
of one's behavior, facilitory attributions, and positive specific use of
feedback.

Meichenbaum suggests another method of analysis that involves clinicians' introspection. He suggests that in order to speculate about what leads to poor performance, clinicians themselves
perform the task and upon completion introspect about the
thoughts, images, and behaviors employed in order to perform adequately on the task.

A related strategy involves manipulating the task demands to
better illustrate the sequential processing involved. The manipu-
lated variables can be of three types: (1) those variables inherent in
the task itself, e.g., salience of certain cues in the stimulus, required
speed of the task or rate of presentation or type of modality; (2)
nontask or environmental variables, such as distracting stimuli, reducing anxiety, etc.; (3) provision of support for the client in the
form of direct task aides (prompts, breakdown of the task into component parts, feedback, or instructional aids to help the client ap-

praise the task, focus attention, self-evaluate, etc.). This latter strategy would allow generation of rules to cover a range of situations varying on the dimensions involved in the manipulation process. The technique outlined by Meichenbaum would allow the therapist to discriminate between different situations that cause difficulty for the client. Perhaps a client can make a request if the stimulus person is a peer but not an authority figure or can express feelings if he is relaxed but not when he is anxious. Meichenbaum indicates one advantage of this method is that it elucidates the situational factors that may inhibit performance when the client actually has the appropriate response in his repertoire. He gives the example of a client who is unable to perform the adaptive response but later is able to offer a *post hoc* strategy that, if followed, would have led to an adequate performance. In this case the client may have an incorrect rule for the focus of attention, i.e., he is focusing on internal cues to the degree that it impairs his performance on the task. A correct rule, according to Meichenbaum, would be to use arousal as a cue for coping strategies rather than as a cue for obsessive self-criticism.

A third possible method of identifying underlying rules of competence is suggested by the research literature on problem-solving generated by Spivak and his colleagues (Spivak and Shure, 1974). They present subjects with interpersonal tasks and successful behavioral outcomes; the subject must determine the middle steps or means to the successful solution specified. Their research indicates that less socially competent individuals produce fewer relevant means than do competent individuals (Platt and Spivak, 1972; Shure and Spivak, 1972). However, they do not report differences in the types of means other than relevant or irrelevant used by the competent subjects. Specification of the type of means would seem to be a fruitful way to look for the rules used by the skilled and unskilled persons.

A fourth approach to identifying the underlying rules is a behavioral empirically based method used by Patterson, Weiss, and their colleagues at the Oregon Research Institute (see Patterson, Hops, and Weiss, 1975). Their program combines clinical outcome assessment and laboratory research. On the basis of observation and ideas from social-exchange theory, they have developed specific hypotheses that are then tested on normal and clinical populations (e.g., hypotheses concerning patterns of reciprocal exchange among marital couples were tested by comparing distressed and nondistressed couples' performances on laboratory tasks). "Rules" that the nondistressed couples are using can be inferred from the pattern of results. These "rules" are not necessarily being verbalized by the happy couples but represent strategies that seem to describe their interaction as differentiated from that of the distressed couples. For example, numerous studies show that distressed couples emit fewer positive responses toward each other and more negative responses than do happy couples, even though they have positive behaviors in their repertoires and display them toward strangers (Birchler, Weiss, and Vincent, 1975). Patterson's research on interaction patterns of families with aggressive children provides a second example. Members of the family may be each using different rules of social control, which results in one-sided aversive control or coercion, as he terms it. One member is controlling the others' behavior by negative reinforcement, while the member who always gives in to the demands of the person using aversive techniques is controlling behavior through positive reinforcement.

The close tie between theorizing and empirical data in the Oregon program strengthens their approach; the "rules" that the clinician researchers have derived are all related to empirical results from actual couples. The method might be enhanced by asking couples directly to reveal some of the strategies and rules for dealing with interpersonal problems.

5. and 6. *How is individual knowledge assessed and intervention developed?*

We have presented a brief overview of the various methods psychologists have used to analyze competent and incompetent behavior to determine the underlying rules of competence. The next step is to develop an assessment device that can be used to determine a particular individual's knowledge of the rules involved in social performance.

Our brief overview of the methods that have been used by psychologists to determine the underlying rules of competent social behavior indicates that several existing methodologies offer promise in this respect, but that most efforts so far have focused primarily on "incorrect" rules and dysfunctional processing mechanisms of clients with relatively little attention paid to the "correct" rules and adaptive processes used by more socially skilled individuals.

It is obvious that more empirical work designed to systematically reveal differences in the types of rules used by competent and socially incompetent people is needed. However, the work already done does suggest several types of "incorrect" rules that troubled people may be using. The next question for the clinician becomes one of assessment: What is the most efficient way to determine which rules the client does and does not know? Behavioral assessment usually reveals what a client can or cannot do. We argued earlier that the specification of behavioral deficits alone is not sufficient to decide what the learner needs to learn. An adequate assessment should include what the client can and cannot do but also what the client does or does not know. In addition, a clinically useful device provides for individualized instructional goals.

Many criterion-referenced forms of testing fail to provide an explicit means of dealing with the relationship between behavior and competence. The structural-learning model provides the means to accomplish the dual form of performance testing. We will provide a brief description of an overall testing procedure as it could be used by a clinician and then cite specific cognitive assessment devices that could be used to implement the general assessment strategy. In structural-learning theory, "rules of competence introduced to account for performance on given behavioral objectives provide an instrument of sorts with which to measure human knowledge. The theory tells how, through a finite testing procedure, one can identify which parts of to-be-taught rules *individual* subjects know. The *rules* in a very real sense serve as *rulers of measurement* and provide a basis for the operational definition of human knowledge" (Scandura, 1977, p. 39).

Use of this form of testing presupposes knowledge of the rule in question by the tester. Unfortunately, research on the rules used by socially competent people is often lacking. However, Meichenbaum's suggestion to use introspection would be quite relevant at this point. As noted above, several different rules may be used to accomplish the same behavioral objective. Thus, knowledge of several rules to accomplish the same behavioral goal would be optimal; the therapist would have flexibility in terms of deciding which rule he might want to teach the client in order to overcome a particular difficulty. However, in the absence of knowledge on the therapist's part of multiple rules, use of the particular rule he himself employs would serve the purpose. It should be noted here that the arbitrary selection of a rule that a skilled person is using differs from the arbitrary selection of a behavior a skilled person is using as a therapy goal in two important respects. First, no claim is made that one rule is any better than another if they both result in successful performance, and secondly, the error of assumed essence made when one behavior is selected as the distinguishing characteristic between skilled and unskilled groups is not being made in this case.

The performance testing is accomplished by breaking the rule or procedure/algorithm down into steps that are so simple that each individual subject from the population of interest may be assumed able to perform either perfectly on each step or not at all. Each step acts as a unit, or in atomic fashion. What are atomic units relative to one population may not be atomic units with respect to another (e.g., less sophisticated). "Express a greeting" may be a unit for a college population while a long-term psychiatric population may require "look at the person," "say hello," "ask a question," etc. Many of the tasks covered in assertiveness-training literature, for example, must be further broken down due to the novelty of the responses for different populations based on their previous histories (e.g., expressing emotions and feelings for some male clients; express your own needs, make a request, etc., for some female clients). Successful attainment of the goal requires success on each of the atomic components. Scandura cites the example of a subtraction algorithm or rule made up of several steps. There are only a finite number of behaviorally distinct paths. A social example might be the rule for the "minimally effective response" used in assertiveness training to teach clients how to escalate the intensity of their demands if the situation requires it (Rimm and Masters, 1974).

Collectively, the paths of a rule impose a partition on the domain of problems; that is, they define a set of distinct, exhaustive, and homogeneous "equivalence classes" of problems such that each problem in any given class can be solved via exactly one of the paths. The fact that each path is associated with a unique subclass of problems makes it possible to pinpoint exactly what it is that each subject knows relative to the initial rule through a finite testing procedure. It is sufficient for this purpose to test each client on one item selected randomly from each subclass. According to the assumptions of the model, success or failure on any one item implies success or failure respectively on any other item chosen from the same equivalence class. Thus, the behavior potential or individual knowledge can be represented in terms of rules, or specifically in terms of subrules of the given rules of competence. Individual differences may emerge even if only one rule of competence is being used to index behavior potential. Individuals may vary, for example, in terms of the number of paths on which they succeed. Each person's knowledge is represented by the number of paths he is able to complete.

The model has been tested with a variety of subjects ranging from preschool children to graduate students on mathematical tasks but remains to be tested on social tasks. Efforts to predict performance on subsequent items (math problems) in the equivalence class were successful (Scandura, 1973a; Scandura and Durin, 1978).

Obviously, a prerequisite for using this model is the development of rules and the development of equivalence classes. The techniques already in use by cognitive therapists offer suggestions for both of these requirements. Types of rules that might be incorporated in the testing procedure include belief systems (rational versus irrational, assertive versus aggressive or nonaggressive), rules for attending, encoding, and processing social stimuli, rules for use of feedback from others, etc. Equivalence classes could be partitioned out on the basis of type of stimulus person (sex, status, relationship, etc.) or according to situational demands (distractions, anxiety). Meichenbaum has recently reviewed the various cognitive behavioral approaches to clinical assessment (1976). He notes that this type of assessment approach is designed to directly measure a client's affect, cognition, and volition. A careful reading of his article indicates that some of these measures could be used by the therapist to infer the client's rules or strategies, but most of them are not direct measures of a client's knowledge of rules. However, several of these techniques might be helpful as means to elicit rules indirectly. For example, several of the cognitive techniques for assessment focus on clients' affect, particularly as expressed in imagery. Often the affect concerns anticipated consequences. The client may be primarily concerned with his negative affect that is the most salient aspect of the situation to him. However, implicit rules such as "avoidance of the situation will prevent negative affect" may be operating. The same argument can be made for irrational thoughts as identified by Ellis; often the thought implies a rule, e.g., "everyone must like me or it will be terrible" could imply "I will be passive and submissive in order to be liked."

The cognitive-assessment model outlined above would be very interesting to use in a clinic or research center where large numbers of people both socially skilled and not skilled could be assessed on a range of interpersonal situations. The individual therapist can obtain much of the same information from his client, although perhaps more indirectly and less systematically, by using one or more of the existing techniques employed by cognitive behaviorists. Meichenbaum's review of cognitive-assessment techniques includes interviews and imagery procedures, videotaping, TAT-like tests, behavioral assessments, homework assignments, and group assessments. We will briefly discuss the way each of these techniques could be used to reveal the underlying rules or subrules the client is using.

Cognitive processes can be assessed in a clinical interview by having the client "run a movie through his head" of the problematic situation. While closing his eyes and using his imagination the client is asked to focus on feelings, thoughts, images, and fantasies that occur to him before, during, and after the event. The client is asked to verbalize the thoughts that occur to him. A variation that is useful in discovering the client's expectations concerning consequences is to ask him to imagine the worst possible outcome and his own reaction in great detail. Meichenbaum notes that faulty cognitions can be expressed visually as well as verbally; a person might have an image of people laughing after she makes a serious statement at a cocktail party or may see an approving look on her companion's face when she imagines her usual passive response. Further probing by the therapist would be necessary to articulate the specific rule that a client is using in a situation. In the above example the woman could be assuming that "I can get people to like me if I am quiet" and/or "people will like me if I dress attractively."

Behavioral tests can involve role-playing or behavior in a naturalistic scene (giving a speech) either live or videotaped. Immediately after the role-playing or while viewing the previously made videotape, the therapist urges the client to reconstruct his thoughts and feelings. It is interesting that role-playing has been used very frequently in research on assertiveness training but that researchers rarely report use of subjects' thoughts and feelings as part of the assessment.

One exception is measurement of internal dialogues (e.g., cognitions, negative self-statements and images) on a questionnaire administered immediately after a behavioral role-playing test. Schwartz and Gottman (1974) developed a list of 17 positive self-statements that would make it easy to accomplish the social task of refusing a request and 17 negative self-statements that would make it harder to refuse the request. Subjects were asked to indicate how frequently each of the thoughts occurred to them during the role-playing. It is important to note that their measure included positive as well as negative self-statements ("I was thinking that it doesn't matter what the person thinks of me" or "I was thinking that the other person might be hurt or insulted if I refused"). It is interesting that the high assertive subjects had significantly more positive than negative self-statements while the low assertive subjects had about an equal number of both, which could be conceptualized as a conflicting dialogue. Another way to conceptualize this finding is to consider the contradicting statements as examples of two subrules that the low assertive subjects were not able to combine through the use of a higher-order rule. The higher-order rule governing assertive behavior can be considered to be "respect the rights of both the other person and yourself." The application of either half of this rule results in either passive or aggressive behavior while a successful combination results in assertive behavior. The use of spontaneously generated reports of thoughts after an actual role play may be more informative than the measure of thoughts on standardized questionnaires such as the Social Avoidance and Distress Scale (Watson and Friend, 1969).

A third method involves the presentation of pictures or slides of events relevant to the presenting problem. This method has been used to elicit strategies (e.g., what the person in the picture could do to handle the situation) as well as thoughts and feelings the client attributes to the character in the scene. Meijers (1974) was able to successfully discriminate between socially withdrawn and socially outgoing children by using this method with a set of slides depicting socially isolated children.

Groups can also be used for assessment by using the client's behavior in the group as one interpersonal situation to be analyzed by the therapist and patient together or by using the group to create a climate conducive to self-disclosure and sharing.

Homework assignments involving written records and specific thoughts and images can also be given. Meichenbaum notes that general instructions to monitor may be as useful as more specific detailed instructions that may in themselves generate concern about whether the assignment is being done correctly. He mentions that patients are requested to record negative thoughts and images; the inclusion of positive thoughts or feelings associated with desired outcomes might also be useful.

Other procedures include two written measures that have already been mentioned: the Assertive Self-Statement Test (Schwartz and Gottman, 1974) and problem-solving test (D'Zurilla and Goldfried, 1971). The Means End Test (Spivak and Shure, 1974) is particularly relevant because it concerns problem-solving in interpersonal situations. The general format of providing the subject with the successful outcome and the initial problem and requesting him to produce the intermediate steps might be adapted by a therapist. He could develop an array of outcomes related to the patient's global goal and then present them to see which particular subrules the client does not know. Another written measure is the true–false test derived from the irrational belief set used by Ellis (Jones, 1968). For further examples of cognitive behavioral assessment techniques, see Hersen and Bellack (1976).

We will now consider question six, how the necessary knowledge is taught and learned. Following is a brief overview of the cognitive techniques that may be used to teach rules underlying effective social performance. Although there is some overlap, the techniques have been grouped according to the response mode that is the prime target of change; i.e., cognitive, affective, or behavioral. The close relationship between affect and cognition makes any division of interventions according to this dimension somewhat arbitrary; therefore, we have discussed them together. Cognitive-affective techniques are those designed to reduce or change negative feelings, to provide the client with more information, or to change thoughts, attitudes, expectations, and goal setting. Cognitive-behavioral techniques include the interventions designed to facilitate the client's actual performance of a desired behavior.

COGNITIVE TECHNIQUES FOR COGNITIVE-AFFECTIVE CHANGE

1. Collection of Automatic Thoughts (Beck, Rush, and Kovacs, 1976). Automatic thoughts are self-statements or images that precede a negative affective state. Four methods of collection are mentioned by Beck: (a) assigning the clients a half hour each day to think about them and write them down; (b) have the client record thoughts accompanying increased negative affect; (c) collect thoughts in association with negative affect and precipitating environmental events; and (d) collection during the therapeutic interview. To this list we might add collection during role-play, group therapy, marital therapy, or through the use of structured projective techniques such as in complete sentences or TAT-like pictures. Initially, the purpose of this technique is to get the client to recognize the association of affect with negative self-statements or images that the therapist can then correct. Ultimately, the client will learn to reason with or modify cognitions that generate negative affect through use of related methods, the *Double or Triple Column Technique,* testing cognitions empirically, and positive self-statements.

Examples of questions to elicit and pinpoint automatic thoughts:

What did that mean to you?

How did you feel about yourself during today's session?

What have you been thinking about me (or about spouse in marital therapy or about other group member in group)?

Are there any thoughts or images you have when you're feeling rejected?

Another method for collecting automatic thoughts might be a sentence-completion task devised by the therapist. Examples used with children include: When someone teases me I feel _____ because _____ .

Examples of automatic thoughts:

If you felt neutral to me it would be awful. I couldn't stand another rejection. How could you help me if you don't care for me?

If only he would be different (see my point of view).

I am wasting your time.

Key words in automatic thoughts:

should	can't stand	awful	always
ought	no right	terrible	never
must	unfair	mean	if only
have to			

2. Technique for Disputing Irrational Beliefs (DIBS) (Ellis, 1971). The client is instructed to spend at least 10 minutes asking himself the following questions, carefully thinking through the answers, and recording both questions and answers either in written form or on a tape recorder:

1. What irrational belief do I want to dispute and surrender?
2. Can I rationally support this belief?
3. What evidence exists for the falseness of this belief?
4. Does any evidence exist of the truth of this belief?
5. What worst things could actually happen to me if I don't get what I think I must (or do get what I think I must not)?
6. What good things could I make happen if I don't get what I think I must (or do get what I think I must not)?

3. Rational Emotive Imagery (REI). Rational emotive imagery is a technique that has been developed by Maultsby and Ellis (1974). It involves having the client imaging or fantasying as vividly as he can an unpleasant, disturbing, or upsetting experience. The client is then instructed to "push" himself into changing the intense emotion (i.e., anxiety, depression, guilt, or hostility) into a less intense emotion such as disappointment, regret, annoyance, or irritation. The client is then asked to look at how he has succeeded in doing this. Maultsby and Ellis contend that this method usually results in a change in belief system or self-statements.

4. Identifying Cognitive Distortion Patterns (Beck et al., 1976).

When the client has collected a sufficient number of cognitions, he can be directed to look for underlying themes, such as being inadequate, expecting rejection, feeling unfairly treated. He then learns to test his cognitions, identify logical errors and patterns of distortion.

5. *Double- and Triple-Column Techniques (Beck et al., 1976)*. As the patient collects his cognitions he is asked to write responses to them. In the left-hand column he writes the automatic thought, in the right column he writes several alternative positive responses. He may also make use of a third column in which he reinterprets the environmental event.

Examples of double- and triple-column techniques:

Unreasonable thinking	*Reasonable thinking*	*Reinterpretation*
I'm a bad mother because my son failed English.	The fact that my son failed English does not reflect on my abilities as a mother, but maybe I can help him improve.	He may have failed because he did not exert enough effort or because the teacher did not give him enough help.
If I'm quiet, people will think I'm strange, but if I speak up they will think I'm stupid and that would be terrible.	People won't necessarily think I'm strange if I am quiet; they may not even notice how much I'm talking.	People enjoy small talk. It doesn't matter whether every remark is clever.

6. *Testing Cognitions (Beck et al., 1976)*. Testing cognitions is done by learning (a) to distinguish ideas from facts and (b) to check observations for possible cognitive distortions. Clients are taught to discriminate between thought and reality and to shift from deductive to inductive analysis of experience, i.e., to treat thoughts as theories or hypotheses to be tested rather than as statements of fact.

Example of testing cognitions:

A client said that she was an awful person because she hurt people. The following test was devised for this cognition.

1. She was to ask each of her friends who were not awful people whether they ever hurt another person. (Out of 12, only one denied ever having hurt anyone.)

2. She was to ask people whether they thought that people who hurt other people were awful.

3. She was to ask people whether she had done more to hurt them or to be nice to them.

Another test is to have the client deliberately perform the most serious error he is afraid of making (providing the therapist judges it as being relatively safe). One client was afraid of appearing foolish when being teased. He deliberately agreed to play the fool and see how others reacted.

7. *Alternative Therapy* (*Beck et al., 1976*). This technique involves the client in reconceptualizing insolvable problems in ways that encourage action and mastery.

8. *Disattribution.* This technique involves teaching the client to stop attributing all blame to himself by recognizing the role played by fate and others in his outcomes.

9. *Decatastrophizing.* The client and therapist logically explore the consequences of some anticipated catastrophic event following a "what if" format.

10. *"Prove to Me That Disaster Will Occur."* The patient is asked to prove to the therapist that a disastrous event will occur. The therapist then makes use of any doubts stated by the client to undermine his proof.

11. *Implosive Therapy* (*Overt*). The client is asked to imagine himself performing in the worst possible manner in a social situation that evokes anxiety. He then can be asked to role-play this situation, deliberately exaggerating his inadequacies.

12. *Positive and Negative Self-Statements.* One method to develop self-confidence is through the use of positive self-statements. Clients are required to keep a list of their good qualities to which they add a specified number each day. Another technique is to change negative self-statements to positive ones and mentally rehearse them.

Negative statement	Positive statement
I'm dull.	I can be interesting.
I never know what to say.	I can think of something.
I'm hopeless.	I can change.
I'm wishy-washy.	I can be firm.

13. *Emotive Imagery.* Negative affect can be reduced through incompatible imagery. The client is asked to identify imaginary scenes that produce positive feelings such as mirth, happiness, self-pride, or confidence. This imagery is then rehearsed to the point

that it can be automatically elicited to counteract negative affect at times of stress (Lange and Jakubowski, 1976).

14. The Card Game. The card game was developed by Knox (1975) for use in marital situations where anger is a problem. It involves instructing the client to write his or her partner's aversive actions on index cards when they occur and to also write a desired alternative. The client then hands the cards to the spouse and walks away. This method is designed to avoid verbal confrontations in the heat of passion.

15. "Funny Faces." Another method developed by Knox involves one partner cueing the other when he is becoming angry. The angry partner is instructed to go into the bathroom and make funny faces at himself until he is calmed down. If he does not immediately do this on request, his partner is instructed to leave the scene.

16. Substituting Rational Self-Statements for Irrational Statements to Control Anger and Blaming. One method that the authors have found particularly useful in teaching clients to control destructive blaming of self and others and associated anger or guilt is based on Hauck's R.E.T. analysis of anger (1977). His basic thesis as we have adapted it is that people become angry because they make the following type of self-statements:

1. I want something and I should or must have it, or it's my right to have it.

2. I didn't get what I want and that is awful and terribly unfair and I'm entitled to feel hurt and angry.

3. You have no right to frustrate me and you are bad, mean, unfair, etc., for doing it or I am despicable for having failed to get what I want.

4. Bad people (whether you or I) deserve to be punished or should be punished by me.

Once the client is able to identify that this or a similar series of self-statements (which he identifies with the aid of the therapist's directive questioning) accompanies his experience of anger at others or himself, he will often ask what else he could say to himself or assert that these beliefs are true and that he is entitled to be angry. It is at this time that an alternative set of cognitions is offered, again adapted from Hauck.

1. Because I want something very badly does not mean I must have it, or that friends, lovers, parents, or significant others must give it to me. I am entitled to ask for it or to try to get it by any means that respects others' rights. However, one of the rights (of myself and others) is to refuse any request without justifying myself.

2. I didn't get what I wanted and that's frustrating. Is it possible to still find a way to get it? Is it worth the effort or do I want to go on to other things?

3. I don't like your frustrating me and I feel annoyed but that does not mean that you are evil or malicious. There are five good reasons you or I would do something that is annoying or fail to do something that is pleasing: (a) stupidity or lack of ability, (b) ignorance or lack of skill, (c) disturbance or upset, (d) habit, and (e) self-interest.

(Surprisingly, it usually takes little persuasion to get clients to agree that none of these motives are worthy of blame.)

4. Even if your (or my) behavior is not blameworthy, I do not like it and do not want to suffer it again.

   a. When I am hurt because of stupidity, I may want to *avoid* that person or situation.
   b. When I am hurt out of ignorance or lack of skill, I may want to *educate* or *train* myself or others.
   c. When I am hurt out of disturbance, I want to *help the other person to calm down* or *avoid them until they do calm down*.
   d. When I am hurt from habit, I may want to *learn* or *help the other person learn alternative habits*.
   e. When I am hurt by a conflict of interest, I may want to *negotiate a workable compromise*.

17. Discrimination Training. Discrimination training is a process of teaching clients ways of classifying and labeling that may later serve as valuable cues for appropriate behaviors.

An example from marital therapy is the training in "pinpointing." Couples are taught to translate abstract statements of blame ("You don't love me") into operational statements ("You interrupted me"). One ploy that Weiss (1973) reports using is pretending to be a "Martian" and having clients describe their problems to him, taking this into account. Programs for low-frequency daters have attempted to teach students how to discriminate approachable and unapproachable partners.

An example from assertion training covers the difference between assertive, aggressive, and nonassertive (i.e., passive or indirect) behavior usually in a short lecture by the therapist. Another teaching device is the Discrimination Test (Jakubowski, 1975), which consists of short descriptions of interpersonal situations followed by a possible response. Clients are asked to read each situation and classify the response as assertive, aggressive, or nonassertive. A score of 90% or better by the client is taken to indicate understanding of the concepts. A sample item is given below:

Situation	*Response*
You have set aside 4:00 to 5:00 for things you want or need to do. Someone asks to see you at that time. You say:	Well, uh, I can see you at that time. It's 4:00 Monday then. Are you sure that's a good time for you?

The above example is correctly scored as passive.

The test can be given to clients in written form or the test can be administered through a tape recorder and used as a stimulus for group discussion. Each member of the group is asked to write his response individually and then share it with the group. The therapist emphasizes that the concepts are easy to understand in the abstract but difficult to apply in specific situations. The individuals who misidentified a response are questioned to determine the source of their misunderstanding. The therapist can then provide the correct label for the response, and most important, provide the rationale. Common confusions that the therapist can explain include labeling nonassertion as politeness, seeing the failure to respond to another's request as aggressiveness, etc.

18. Development of an Assertive Belief System. An assertive belief system is composed of two basic beliefs: (1) that assertive rather than manipulative, submissive, or hostile behavior ultimately leads to effective interpersonal relationships; and (2) that everyone, including the client, has certain basic rights, including the right to act assertively and express honest thoughts, feelings, and beliefs (Lange and Jakubowski, 1976, pp. 64–65).

A convenient way to define styles of influence is in terms of at-

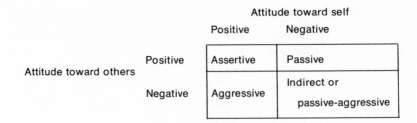

Figure 2. Styles of interpersonal behavior.

titudes toward self and others. Our conceptualization (see Figure 2) generates four styles of behavior defined as follows: *Assertive behavior* is that which involves both a high degree of respect for one's own rights and needs in a situation and respect or acknowledgment of the rights and needs of the other person involved. It should be noted that respect for the rights of others is not always the same as agreement with the other's wishes but implies acceptance of the other person's needs as legitimate and worthy of consideration. *Aggression* refers to a behavioral style that is high in respect for one's own rights or wishes but low in respect for the other person. In other words, aggressive behavior involves both an effort to have one's own rights prevail and a failure to acknowledge the legitimacy of the other person's needs. Such behavior may include put-downs, hostility, humiliation, etc. *Passive behavior* includes actions that acknowledge the rights of the other person but fail to include one's own rights. Passive behavior is characterized by the fact that the other person's needs or wishes always take precedence over the individual's. *Indirect* or *passive-aggressive behavior* involves lack of respect for the rights of both oneself and the other person. A person displaying this style of behavior does not express his needs and wishes in a forthright manner, but rather does so in an indirect or manipulative way. In addition, the behavior often has aggressive components directed toward the other person, such as compliments that are in fact put-downs, etc.

One technique to introduce an assertive belief system is *therapist lectures* about the consequences of different behavioral styles. For example, the belief that passive behavior leads to liking or that aggression is the most effective way to elicit cooperation can be challenged. The therapist can suggest that passive behavior may cause others to lose respect for a person rather than like him, and that aggression may lead to initial cooperation but ultimate sabotage from others. *Therapist modeling* can also be employed to help clients develop a responsible assertive belief system. The therapist models assertive behavior in the group and engages in behavior that supports the principle that everybody has a right to have their feelings considered and respected.

19. Identifying Rights. Specific strategies for identifying rights include *bibliotherapy,* assigning readings such as *Your Perfect Right,* by Alberti and Emmons (1974) and group discussions wherein members can support each other in accepting a new right. Group feedback can be used to challenge "socialization messages" (Lange and Jakubowski, 1976, p. 86). These are assertion-inhibiting ideas that people have internalized, e.g., thinking of others first, give to others even if you are hurting.

If members appear to accept rights intellectually but feel uncomfortable about them emotionally, more involving *Gestalt techniques* such as the Perls's empty chair, in which the client alternates between two chairs in conducting dialogue with herself (see Lange and Jakubowski, 1976), can be used.

20. Identifying Arousal. Techniques to correctly identify arousal are often used as preliminary exercises in assertiveness-training exercises with clients who are generally unaware of their internal states until they reach disturbing proportions, or clients who attribute their anxiety symptoms to medical causes (e.g., assuming that stomachaches indicate ulcers, etc.). Clients are instructed that these symptoms may actually be indicators of anxiety and are given a list to help them identify motor symptoms (e.g., flushing, sweating, dry mouth, startle reaction, pounding pulse) and affective and cognitive symptoms (e.g., panic, depression, dread, inattention, forgetfulness); see Cotler and Guerra (1976) for a complete list.

21. Subjective Units of Disturbance Scale (SUDS). In order to help clients become aware of their internal arousal states, Wolpe developed the SUDS scale (1969). Clients are asked to think of a situation in which they felt very relaxed and comfortable and to give that situation a rating of zero. They are then asked to imagine a scene at the other end of the continuum that would result in a feeling of high anxiety or panic and give that situation a rating of 100. They are then asked to rate their current feelings with a specific number.

If the client responds with a range, e.g., 20–30, he is asked to be more specific. To enhance understanding of the scale, clients can be asked to think of eight additional situations that fall between the 0 and 100 mark.

22. *SUDS Diary*. The SUDS Diary is a record sheet used to train clients to recognize relaxation and anxiety and to show them the relationship between daily situations and their internal states. Clients are given a written sheet as a homework assignment. They are asked to record specific situations along with a number on the SUDS scale and a description of their specific physiological responses. For example, "opened a bill I knew would be high," SUDS = 40, "hands sweating, stomach tight" (see Cotler and Guerra, 1976).

23. *Thought-Stopping*. The client is asked to focus on the anxiety-inducing repetitive thoughts that have been disturbing him. The therapist waits a short period of time and then shouts, "Stop!" or makes a loud noise. After several repetitions of this procedure, when the client reports that his thoughts were interrupted, the locus of control is shifted to the client. He is asked to say, "Stop!" to himself when the obsessive thoughts occur. He can do this out loud at first and then subvocally.

24. *Changing Language*. The client is asked to substitute assertive phrases such as "I want" or "I would like to" instead of absolute phrases such as "I must," "I have to," or "I need to" during everyday conversations to increase self-perceptions of assertiveness. Other people in the client's environment may perceive the client as more assertive following such relatively minor language changes (Sorenson and Cavior, 1977).

25. *Perspective-Taking or Role Reversal*. Role reversal is useful in teaching a client the impact her behavior has on other people. Usually the therapist plays the part of the client while the client plays the part of the other person in a problematic interpersonal situation (e.g., boss, friend, parent). The technique has been used to develop trust.

A variation used in social-skills training with children involves the alternate use of a doll by the child and the therapist. The doll plays the role of the child protagonist, teacher, or peer while the other person responds to the doll in the reciprocal role. The consequences of both appropriate and inappropriate social behavior are role-played and discussed (Slaby, 1976).

26. Symbolic Modeling on Films and Tapes. By devising a careful film sequence, the therapist can present rather complex social interactions in a dramatic manner that controls the viewer's attention to relevant cues. The exclusion of extraneous events and the enthusiastic and emotionally expressive behavior of the models can enhance attention and vicarious learning in the viewer. Two important components of this technique are presentation of positive consequences to the filmed model and the use of a narrator to explain the rules the socially competent models are employing. The reader is referred to O'Connor's work on the modification of social withdrawal in nursery-school children (O'Connor, 1969; 1972). Films can also be used to teach assertion (see Research Press, *Actualization Through Assertion*). A particularly comprehensive set of modeling tapes for use with a diverse client population, including lower- and working-class patients, has been prepared by Arnold Goldstein; the reader is referred to his book *Structured Learning Therapy: Towards a Psychotherapy for the Poor* (1973).

27. Instructions and Information. Rules for effective interaction can be presented to clients in written form, for example, giving shy males and females a dating manual (McGovern, Arkowitz, and Gilmore, 1975).

28. Counter Attitudinal Advocacy. Based on the research in cognitive dissonance theory, this technique involves the client reciting the counterarguments to his present position. By having the client think up counterarguments and present them orally to the therapist, the client may convince himself of the reasonableness of the position he is arguing. For instance, a person could be asked to give all the arguments why he could attend a party even though he is anxious.

COGNITIVE TECHNIQUES FOR BEHAVIOR CHANGE

1. Graded Task Assignment (Success Therapy). This technique is designed to combat passivity and overgeneralized beliefs of personal inadequacy and incompetence. The therapist begins by assigning the client a task that he can handle successfully. As long as an effort is made, the therapist interprets it as a success. As the client's competence increases, more complex and demanding activities are included. This technique is useful both in the therapeutic session and for homework assignments. The utility of this technique may be increased by asking the patient to make note of his/her cognition while performing the tasks. Cognitions that interfere with successful task performance may then be explored by client and therapist.

2. *Guided Rehearsal.* During the initial stages of behavioral rehearsal, or when a situation is particularly difficult for the client to handle, more intense prompting may be given by the therapist. One technique for guided rehearsal is *doubling* (Liberman, King, DeRisi, and McCann, 1975). Doubling begins with the therapist standing just to the rear of the client and actually playing the client's role in the behavioral rehearsal scene. The therapist gradually reduces his participation and allows the client to take over. A similar result may be achieved by delivering prompts to the client by way of a "bug in the ear" device.

3. *Modeling.* The therapist or other competent individual may demonstrate for the client ways to manage a problem situation in an effective manner. Modeling has proven to be an efficient way to teach relatively complex behaviors, especially the nonverbal and expressive components. A model will be more effective if he is seen as having high status and competence; if he is similar in age, sex, and other characteristics to the client; and if he is rewarded for the behavior displayed (Bandura, 1969; Goldstein, 1973). Learning of the rules involved would be enhanced by use of multiple models and by requesting the client to verbalize the rule governing the completed performance of the model.

4. *Coaching.* A coach serves to provide feedback and positive reinforcement to the client as well as prompting him or her when he or she encounters difficulties. The role of the coach is an active one; verbal and nonverbal feedback is given continually by the coach as the client practices new behavior. In the initial stages, the coach may essentially be providing all of the words for the client. As the client becomes more skillful, the role of the coach shifts to providing positive reinforcement and feedback. More effective coaching would involve emphasis of underlying rules such as "increased eye contact indicates interest in the other person."

5. *Behavioral Rehearsal*. Behavioral rehearsal involves the role-playing of a previously experienced or anticipated situation that has been or is expected to be difficult for the client to handle. The focus is the client's verbal and nonverbal behavior. Behavioral rehearsal is one of the basic components of assertiveness training (Liberman *et al.*, 1975; Cotler and Guerra, 1976). This technique combines *in vivo* desensitization and skill training.

6. *Homework*. Specific assignments may be given the client between therapy sessions. Generally, these assignments consist of practicing behaviors or coping strategies and keeping records of the client's progress. Homework assignments are given in hierarchical order with the least difficult tasks being assigned first in order to maximize the probability of success (Liberman *et al.*, 1975; Cotler and Guerra, 1976). Maultsby (1971) has suggested the following rationale be given to the client for homework assignments: (1) By doing homework, the client can rehearse and practice more appropriate ways of talking to himself; (2) it increases the probability of more adaptive behaviors; (3) it provides appropriate self-counseling around the clock; (4) it extinguishes undesirable thinking habits by making the client more aware of self-defeating habits; (5) it reinforces self-change by increasing the client's skill in realistic thinking, decreasing the frequency of emotional conflict, and increasing the client's ability to control his behavior; (6) it provides tools for handling future problems; (7) it provides an understanding of one's problems; and (8) regular homework is prophylactic against temptations to give in to self-defeating ideas.

Gary Emery has proposed a set of useful guidelines for making homework assignments in cognitive behavior therapy (see Beck *et al.*, 1976). Briefly, he suggests that the patient has to believe that the homework is meaningful. The reasons for doing the homework, as well as the instructions for how to do it, should be extremely clear. In addition, the patient should feel that he has some input into the assignment. He suggests that an experimental set is more appropriate than a prescriptive set; i.e., instead of saying, "This will work for you," say "Why not try it on for size?" or "What do you have to lose and what do you have to gain?" Homework should be individual and possible problems and alternatives anticipated and discussed. Homework should be specific enough to determine whether the homework goal was attained. Both therapist and client should have a written copy of the assignment, including responsibilities of the therapist and his or her homework. He suggests that bibliotherapy makes excellent homework assignments. Another suggested assignment is listening to the sessions' tapes.

In reviewing homework, Emery suggests that all homework be checked at the beginning of the session to determine completion. In addition, the client's cognitions concerning the homework are requested, e.g., was it too simple, too difficult, or did he think it was busy work? Any attempt to complete this assignment is treated as a success.

When assignments are not completed, Emery suggests to first check to see if the instructions were clear and meaningful. If they were, the therapist may wish to teach the client some homework aids. These aids include stimulus control procedures, the use of cognitive self-therapy, and the use of the Premack principle to program external self-reinforcement. Follow-up calls by the therapist may be used either as cues or reinforcers. For the most difficult cases he suggests contingency contracting, i.e., if the client does not complete his assignment, then the therapist implements a response cost, i.e., paying for the therapy hour but not being allowed to attend.

7. Stress-Inoculation Training. Stress-inoculation training is a self-instructional method developed by Meichenbaum for the purpose of teaching clients to cope with anxiety (Novaco and Turk discuss similar methods for coping with anger and pain in this volume). It involves discussing the nature of emotion and stress reactions, rehearsing coping self-statements and relaxation skills, and testing these skills under actual stress conditions. The focus is on coping and functioning despite the aversive affect rather than completely mastering the affect.

8. Systematic Rational Restructuring. Goldfried developed this procedure based on Ellis's rational-emotive therapy. After exposure to an imagined upsetting experience, the client is asked to label the degree of arousal and to use his negative affective state as a cue for exploring and describing self-defeating attitudes or expectations about the affect-arousing situation. The self-defeating statements are then reevaluated rationally, first with the therapist and then by the client himself, and reduction in affect is noted after rational reevaluation has taken place. The affect-provoking situations are arranged hierarchically as in desensitization. Goldfried, Decenteceo, and Weinberg (1974) describe this procedure as one in which the client learns to control his affect by modifying the cognitive set he adopts in approaching upsetting situations.

9. *Covert Modeling*. In covert modeling, the client imagines a model performing the desired behavior rather than actually observing a live or filmed model. For example, a client might imagine a peer introducing himself to a group or asking his boss for a raise. Kazdin (1973; 1974) has demonstrated that covert modeling can be effective for both reducing anxiety and developing new response patterns. As with overt modeling, the characteristics of the model contribute to the effectiveness of the technique; i.e., models of the same age and sex as the client are most effective. Visualization of multiple models is more effective than visualization of a single model, and the effect is greater if the models are reinforced than if no consequence is visualized. Better results are obtained when the client imagines coping models as opposed to mastery models.

10. *Being Coach for Another*. This technique calls for the client to serve as coach while two others role-play a situation. As the actors play the scene, the coach suggests lines to the antagonist. Cognitions that interfere with successful task performance may then be explored by client and therapist.

11. *Stimulus Control*. The objective of stimulus control is to set up environmental conditions in a way that makes it impossible or unfavorable for the undesired behavior to occur. As a cognitive technique, stimulus control consists of training self-generated verbal responses while making no changes in the physical environment. These self-instructions may include statements about resisting temptation, putting up with aversive situations, handling a situation effectively, or controlling anxiety or anger. Self-rewarding statements about effective behavior and similar verbal cues can serve as stimuli that can exert control over future behavior.

12. *Cognitive Modeling*. Cognitive modeling was originally developed by Meichenbaum and has been greatly expanded by Goldstein in his Structured Learning tapes for psychiatric patients. Essentially it involves the model thinking out loud. It appears to be an excellent method for the direct teaching of relevant underlying

TABLE II. EXAMPLE OF TAPE TRANSCRIPT

Social Interaction—Cognitive Modeling: Type I
Scene I
P: Hello, my name is Tom. How are you?
M: Hmm, let me see, what am I supposed to do? I'm new here and I don't know
    anyone yet, but I do want to get to know the other people on the floor. So what
    should I do? There are four things I'm supposed to do. (1) I'm supposed to an-
    swer questions when somebody asks me something, try to make conversation
    when someone comes over to me. (2) I'm supposed to also talk to them, ask
    them questions. O.K. so far. (3) I'm supposed to make sense, talk so that Tom
    here can understand me. (4) I'm supposed to talk a lot, not just say yes or no.
    O.K., I think I know what to do. I'll talk to Tom now. That way, I can get to
    know him. I'll answer the questions he asked me. First, I'll tell him my name,
    then I'll tell him that I feel fine. That will answer his questions. I could also ask
    him questions about himself . . . that'll start a conversation. But I have to
    remember to ask good questions, something that he'd be interested in. I'll ask
    him how long he's been here at the hospital and how he likes it. Those are good
    questions. He'll understand what I'm saying. Hey, that's pretty good, I figured
    it all out. Pretty smart of me.

---

[a] From Goldstein, 1973 with permission.

rules. An example from the transcripts of one of Goldstein's tapes is given in Table II (Goldstein, 1973, p. 26).

Focusing–experiencing is a method of helping a client increase his awareness, accurate perception, and use of his ongoing affective experience. It was originally developed by Gendlin and his co-workers (Gendlin, Beebe, Cassens, Klein, and Oberlander, 1968; Gendlin, 1969). Goldstein has adapted the method and incorporated it into his structured-learning therapy.

13. Scripting. "Scripting" is a label that may be given to a variety of methods that have been used to help restructure problematic interpersonal behaviors into constructive interaction by providing a script that serves a cueing function for constructive behaviors. Examples are Weiss's Flow Chart for Conflict Resolution (1976) and Bower and Bower's (1976) DESC Scripts. These scripts may be provided by the therapist or written by the clients themselves.

The above catalog of techniques was presented to indicate the wide range of interventions available. The reader is referred to the original sources for greater detail.

SUMMARY AND CONCLUSIONS

Our attempt to use a structural-learning model to conceptualize the task of the therapist who seeks to improve the social performance of his client indicates that such a model may provide a helpful unifying framework. However, much more data on social interaction is needed in order to use the model systematically. Marital therapy research and its clinical applications is probably the best example of the way the model could be used. The extensive amount of data in this area has identified the tasks that make up a successful marriage as well as specified behavioral objectives derived from the tasks and the underlying rules that happily married couples use. On the basis of this information, several comprehensive training packages have been developed (see Jacobson and Martin, 1976). It is here that the structural-learning model might provide a framework for future efforts toward combining research and clinical experience productively.

A second conclusion to be drawn from our paper is similar to the point made by Wilson earlier in the volume concerning the distinction between treatment procedure and theoretical process. Although cognitive processes play a crucial role in social behavior, cognitive techniques are not necessarily the most effective techniques for bringing about behavior change. Instead, we have argued that cognitive factors are involved in specifying the underlying rules governing social performance and that these rules can be taught through a variety of techniques, both cognitive and behavioral. In fact, it is the combination of interventions that may offer the most promise.

REFERENCES

Alberti, R.E., and Emmons, M.L. *Your perfect right: A guide to assertive behavior* (2nd ed.). San Luis Obispo, Calif.: Impact Press, 1974.

Bandura, A. *Principles of behavior modification.* Holt, Rinehart and Winston, 1969.

Bandura, A. Self-efficacy: Toward a unifying theory of behavioral change. *Psychological Review*, 1977, *84*, 191–215.

Beck, A.T. Cognitive therapy: Nature and relation to behavior therapy. *Behavior Therapy*, 1970, *1*, 184–200.

Beck, A.T., Rush, A.J., and Kovacs, M. *Individual treatment manual for cogni-*

tive/behavioral psychotherapy of depression. Philadelphia, Pa.: University of Pennsylvania, 1976.

Bellack, A.S., and Hersen, M. Behavior modification: An introductory textbook. Baltimore, Md.: Williams and Wilkens Co., 1976.

Birchler, G.R., Weiss, R.L., and Vincent, J.P. A multimethod analysis of social reinforcement exchange between maritally distressed and nondistressed spouse and stranger dyads. Journal of Personality and Social Psychology, 1975, 31 (2), 349–360.

Bower, S.A., and Bower, G. Asserting your self. Reading, Mass.: Addison-Wesley, 1976.

Cotler, S.B., and Guerra, J.J. Assertion training. Champaign, Ill.: Research Press, 1976.

D'Zurilla, T.J., and Goldfried, M.R. Problem solving and behavior modification. Journal of Abnormal Psychology, 1971, 78, 107–126.

Ellis, A. A guide to rational living. London: Prentice-Hall, 1961.

Ellis, A. The essence of rational psychotherapy: A comprehensive approach to treatment. New York: Institute for Rational Living, 1970.

Ellis, A. Rational-emotive therapy. In R.M. Jurjevich (Ed.), Directive psychotherapy. Miami: University of Miami Press, 1971.

Festinger, L. A theory of cognitive dissonance. Evanston, Ill.: Row, Peterson, 1957.

Freedman, M.P. An analysis of social-behavioral skill deficits in delinquent and nondelinquent adolescent boys. Unpublished doctoral dissertation, University of Wisconsin at Madison, 1974.

Gendlin, E.T. Focusing. Psychotherapy: Theory, Research, and Practice, 1969, 6, 4–15.

Gendlin, E.T., Beebe, J., Cassens, J., Klein, M., and Oberlander, M. Focusing ability in psychotherapy, personality and creativity. In J.M. Shlien, H.F. Hunt, J.D. Matarazzo, and C. Savage (Eds.), Research in Psychotherapy (Vol. 3). Washington, D.C.: American Psychological Association, 1968, 217–241.

Goldfried, M.R., and Davison, G.C. Clinical behavior therapy. New York: Holt, Rinehart and Winston, 1976.

Goldfried, M.R., and D'Zurilla, T.J. A behavioral analytic model for assessing competence. In C.D. spielberger (Ed.), Current topics in clinical and community psychology (Vol. 1). New York: Academic Press, 1969.

Goldfried, M.R., Decenteceo, E.T., and Weinberg, L. Systematic rational restructuring as a self-control technique. Behavior Therapy, 1974, 5, 247–254.

Goldsmith, J.B., and McFall, R.M. Development and evaluation of an interpersonal skill-training program for psychiatric inpatients. Journal of Abnormal Psychology, 1975, 84, 51–58.

Goldstein, A.P. Structured learning therapy: Toward a psychotherapy for the poor. New York: Academic Press, 1973.

Hauck, P.A. Overcoming frustration and anger. Philadelphia, Pa.: Westminster Press, 1977.

Hersen, M., and Bellack, A.S. (Eds.). Behavioral assessment: A practical handbook. Oxford: Pergamon Press, 1976.

Jacobson, N.S., and Martin, B. Behavioral marriage therapy: Current status. Psychological Bulletin, 1976, 83, (4), 540–556.

Jakubowski, P.A. A discrimination measure of assertion concepts. Unpublished manuscript, University of Missouri, St. Louis, 1975.

Jones, E.E., Kanouse, D.E., Kelly, H.H., Nisbett, R.D., Valins, S., and Weiner, B. Attribution: Perceiving the causes of behavior. Morristown, N.J.: General Learning Press, 1972.

Jones, R.G. A factored measure of Ellis' irrational belief system with personality and maladjustment correlates. Ph.D. Thesis, Texas Technological College, 1968.

Jourard, S.M. The transparent self: Self-disclosure and well being. Princeton, N.J.: Van Nostrand, 1964.

Kazdin, A.E. Covert modeling and the reduction of avoidance behavior. Journal of Abnormal Psychology, 1973, 81, 87–95.

Kazdin, A.E. Effects of covert modeling and model reinforcement on assertive behavior. Journal of Abnormal Psychology, 1974, 83, 240–252.

Knox, D. Dr. Knox's marital exercise book. New York: David McKay Co., Inc., 1975.

Lange, A., and Jakubowski, P. Responsible assertive behavior. Champaign, Ill.: Research Press, 1976.

Liberman, R.P., King, L.W., DeRisi, W.J., and McCann, M. Personal effectiveness: Guiding people to assert themselves and improve their social skills. Champaign, Ill.: Research Press, 1975.

Mager, R.F., and Pipe, P. Analysing performance problems. Fearon, 1970.

Mahoney, M.J. Cognition and behavior modification. Cambridge, Mass.: Ballinger Publishing Co., 1974.

Mahoney, M.J. Reflections on the cognitive-learning trend in psychotherapy. American Psychologist, 1977, 32, 5–13.

Maultsby, M. Systematic written homework in psychotherapy. Rational Living, 1971, 6, 17–23.

Maultsby, M.C., and Ellis, A. Technique for using rational-emotive imagery (REI). New York: Institute for Rational Living, 1974.

McFall, R.M. Behavioral training: A skill-acquisition approach to clinical problems. Morristown, N.J.: General Learning Press, 1976.

McGovern, K., Arkowitz, H., and Gilmore, S. Evaluation of social skills training programs for college dating inhibitions. Journal of Counseling Psychology, 1975, 22, 505–512.

Meichenbaum, D. A cognitive-behavior modification approach to assessment. In M. Hersen and A.S. Bellack (Eds.), Behavioral assessment: A practical handbook. Oxford: pergamon Press, 1976.

Meijers, J.A. A cognitive assessment of socially withdrawn children. Cited as personal communication, 1974, in M. Hersen and A.S. Bellack (Eds.), Behavioral assessment: A practical handbook. Oxford: Pergamon Press, 1976, 170.

O'Connor, R.D. Modification of social withdrawal through symbolic modeling. Journal of Applied Behavior Analysis, 1969, 2, 15–22.

O'Connor, R.D. Relative efficacy of modeling, shaping, and the combined procedures for modification of social withdrawal. Journal of Abnormal Psychology, 1972, 79, 327–334.

Patterson, G.R., Hops, H., and Weiss, R.L. Interpersonal skills training for couples in early stages of conflict. Journal of Marriage and the Family, 1975.

Patterson, G.R., Reid, J.B., Jones, R.R., and Conger, R.E. A social learning approach to family intervention: Families with aggressive children (Vol. 1). Eugene, Ore.: Castalia Publishing Co., 1975.

Patterson, M. An arousal model of interpersonal intimacy. Psychological Review, 1976, 235–245.

Platt, J., and Spivak, G. Social competence and effective problem-solving thinking in psychiatric patients. *Journal of Clinical Psychology*, 1972, *28*, 3–5.

Rich, A. R., and Schroeder, H. E. Research issues in assertiveness training. *Psychological Bulletin*, 1976, *83* (6), 1081–1096.

Rimm, D.C., and Masters, J.C. *Behavior therapy: Techniques and empirical findings*. New York: Academic Press, 1974.

Scandura, J.M. *Structural learning I: Theory and research*. New York: Gordon and Breach, Science Publishers, 1973a.

Scandura, J.M. Structural learning and the design of educational materials. *Educational Technology*, 1973b, *13*, 7–13.

Scandura, J.M. Structural approach to instructional problems. American Psychologist, 1977, *32*, 33–53.

Scandura, J.M., and Durin, J.H. Assessing behavior potential: Adequacy of basic theoretical assumptions. *Journal of Structural Learning*, 1978.

Schwartz, R., and Gottman, J.M. A task analysis approach to clinical problems: A study of assertive behavior. Unpublished manuscript, Indiana University, 1974.

Shure, M., and Spivak, G. Means-ends thinking, adjustment and social class among elementary school-aged children. *Journal of Consulting and Clinical Psychology*, 1972, *38*, 348–353.

Slaby, D.A. Day treatment and parent training programs. Unpublished manuscript, Children's Orthopedic Hospital and Medical Center, Seattle, Wash., 1976.

Sorenson, R.H., and Cavior, N. The effects of specific word usage on experienced and perceived assertiveness. Paper presented at the 57th Annual Western Psychological Association Convention, 1977.

Spivak, G., and Shure, M.B. *Social adjustment of young children: A cognitive approach to solving real-life problems*. San Francisco: Jossey-Bass Publishers, 1974.

Watson, D., and Friend, R. Measurement of social-evaluative anxiety. *Journal of Consulting and Clinical Psychology*, 1969, *33*, 448–457.

Weiss, R.L. Strategies for couples' therapy. Workshop presented at the Association for Advancement of Behavior Therapy, December, 1976.

Weiss, R.L., Hops, H., and Patterson, G.R. A framework for conceptualizing marital conflict, a technology for altering it, some data for evaluating it. In L.A. Hamerlynck, L.C. Handy, and E.J. Mash (Eds.), *Behavior change: Methodology, concepts, and practice*. Champaign, Ill.: Research Press, 1973.

Weiss, R.L., and Isaac, J. Behavioral vs. cognitive measures as predictors of marital satisfaction. Paper presented at Western Psychological Association, April, 1976.

Wolpe, J. *The practice of behavior therapy*. New York: Pergamon, 1969.

3

Cognitive Behavioral Strategies in the Treatment of Sexual Problems

JEFFREY C. STEGER

The importance of cognitive mediation in the experience of sexual sensations has long been an accepted, albeit marginally comprehended, tenet among scholars and laymen. The symbolic nature of most aphrodisiacs, designed to stimulate the imagination more than the physiology (e.g., ground rhinoceros' horns, powdered lions' penises), further attests to the significance of cognitive processes in sexual activities. The progression of systematic investigation regarding sexuality has followed that of the other behavioral sciences: beginning with external, more easily observable events and eventually including thoughts, feelings, or attitudes as part of the investigatory realm. This strategy has yielded a set of effective

JEFFREY C. STEGER • Department of Rehabilitation Medicine, University of Washington School of Medicine, Seattle, Washington 98195. This project was supported in part by a Rehabilitation Services Administration Grant 16P-56818/0-15 to the Physical Medicine and Rehabilitation Department, University of Washington School of Medicine.

therapeutic techniques focusing primarily upon sexual behavior change, which only recently have included specific cognitive interventions.

Classic behavioral intervention strategies have been extensively described by Bandura (1969), Lazarus (1972), Ullmann and Krasner (1965), and Wolpe (1969), and usually involve techniques based on operant conditioning, classical conditioning, and social learning theory applied to overt behavior problems. Cognitive behavioral strategies are generally those techniques designed to alter covert behavior (e.g., thoughts, feelings) and not necessarily relying on external rewards or punishments.

The purpose of this chapter is to briefly review the efficacy of various strategies in the treatment of commonly occurring sexual problems and to identify and illustrate the cognitive techniques used in these various approaches. For the purposes of this chapter, cognitive procedures are conceptualized as the ways sex therapists mobilize expectations, attitudes, and cognitive sets of self-instruction to facilitate and maintain therapeutic gains in people with sexual difficulties.

Many of the cognitive techniques presented in these pages have been applied to the treatment of various nonsexual psychological problems (e.g., test anxiety, speech phobia) and their efficacy for these difficulties has been evaluated (e.g., Cautela, 1967; Meichenbaum, 1972; Sarason, 1973). In addition, certain cognitive techniques have been used in directly modifying sexual behavior (e.g., Ellis, 1975; Flowers, 1975; and Wish, 1975), while other techniques described in this chapter have been included based on the assumption that they will prove valuable adjuncts to treatment when the appropriate research studies have been completed. In this way, an attempt has been made to present the efficacy of those cognitive behavioral strategies that have been evaluated in the treatment of sexual difficulties, while describing those untested cognitive techniques. It is hoped, therefore, that sex therapists and sex therapy researchers in the immediate future will include these strategies in their treatment and research paradigms to facilitate evaluation of each technique's utility in the treatment of various sexual problems.

Definition of Sexual Difficulties

Kanfer and Saslow (1969) have suggested a succinct behavioral analysis system for determining appropriate target behaviors prior to initiating therapy. This system classifies behaviors into assets, excesses, and deficits and can be applied to overt and covert behavior. Applied to sexual behavior, the following definitions are consonant with their framework:

1. *Behavioral Assets.* These are defined as those nonproblematic sexual areas in which the person does well. These behaviors are usually taken into account during treatment, but rarely constitute the focus of treatment.

2. *Behavioral Excesses.* This term describes those sexual activities described as problematic by the client or an informant due to an excess in frequency, intensity, duration, or occurrence in socially unsanctioned situations. Examples of sexual excesses would be exhibitionism, masochism, and pedophilia.

3. *Behavioral Deficits.* Those sexual behaviors seen as problematic due to insufficient frequency, inadequate intensity, inappropriate form, or lack of occurrence in expected conditions are referred to as behavioral deficits. Examples of sexual deficits would be erectile failure, orgasmic dysfunction, and premature ejaculation (a lack of desired control).

Within this system, problematic homosexual behavior can involve both excesses (soliciting sexual activities in public with the same sex) and deficits (no erection or arousal in heterosexual activity, infrequent approaching of the opposite sex).

In a recent publication, Annon (1975) reviewed the effective treatment strategies for sexual-behavior excesses. He concluded that longer-term intervention (more than 15–20 sessions) and aversive conditioning paradigms were generally necessary to yield adequate improvement for such problems (e.g., fetishism, exhibitionism, transvestism). While some cognitive modification techniques have been posited as useful in treating sexual excesses (i.e., those that increase avoidance responses), the major source of outcome variance in such cases appears due to aversive conditioning techniques like electric shock (Max, 1935) or aversive drugs (James,

1962). Given this trend, the lack of controlled studies comparing cognitive and noncognitive approaches in this area, and the limited scope of this chapter, sexual excesses will not be discussed (see Annon, 1975, for an excellent review). This chapter will focus on the treatment of behavioral deficits (often referred to as sexual dysfunctions) and those homosexual behaviors that interfere with a person's desire to engage in satisfying heterosexual activity.

It has been reported that sexual dysfunction may be related to some organic component in 3–20% of individuals referred for sexual treatment (Kaplan, 1974). This same author reported that in her therapeutic practice, only about 10% of the individuals seeking relief from sexual dysfunction were found to have some organic component to their difficulty (e.g., early diabetes, narcotics use, alcohol abuse, genital pathology, or neurological disease). Masters and Johnson (1970) also reported that less than 10% of the sexual problems treated in their program were primarily caused by organic difficulties. The treatment of clients with organically based sexual dysfunctions generally requires specific medical expertise and interventions that are beyond the scope of this paper. The focus of this chapter will be on those sexual difficulties with a primarily psychological etiology. Kaplan (1974) has summarized the opinion among sex therapists regarding the etiology of sexual dysfunction as follows:

> It is generally agreed that by far the great majority of sexual difficulties is created by experiential factors. There is, however, no agreement regarding the nature of these factors and considerable controversy and confusion exists in the field because many different and even contradictory "specific" psychological causes have been advanced by various authorities. (p. 117)

In other words, researchers agree that most sexual problems can be treated through psychological intervention, but few can agree regarding the appropriate treatment for a given difficulty. Part of this disparity lies in diagnostic confusion while the remainder appears related to theoretical differences in the approaches to therapy.

There are varying terms used to describe and label the different sexual difficulties. For the purposes of this chapter, the following definitions have been adapted and are primarily based upon those presented by Masters and Johnson (1970) and Annon (1974).

Premature Ejaculation. This diagnosis can be very subjective, but usually refers to the situation where a man cannot control his ejaculatory process for a sufficient length of time during vaginal containment to satisfy his partner in approximately 50% of their coital opportunities (with the stipulation that the female partner is not persistently inorgasmic for reasons other than the rapidity of the male's ejaculation).

Primary Erectile Failure (Also Referred to as Primary Impotence). This diagnosis applies to any male who had *never* been able to achieve and maintain an erection sufficient to accomplish successful coitus. Primary erectile failure does not apply to men who have at any time obtained an erection sufficient for intromission, whether in homosexual or heterosexual activities.

Secondary Erectile Failure (Secondary Impotence). This category refers to men who have experienced an erection sufficient for coitus (for example, during masturbation, homosexual encounters, or previous heterosexual intercourse), but who currently cannot obtain an erection adequate for initiating and maintaining coitus consistently (i.e., if failure to successfully complete coitus approaches 25% of the coital opportunities). This definition is not intended to apply to exclusively homosexual males who are not sexually aroused by females, but who consistently experience no erectile difficulty in their homosexual contacts and consider this pattern nonproblematic.

Vaginismus. This term refers to the situation where a woman experiences spastic contractions of the outer third of the vaginal muscles (this muscle contraction activity may also involve the pelvic musculature as well as the perineum) that are of sufficient strength and duration to prohibit entry of the penis into the vagina. Dyspareunia (painful entry or intercourse) is usually associated with vaginismus in women and these two diagnostic categories are generally treated in the same manner behaviorally.

Primary Orgasmic Dysfunction (Frigidity). This is a common sexual difficulty and refers to women who have never experienced an orgasm through any source of stimulation (i.e., masturbation, intercourse, heterosexual petting, or homosexual encounters).

Secondary or Situational Orgasmic Dysfunction (Sometimes Referred to as Low Libido or Low Sex Drive). This category refers to women who have experienced orgasm through some modality (e.g., masturbation, homosexual petting, or past heterosexual intercourse), but who currently experience sporatic or no orgasmic response with their established sexual partners. It should be noted that Masters and Johnson (1970) separate this category into three types of situations: (1) masturbatory orgasmic inadequacy (orgasmic release with a partner but not during masturbation); (2) coital orgasmic inadequacy (the ability to experience orgasm from some noncoital stimulus, but an inability to have an orgasm during coitus); and (3) random orgasmic inadequacy (women who have experienced an orgasm at least once during both masturbation and coitus but this response occurs very infrequently and apparently at random).

Since these three situations have not been consistently differentiated by other authors in the available research, the term "secondary inorgasmic dysfunction" will be used in this chapter to refer to any situational orgasmic difficulty.

Ejaculatory Incompetence (Retarded Ejaculation). This diagnosis refers to the inability of a male to ejaculate during heterosexual intercourse. Two types of difficulty have been specified: (1) primary ejaculatory incompetence (having never ejaculated intravaginally); and (2) secondary ejaculation incompetence (a past ability to ejaculate intravaginally, but currently no ejaculation occurs during coition).

The relative rarity of ejaculatory incompetence (17 out of 448 of Masters and Johnson's male patients were referred with this difficulty) vitiates the evaluation of any treatment strategy's efficacy with this problem. Annon (1974) further notes the rarity of this malady and points out that it is occasionally included under the category of male impotence (an erroneous inclusion, since most men who suffer from ejaculatory incompetence experience erections sufficient to allow intercourse).

Homosexual Orientation. In the context of this chapter, this phrase applies to a man or woman whose arousal to same-sexed stimuli (whether *in vivo* or fantasized) in some way prohibits or decreases his or her interest or arousal in heterosexual activities. This category applies only to those individuals desiring to decrease their homosexual orientation in a way designed to facilitate increased heterosexual satisfaction. The inclusion of this category is not meant to imply that homosexual orientation needs to be decreased in general. This set of behavior is most frequently reported to be problematic in cases of erectile failure, ejaculatory incompetence, and secondary orgasmic dysfunction.

It is important to note that many of these sexual dysfunction categories occur concomitantly with each other (e.g., premature ejaculation is often associated with primary orgasmic dysfunction, while primary and secondary erectile failure often correlate with the existence of vaginismus). In a clinical situation, therefore, the treatment strategies often deal with these different sexual difficulties simultaneously. Accordingly, in many of the clinical case reports, it is not always possible to accurately separate the specific efficacy of a given treatment technique for a specific sexual problem. In addition to symptom overlap, another factor that permeates the sexual treatment literature and yields specious outcome results is that of varying success criteria. In an attempt to circumvent this analysis problem, the following terms and definitions apply in this chapter (unless reported otherwise):

Cure—relatively complete amelioration of the target symptom (e.g., 75% or "most" of one's sexual encounters yield no evidence of the problem).

Improvement—a persistent, though occasional, occurrence of the symptom (i.e., during more than 25% of one's sexual encounters), but posttreatment analysis indicates at least a 50% decrease (or increase where appropriate) in the target symptom when compared with baseline frequencies.

In this way, an attempt has been made to separate "cure" and "improvement" rates as well as differentiate strategies and their effectiveness for the various sexual problems.

Overview of the Strategies for the Treatment of Sexual Dysfunction

Long-Term Strategies. Long-term intervention has frequently been the strategy of choice in the history of psychotherapy. In the treatment of sexual difficulties, Freud (1938), Knight (1943), and Kaplan (1974) have suggested the psychoanalytic model as an effective therapeutic intervention. It is, therefore, not surprising that psychoanalysis is currently being applied as a major treatment strategy for various sexual difficulties. For example, O'Connor and Stern (1972) reported that 77% of their primary and secondary erectile failure (impotence) cases were "cured" following two years of psychoanalysis. In this same study, a comparison with a less psychoanalytically oriented strategy (i.e., Rogerian insight psychotherapy) yielded only a 46% cure rate after two years of treatment for this same type of sexual difficulty. Similarly, Friedman (1968) reported a cure rate of approximately 50% for 22 cases of male erectile failure (both primary and secondary) following an extended intervention with insight-oriented psychotherapy. In these studies, it appears that psychoanalysis has "an edge" over insight psychotherapy when treating male erectile failure.

Long-term psychotherapy has not fared as well with other sexual problems. For example, in the treatment of primary and secondary orgasmic dysfunction, O'Connor and Stern (1972) reported only a 25% cure rate following three to five years of psychoanalytic or insight-oriented psychotherapy. These results are consistent with a recent review of the literature suggesting that traditional psychotherapy has failed to help certain specific sexual difficulties (e.g., vaginismus, premature ejaculation, and orgasmic dysfunction) to the extent that some of the more recent brief therapy approaches have (Kaplan, 1974). Additional references regarding the effectiveness of long-term psychotherapy for various sexual difficulties are: impotence (Ovesey and Myers, 1968), primary and secondary inorgasmic dysfunction (Wittels, 1951), and ejaculatory incompetence (Friedman, 1973).

Short-Term Intervention—Nonbehavioral Approaches. Several short-term strategies have been applied to the treatment of sexual difficulties that do not fall within a behavioral or cognitive behavioral frame of reference. These include hypnosis, medical intervention using medication, and medical–mechanical strategies. Few controlled studies exist comparing the differential efficacy of these procedures with an alternative and most of the following reports are based on single-subject or multiple-case study reports.

Mirowitz (1966) reported a 52% cure rate with 42 male erectile failure cases following an hypnotic intervention requiring from 10 to 54 hours of therapy. While no control procedures were employed, these results are consistent with those of other hypnotic interventions in suggesting the general utility of hypnosis with respect to anxiety reduction and any psychological problem with some anxiety component (Hussain, 1964; Kaufman, 1967; and Kroger, 1969). Other hypnotic interventions have required an average of less than 10 hours of treatment and have occasionally resulted in as high a cure rate as 60%, with improvement in 94.7% of the cases, in the treatment of primary and secondary orgasmic dysfunction (August, 1959; Coulton, 1960; and Richardson, 1963).

Even more short-term oriented than the hypnotic intervention procedures are the medication and mechanical approaches. For example, in one case of premature ejaculation, a man was treated with Thioridizine on several occasions with reported success in delaying his ejaculatory latency (Singh, 1963). In a similar study, Friedman (1968) reported that testosterone injections had been effective in treating two of 12 cases of primary and secondary erectile failure. A single case study and a 16% cure rate are far from encouraging results; however, many mechanical and medical approaches have been tried with little more success. Specifically, erectile failure has been treated through means of splints and artificial phalluses (Kelly, 1961; Rubin, 1965) and primary and secondary orgasmic dysfunction have been treated with injections of androgen-estrogen compounds followed by antidepressant injections, explanation of sexual mechanisms, and techniques for clitoral stimulation (Bailey, 1973). Unfortunately, none of these techniques has been incorporated into a controlled study and the results of single case studies have not been overwhelmingly positive. There has, however, been one exception to this generalization and that relates to the efficacy of a physical exercise procedure referred to as the Kegel exercises (Kegel, 1952). That is, Deutsch (1968) reported a 65% improvement rate for inorgasmic women following systematic use of Kegel exercises at home. While this report was like the others in its lack of adequate controls, the improvement rate from a simple physical exercise is certainly impressive given the simplicity of such a procedure.

The final nonbehavioral treatment strategy to be reviewed is short-term group therapy. While most of the treatment populations for such short-term or "encounter" group procedures have been "normal or nonpathological" with respect to sexual functioning, several researchers have reported improved sexual functioning and sexual satisfaction as a result of these interventions. For example, Bindrim (1968, 1969) described nude encounter marathons where he reported having enhanced the sexual satisfaction of group members through nudity and sensitivity procedures. Similarly, Gunther (1971) advocates group sensory awareness training as a means for increasing sexual satisfaction. While these authors have reported positive results (with respect to increases in sexual satisfaction of the group members), there was no formal assessment and the actual long-term outcome of these procedures is uncertain. Short-term, intensive group experiences have been designed specifically for treating sexual dysfunctional individuals (Hartman and Fithian, 1970) and the more traditional group therapy approach (e.g., Stone and Levine, 1950) has also been used with sexual problems. As in the previous reports, the evaluation of the efficacy of these strategies was based mainly on subjective impressions of the therapists and further research is necessary before such approaches can be deemed effective in the treatment of specific sexual difficulties.

Short-Term Intervention—Behavioral Strategies. Within the past few years, much evidence has accumulated to support the utility of behavioral techniques in the treatment of various sexual difficulties. Such sexual dysfunctions as erectile failure and premature ejaculation in men and orgasmic dysfunction in women have been effectively treated by the behavior therapist where previous therapeutic intervention had failed (Kaplan, 1974; LoPiccolo and Lobitz, 1972; Masters and Johnson, 1970; Wolpe and Lazarus, 1966). Annon (1974) has summarized that "behavior therapists have made considerable progress in an area that has long been known for its resistance to treatment by other approaches" (p. 16). While the specific procedures for each behavioral intervention differ, most researchers agree that the general treatment strategy focuses on skill training in effective sexual behavior, reduction in performance anxiety concerning sexual interaction, and occasionally increasing communication between partners (e.g., Annon, 1974; LoPiccolo and Miller, 1975; Masters and Johnson, 1970).

The most commonly used strategies for the treatment of sexual dysfunctions are based on those techniques developed by Masters and Johnson (1970). These techniques involve desensitization procedures (through *in vivo* successive approximation) where each couple is instructed to progressively and systematically engage in more complicated and arousing behavior designed to build in new and more functional sexual interaction patterns. In addition to the desensitization techniques, specific sexual skill training and sexual-information presentation are combined to decrease sexual-performance anxiety, increase sexual appreciation (sensate focus), and facilitate sexual attitude change. Since it has been reported that most of the sexual-treatment programs utilizing an *in vivo* desensitization and skill learning approach (like that of Masters and Johnson) appear to be reporting similar results (Annon, 1974; Kaplan, 1974), a brief review of the efficacy of the Masters and Johnson program (and several similar programs) will suffice to summarize the efficacy of most of the behavioral strategies with respect to the treatment of commonly occurring sexual problems.

A variant of the "squeeze" technique (Semans, 1956) has been used by Masters and Johnson in the treatment of premature ejaculation. This method usually combines a series of extended sexual activity sessions (graded sexual responses) with prolonged penile stimulation (facilitated by the "squeeze" or "pause" procedure) that gradually approximate penile–vaginal coitus. This successive approximation approach has proven very effective, with cure rates of 98% (Masters and Johnson, 1970) and 100% (Kaplan, 1974; LoPiccolo and Lobitz, 1973) having been reported for over 200 cases.

While these statistics for premature ejaculation are difficult if not impossible to improve upon, another behavioral intervention that has been successfully employed with premature ejaculation involves systematic desensitization and yielded success rates averaging over 80% (Friedman, 1968; Kraft and Al-Issa, 1968).

The behavioral treatment of erectile failure generally consists of graded sexual responses in the actual sexual situation (Wolpe, 1958) and sensate focus techniques (Masters and Johnson, 1970). Systematic desensitization has also been employed when no male arousal is reported to any sexual activity (Lazarus and Rachman, 1960; Wolpe, 1969). While not as effective with this problem as they have been with premature ejaculation, Masters and Johnson reported a cure rate of 59% for primary erectile failure and 74% for secondary erectile failure. Again, the results are relatively consistent across different behavioral strategies employing methods similar to those of the St. Louis group. Specifically, cure rates from 68% to 100% (depending on the criteria for success) have been reported in the treatment of primary and secondary erectile failure (e.g., LoPiccolo and Lobitz, 1973; Wolpe and Lazarus, 1966).

The treatment of vaginismus (and dyspareunia, since it usually accompanies vaginismus), like that of premature ejaculation, has proven amenable to the specific, behavioral strategies employed in recent years. The particular treatment strategy for vaginismus generally utilizes a set of *in vivo* successive approximation tasks (introduction of progressively larger dilators into the vagina) to systematically desensitize muscle contraction responses (Haslam, 1965). In addition, partial insertion of the penis into the vagina and other graded *in vivo* exercises are often recommended (Masters and Johnson, 1970). Following this type of short-term, behavioral intervention, success has been reported to be virtually 100% (Kaplan, 1974; Masters and Johnson, 1970). Additional behavioral strategies for vaginismus and dyspareunia have included traditional systematic desensitization to reduce anxiety (Eysenck and Rachman, 1965; Lazarus, 1963) and these also have met with generally good results (average cure rates greater than 90%).

The final categories to be reviewed are primary and secondary orgasmic dysfunction. The learning theory approaches to treating these problems generally combine sexual anxiety reduction procedures with specific sexual technique training. Anxiety reduction in sexual encounters is often facilitated through *in vivo* desensitization and successive approximation procedures, while some commonly taught techniques are female masturbation, intercourse positions to maximize clitoral stimulation, sensate focus, and the use of vibrators. Using Masters and Johnson's results as the standard, the efficacy of behavior therapy appears to be 85% for primary and 77% for secondary orgasmic dysfunction (Masters and Johnson, 1970). LoPiccolo and Lobitz (1972) demonstrated the utility of a nine-step masturbation program in successfully treating 100% of their primary inorgasmic women. As with other types of sexual problems, a combination of systematic desensitization procedures and other operant conditioning strategies has been used (e.g., specific desensitization hierarchies, assertive training, behavioral rehearsal, automated desensitization with instructional aids) to treat primary and secondary orgasmic dysfunction and all have yielded outcome statistics comparable to those reported by Masters and Johnson (e.g., Brady, 1966; Lazarus, 1963; Tinling, 1969; Wolpe, 1969; Wolpe and Lazarus, 1966). Behavior therapy groups have also been demonstrated to yield cure rates (with respect to the occurrence of female orgasm) of between 90% and 100% in the treatment of primary orgasmic dysfunction (e.g., Barbach, 1974; LoPiccolo, 1973). Therefore, it can be gleaned from this review that behavioral techniques (whether with individuals, couples, or groups) have generally been effective in the treatment of sexual dysfunction. There is, however, some room for improvement.

Close scrutiny of the cure rates reported for behavioral interventions suggests that while premature ejaculation, vaginismus (dyspareunia), and primary orgasmic dysfunction are not likely to be more effectively treated with nonbehavioral strategies, erectile failure (primary and secondary) and secondary orgasmic dysfunction are equally well treated by certain behavioral and nonbehavioral approaches.

In an attempt to explain the differential efficacy of behavioral strategies for primary and secondary orgasmic dysfunction, McGovern, Stewart, and LoPiccolo (1975) compared treatment strategies and pretreatment personality characteristics for primary and secondary inorgasmic women. The results of this analysis showed that primary and secondary inorgasmic women have similar specific sexual problems prior to treatment, yet all the primary inorgasmic women achieved orgasm that generalized to intercourse with their partners, while the secondary inorgasmic women demonstrated no significant change in their orgasmic patterns at posttreatment assessment (McGovern et al; 1975). However, a significant pretreatment difference did appear between primary and secondary women in terms of their marital adjustment scores. Specifically, the primary inorgasmic women had consistently higher marital adjustment scores than did the secondary inorgasmic females. This led these researchers to speculate that emotional involvement and relationship issues were significantly related to treatment outcome for secondary inorgasmic women, but not for primary inorgasmic women.

To verify this hypothesis, Snyder, LoPiccolo, and LoPiccolo (1975) devised a specific treatment strategy for secondary inorgasmic women. This strategy involved sexual technique training designed to generate orgasmic responses in those women who had inconsistently experienced these and instruction in methods for generalizing the orgasmic response to intercourse. These specific behavioral procedures were the same as those used in the primary inorgasmic treatment program, but a specific marital adjustment intervention procedure was implemented to facilitate therapeutic success. The results of this study suggested that a treatment approach combining specific sexual techniques and a strategy that could be viewed as a manipulation of cognitive sets (marital communication training) succeeded in increasing orgasmic response during intercourse from 50% to 100% for a secondary inorgasmic woman. This type of finding suggests the importance of cognitive factors in certain kinds of sexual dysfunction, which is consistent with other reports regarding the importance of relationship issues in the treatment of erectile failure (Willy, Vander, and Fisher, 1967). This model, the combination of specific behavioral techniques with cognitive and emotional intervention, is a relatively recent approach to the treatment of sexual dysfunction and appears to be a future trend. As one sex therapist has remarked: "Cognitive-behavior therapy more and more keeps winning out over primarily cognitive or emotive-behavioral therapies, and I think that this same approach will win the day in sex therapy as well" (Ellis, 1975b, p. 13). While this statement may be premature, the following review of relevant literature points to the facts and fantasies of a cognitive approach to sex therapy.

DESCRIPTION AND UTILITY OF SPECIFIC COGNITIVE BEHAVIORAL TECHNIQUES

It has been observed that behavior therapy (as practiced by Wolpe and Lazarus circa 1968) includes indoctrination, teaching and exhortation, all apparently evidenced to provide a rationale for treatment and to enhance motivation (Klein, Dittman, Parloff, and Gill, 1963). Although such procedures are justified as means to enhance compliance with behavioral assignments, these processes likely mobilize the client's expectancies and attitudes toward a positive therapeutic change (i.e., a cognitive manipulation). It is not surprising, then, that a recent development among behaviorists is the trend to move away from limiting treatment theories and interventions to overt behavior and focus more on cognitive and emotional responses or behaviors (Franks, 1970; Kanfer, 1970; Lazarus, 1967; Staats, 1970).

Annon (1974), Cautela (1967), and others refer to thoughts and emotions as covert behavior, and Meichenbaum (1972) posited the use of the term "cognitive modification" as a label for a treatment strategy designed to focus on covert occurrences (e.g., self-statements or thoughts) to enhance therapeutic change. The recent cognitive behavioral approaches to therapy (e.g., Beck, 1970; Kazdin, 1973; Meichenbaum, 1972) are unique in their integration of learning theory and cognitive control techniques, but the notion of modifying one's psychological adjustment through the manipulation and alteration of thoughts and feelings is not new as a therapeutic rationale (e.g., Ellis, 1962; 1967). The important step, however, may have been the marriage between cognitive and behavioral approaches, which broadened the scope of the often-maligned "narrow behavioral approach" and lifted the too-often intuitively developed cognitive–emotional techniques into the ranks of scientific rigor. Finally, it should be remembered that the following list of cognitive procedures is not meant to supplant the existing behavioral treatments for sexual problems; rather, these procedures will most appropriately be viewed as complements to behavioral techniques (Flowers, 1975; Wish, 1975).

Guided Imagining. Cognitive imagery techniques have been posited as useful additions to behavioral sex therapy when any of the following conditions exist:

1. A person has failed to respond to the initial behavioral intervention due to intense sexual anxiety or moral objections.

2. The individual's fear of failure or fear of rejection is sufficiently intense to prohibit that individual from taking the initial step of an *in vivo* desensitization exercise.

3. The person cannot continue a behavioral intervention after starting it due to failure fantasies and preoccupation following a setback in the treatment.

4. An individual has succeeded in the behavioral intervention but failed to reach a desired level of arousal or excitation (Flowers, 1975; Wish, 1975).

In the situation where the individual's initial anxiety levels or fears are sufficiently intense and prohibit beginning an *in vivo* behavioral program, an initial facilatory step can be the use of guided imagery in a cognitive desensitization procedure to decrease this anxiety and allow for participation in the *in vivo* desensitization procedure (e.g., Wolpe, 1969; Wolpin, 1969).

In general, the procedure involving guided imagery consists of the therapist instructing the client through an anxiety hierarchy involving the desired behavioral sequence in an eyes-closed position. However, unlike systematic desensitization, there is no muscle relaxation paired with the anxiety responses and the progression through a hierarchy occurs only in the person's thought processes and imagination. For example, Wolpe (1969) used this type of procedure to facilitate treatment of vaginismus. In this case, the therapist used systematic desensitization to the imaginary insertion of graded dilators and when that was successfully completed, he provided the patient with the actual dilators for *in vivo* insertion. In treating the same problem, Wish (1975) used imaginal desensitization for a women who had failed previously with an *in vivo* approach. This twenty-three-year-old woman was taught relaxation and then imaginally progressed through a hierarchy of increasingly more anxiety-producing sexual situations, ranging from holding hands to having intercourse. He reported that following 10 sessions of imaginal desensitization vaginal spasms had ceased and the client was able to have successful intercourse.

The similarities between systematic, *in vivo*, and imaginal desensitization appear more prevalent than the differences. In an attempt to evaluate the differential efficacy of graded *in vivo* tasks compared to imaginal desensitization, Husted (1975) utilized a no-treatment control paradigm in assessing outcome for female sexual dysfunction. He found that both treatment groups yielded significant clinical improvement in comparison to the controls, but no significant differences accrued between the treatment groups in terms of clinical outcome. That is, both imaginal desensitization and *in vivo* desensitization facilitated decreases in reported sexual anxiety and increases in intercourse frequency, extracoital orgasmic response, and sexual satisfaction. The important finding, however, was not that a cognitive strategy could equal the clinical results of an effective behavioral intervention, but that the imaginal group required significantly fewer treatment sessions to obtain the same results (7.8 sessions versus 13.3 sessions). Given the lack of long-term follow-up data, it is prudent to assume that some *in vivo* behavioral rehearsal would be necessary to yield durable changes in such a procedure. Nevertheless, it appears likely that a combination of cognitive and behavioral strategies may be effective and efficient in producing positive clinical results, at least with orgasmic dysfunction. As Husted (1975) suggested, the essential elements for successful use of this cognitive procedure are accurate identification of the specific anxiety-producing situations, generation of the appropriate hierarchy to be used, and systematic guidance through this hierarchy in the person's imagination prior to attempting any *in vivo* behavioral intervention.

Cognitive Rehearsal (Self-Guided Imagining). Covert self-rehearsal is a cognitive intervention strategy designed to function as a separate behavior technique or be used in conjunction with an ongoing *in vivo* program (Meichenbaum, 1972). This procedure generally is implemented following instruction in the use of guided systematic desensitization, since it is an identical procedure only employed by the individual covertly rather than with the aid of a therapist. That is, if an individual has extreme anxiety about his ability to obtain an erection sufficient to allow intercourse and this anxiety inhibits his active participation in an *in vivo* procedure, he is first instructed in a cognitive desensitization procedure using a hierarchy of specific sexual behaviors related to achieving an erection and relaxing in a sexual situation. Following the successful use of this therapist-aided procedure, the patient is then instructed to self-rehearse the same imagined hierarchy at home until he feels comfortable and relaxed with the thought of engaging in sexual activity. Again, there is no specific muscle relaxation or anxiety reduction technique employed other than the self-rehearsed cognitive desensitization. At this point, the individual is encouraged to begin an *in vivo* treatment procedure and uses this cognitive self-rehearsal technique prior to each *in vivo* behavioral task. This type of covert self-rehearsal has been shown to significantly reduce performance anxiety in behavioral situations for test- and speech-phobic individuals (e.g., Meichenbaum, 1972, 1974).

Covert Reinforcement (Emotive Imagery). Cautela, Walsh, and Wish (1971) define covert positive reinforcement as the imagined presentation of a positively reinforcing scene in an operant paradigm to increase the probability of a desired response. This type of emotive imagery is often used in the following way. If an individual is experiencing anxiety associated with certain sexual scenes, he/she is instructed to first construct in his/her imagination a positive fantasy or image (e.g., skiing down a mountain on a sunny day or lying comfortably on the sand of a warm beach). Then, the person is engaged in a cognitive desensitization hierarchy, but each time a hierarchy item is imagined and presented by the therapist, the individual is instructed to switch to this positively reinforcing scene in his/her imagination. In this way, each level of anxiety-producing behavior is imagined and then paired with a positive image or emotion, resulting in a decrease in the anxiety associated with the item and an increased probability of approaching the situation.

An example of a covert conditioning paradigm applied to a sexual treatment problem is presented by Wish (1975) in his treatment of erectile failure. In this case, a behavioral analysis was conducted to determine the idiosyncratic reinforcing stimuli and images and the client was trained to visualize the reinforcing scene whenever the therapist said the word "reinforcement." The client was then directed through the following scene:

> I want you to imagine sitting in the den with your date (when the client raises his index finger to indicate that the scene is clearly visualized, counselor, say "reinforcement"). You glance over at your date with a smile and she smiles back (counselor reinforces). You get up, walk over, and sit down beside her on the couch (reinforcement). She moves toward you and you kiss (reinforcement). You are feeling calm, relaxed, and confident as you kiss her (reinforcement). Make sure the scene is clear. Try to feel her breasts. See yourself calm and relaxed. (Wish, 1975, p. 54).

In this way, the client was imaginally progressed through an entire sexual encounter in several sessions and instructed to practice this self-reinforcing procedure several times a day at home. The outcome of this covert reinforcement program reportedly yeilded successful treatment of this man's erectile difficulties.

An example of covert negative reinforcement is given by Cautela (1970) in the successful treatment of erectile failure. In this procedure, the client was asked to imagine an aversive scene (such as his boss yelling at him) and then he was instructed to immediately switch to imagining a scene in which he was lying in bed, naked and relaxed, next to his partner. Again, the repetitive use of a self-rehearsed, covert reinforcement process yielded significant improvement in this individual's erectile functioning.

A further use of covert reinforcement principles combines masturbation fantasies with sexual activities to enhance arousal and orgasmic responses in heterosexual situations previously found to be minimally stimulating (e.g., Marquis, 1970). For example, in the treatment of impotence related to male homosexual orientation an *in vivo* desensitization procedure (e.g., Davison, 1968) was combined with covert conditioning of heterosexual imagery during masturbation. More specifically, the male was instructed to use his homosexual fantasies to facilitate erection and arousal during masturbation, but immediately prior to ejaculation, he was to switch to fantasies of sexual activity with his female partner. This procedure was repeated several times a week for several weeks, at which time the interval between switching to fantasies of her and ejaculation was lengthened to 30 seconds. In this treatment phase, the client was instructed to use homosexual fantasies to facilitate erections, but to alternate between homosexual and heterosexual images until 30 seconds before ejaculating, at which time he was to imagine engaging in intercourse with his female partner. Throughout the remainder of treatment, the percentage of time he spent using heterosexual fantasies during masturbation was gradually increased until no homosexual images were used. This pairing of covert and overt behavior (cognitive conditioning) was combined with graded *in vivo* heterosexual activities throughout the duration of treatment. While no specific technique to decrease homosexual behavior was initiated, this cognitive behavioral strategy resulted in increased heterosexual interest and arousal, decreased homosexual activity, and a mutually satisfactory heterosexual relationship (LoPiccolo, Stewart, and Watkins, 1972).

Finally, an innovative usage of covert reinforcement in the

treatment of vaginismus was presented by Wilson (1973). In this study, the woman had failed to engage in *in vivo* desensitization procedures at home with her partner, despite a systematic and graded behavioral approach combined with imaginal systematic desensitization. Also, deep muscle relaxation in addition to the imaginal desensitization had failed to facilitate any portion of the digital insertion procedure at home. The technique used to facilitate eventual success was a form of covert positive reinforcement paired with orgasm. In this procedure the woman was instructed to first imagine and fantasize that she was inserting her finger into the vagina at the moment preceding orgasm (of which she was capable during mutual genital manipulation with her partner). She was then encouraged to gradually increase the time and amount of digital insertion in her imagination as well as increasing the duration between onset of this imagery and orgasm. The final step in the procedure involved instructing her partner to actually insert his finger at the point of orgasm as had been practiced in her imagination previously. While this is not an isolated application of covert positive reinforcement it is a good example of the complementary interaction between a specific cognitive technique, a reinforcing behavior, and graded *in vivo* tasks in generating a successful outcome (Wilson, 1973).

Thought-Stopping. This procedure was originally developed by Wolpe (1969) to decrease obsessive rumination and disruptive or anxiety-producing thoughts. Such a technique can readily be seen to have application in the treatment of sexual dysfunction when the disruptive effects of "spectatoring," Masters and Johnson (1970), and negative self-statements concerning sexual adequacy are considered. As indicated by Masters and Johnson (1970) and Wish (1975), the effects of rumination and preoccupation generally involve distraction from the immediate sexual situation, decreased erotic stimulation, and interference with the natural physiological arousal cycle. It can be seen from this discussion that thought-stopping techniques could have particular applicability to the treatment of sexual dysfunctions susceptible to distracting thoughts and personal preoccupations (e.g., erectile failure and orgasmic dysfunction).

In an attempt to facilitate sensate focus and sexual enjoyment that had been hindered by cognitive preoccupation, covert thought-stopping techniques have been introduced in the treatment of secondary erectile failure (Wish, 1975; Wolpe, 1969) and orgasmic dysfunction (Geisinger, 1969). The specific technique used in the erectile failure treatment program was designed to decrease the husband's preoccupation and concern with the quality of his erection and proceeded as follows:

> Close your eyes and imagine thinking about your penis being flaccid. Also imagine that you say to yourself, "Oh, God, I'll never be able to perform." When you can imagine this clearly, indicate it to me by raising your right index finger. O.K. Go ahead. (Client closes his eyes and then raises his index finger—therapist shouts, "Stop!") O.K. What happened to the thought? (Client usually answers that it went away.) Right! You can't think, "Oh, God, I'll never be able to perform" and hear "Stop!" at the same time. Now close your eyes, think about the thought, but shout, "Stop!" to yourself. Actually, tighten your vocal cords and move your tongue as if you were yelling it aloud. Go ahead and try. (Wish, 1975, p. 53)

This client was then encouraged to practice eliminating his ruminative thoughts about erections by subvocally yelling "Stop!" anytime he began to think negatively about his ability to obtain an erection. This procedure reportedly resulted in a dramatic improvement in frequency and duration of erections that maintained following treatment (Wish, 1975).

An additional use of the thought-stopping procedure can be imagined to apply in the treatment of secondary orgasmic dysfunction. That is, it has been suggested that concern about self-worth, self-acceptance, or the authenticity of a partner's love have contributed to poor marital relationships, which then precipitate secondary orgasmic dysfunction (e.g., Masters and Johnson, 1970; McGovern et al., 1975). In those cases where this appears evident, a specific thought-stopping procedure, to be covertly implemented by the preoccupied partner, could precede or accompany an *in vivo* behavioral program and may increase the effectiveness of the treatment. While this should benefit some, the myriad of serious psychological and marital distresses that can cause similar negative self-statements dictates a comprehensive evaluation before utilizing this approach to the exclusion of others.

Covert Assertion. This procedure is designed to be implemented following a thought-stopping procedure and focuses on eliminating any residual anxiety or preoccupation not dispersed by thought-stopping (Rimm and Masters, 1974). In this approach, after the client has been trained to use the thought-stopping technique and has come to the "Stop" phase, she/he is instructed to insert a more appropriate and forceful assertive statement about herself/himself. For example, in the case illustration mentioned above (Wish, 1975), the covert assertive phase of treatment would begin following the subvocalized "Stop!" and would consist of a self-rehearsed statement such as the following: "My ability to obtain an erection is as normal as anyone's. I can get an adequate erection and maintain it sufficient for enjoyable intercourse."

Another example of covert assertive methodology might be in the case of orgasmic dysfunction where the woman was overconcerned with feelings of asexuality or sensual inadequacy. In this case and after she has been instructed in a thought-stopping technique to be used following each worry about her sexiness, she could be instructed to subvocally self-rehearse the following statement: "I am as sensuous as most women. I can feel relaxed and sexy with my partner." Obviously, this approach can be maximized if the partner is programmed to reinforce such covert statements with overt behavior and verbalizations that are consonant with this impression. As a final adjunct to the use of covert assertion procedures, Wish (1975) suggests that the entire process be culminated by a covert positive reinforcement (e.g., visualizing a pleasant nonsexual but rewarding scene). In this way, the following paradigm evolved: Obsessive thought-STOP-Assertive statement-Positive reinforcement scene, or "I'm not sexy enough"—STOP—"I'm as sexy as most women"—Lying on the beach on a warm sunny afternoon.

Covert Sensitization (Aversive Cognitive Conditioning). This method was initially introduced by Cautela (1967) and is designed to decrease the probability of an unwanted behavior or thought through aversive conditioning techniques. In the treatment of sexual difficulties, this procedure is most often used to decrease arousal resulting from an "inappropriate" stimulus (e.g., undesired homosexual arousal, pedophilial arousal), thereby facilitating new learning and heterosexual arousal patterns. For example, in the treatment of a twenty-eight-year-old married male homosexual who had not consummated his marriage, Cautela (1967) used a form of covert sensitization. One of the reasons for this procedure was the client's insistence that he could not engage in an *in vivo* approach nor would he tolerate the presence of his wife in therapy initially. Therefore, a shift to heterosexual behavior and arousal was facilitated by using aversive imagery associated with the thoughts of male approaches. That is, the client was instructed to imagine vividly a scene where he was being approached by another man for sexual activity and when he raised his finger indicating a clear image of this scene, the therapist instructed him to switch to an aversive image (e.g., vomiting, ridicule, loss of work prestige). The covert sensitization program was initiated with the therapist's description of aversive consequences and scenes following the client's indication of a clear visualization of his homosexual approach. This intervention was designed to decrease the frequency of homosexual thoughts and arousal and was combined with a covert positive reinforcement procedure (where imagined heterosexual scenes with his wife were paired with pleasant and positive images and fantasies). The result of this combined cognitive modification strategy was that he and his wife successfully entered and completed an *in vivo* treatment program (Cautela, 1967).

Additional evidence concerning the utility of a covert sensitization approach in effecting increases in heterosexual arousal and behavior and decreases in homosexual urges and activity have been reported by several authors (Curtis and Presly, 1972; Kendrick and McCullough, 1973; Rehm and Rosensky, 1974). It is important to note that all these treatment techniques combined covert sensitization to decrease homosexual interest and arousal and covert or overt positive reinforcement to increase the likelihood of heterosexual arousal and behavior. In a controlled study comparing the effects of electrical aversive conditioning to covert sensitization in eliminating deviant fantasies in homosexuals, Callahan and Leitenberg (1973) demonstrated that both procedures were equally effective in decreasing homosexual arousal. However, the covert sensitization treatment was significantly more effective in yielding decreased homosexual urges and increased heterosexual behavior. Further controlled studies are needed to replicate these findings.

Implosive Therapy (Covert Flooding). This strategy is presented last since it encompasses several elements of previously described techniques. It was initially devised by Stampfl and Levis (1967) and is designed to increase the probability of a behavior's occurrence through imaginal confrontation between the individual and the feared or anxiety-producing stimuli. Anxiety is purposefully kept at a high level by interspersing the therapist's vivid verbal descriptions of repeated exposure to the feared situation with the person's visualization of this confrontation. It has been suggested that this procedure typically results in a decrease of avoidance behavior through a kind of stimulus satiation or flooding and rapid desensitization to the feared set of responses.

In an application to sexual difficulties, Hogan (1969) used an implosive paradigm to decrease the anxiety associated with heterosexual activities in the treatment of orgasmic dysfunction. This technique facilitated participation in a previously avoided *in vivo* treatment strategy that then yielded success. Another quasi-implosive procedure that has been posited as an effective technique in augmenting the behavioral treatment of orgasmic dysfunction employs imagined and *in vivo* role-playing of an "exaggerated orgasm" (Lobitz and LoPiccolo, 1972). This method involves both cognitive and behavioral rehearsal of an anxiety-producing situation and, as such, contains elements of both behavioral-flooding and cognitive implosion therapy. Furthermore, it has been suggested that in a nonorgasmic woman, such fears as loss of control and personal embarrassment contribute to anxiety and distraction, which interfere with sensate-focusing exercises and sexual arousal, and that these experiences often generate avoidance of heterosexual activities (Lobitz and LoPiccolo, 1971, 1972). The implosive aspects of the "exaggerated orgasm" approach involve instructing the woman to imagine the wildest, most uncontrolled orgasm she can and to vividly rehearse this in her imagination. She is encouraged to envision responses such as physically thrashing about, screaming, panting heavily, and moaning. When these vivid images become tiresome and boring, she is then instructed to role-play all these actions *in vivo*. This cognitive behavioral approach has facilitated orgasmic attainment in several women when embedded in a systematic *in vivo* treatment program (Lobitz and LoPiccolo, 1972).

A final consideration concerning implosive intervention is its apparent relationship to some of the techniques used by rational-emotive therapists (e.g., Ellis, 1974; Maultsby, 1971). That is, rational-emotive therapy (RET) applied to the treatment of sexual dysfunction espouses the use of emotional and imaginal confrontation involving irrational beliefs and negative self-statements (e.g., Ellis, 1975b). Specifically, the client is encouraged to vividly imagine a sexual situation and is aided by the therapist in systematically progressing through all aspects of the sexual activities and feelings in this visualization. The content of this imagery often entails subjectively aversive outcomes (such as no physical arousal occurring, emotional irritability, and depression), and the therapist encourages the individual to vividly fantasize and imagine these negative outcomes. At this point, the therapist asks several questions and elicits statements designed to maximize the discomfort and negative fantasy of the individual in this situation (e.g., Ellis, 1975b). To this point, this particular procedure can be viewed as an implosive method of desensitizing or acclimating the individual to the notion of failure in a sexual situation, and as such is similar to other forms of imaginal desensitization. It is important to note that RET techniques continue beyond this point to attempt facilitation of positive self-statements similar to covert assertion and rational ways of looking at the realistic sexual options available. However, many of the RET therapist's techniques can be equated with one or more of the cognitive procedures (e.g., "anti-awfulizing" is a form of cognitive self-instruction; rational-emotive imagery can be viewed as a combination of thought-stopping and covert reinforcement). This comparison is intended as a catalyst for further research regarding the utility of RET and to promote comprehension of the similarities among most therapies utilizing cognitive mediation. Perhaps the most important similarity between these approaches to the treatment of sexual difficulties is the apparent similarity of effectiveness when comparing the cognitive strategies reviewed above and RET outcome data (e.g., Ard, 1974; Ellis, 1967, 1974; Maultsby and Ellis, 1974). While it is clearly premature to categorically postulate the differential efficacy of RET, cognitive behavioral intervention, and *in vivo* behavioral techniques in treating sexual difficulties, the existing data suggest that an eclectic combination of strategies may be the most efficacious approach.

CONCLUSION

This chapter reviewed different strategies and their efficacy in the treatment of sexual problems. The recent trend toward short-term behavioral intervention or the "new sex therapy" (Kaplan, 1974) was noted and the outcome statistics for these approaches presented. Since different treatment groups employing procedures similar to those described by Masters and Johnson (1970) have generally yielded comparable results in terms of the duration and utility of treatment, it is suggested that these data provide clinically relevant criteria against which other intervention techniques can be measured. In this regard, it appears that any treatment paradigm cannot significantly improve upon the near-perfect outcome of these *in vivo* behavioral procedures in the treatment of premature ejaculation, vaginismus, dyspareunia, and primary orgasmic dysfunction. For these diagnoses, the contribution that cognitive behavioral principles offer relates primarily to facilitating and streamlining the efficacious existing technology.

The remaining diagnostic categories (erectile failure, ejaculatory incompetence, and secondary orgasmic dysfunction) have not responded as dramatically to *in vivo* behavioral approaches, and it is within these areas that covert strategies and cognitive intervening variables tend to exert a significant impact upon treatment outcome. In particular, it has been postulated that cognitive intervention procedures are indicated in the following situations:

1. When anxiety or fear has prohibited initiation of an *in vivo* approach.

2. When an *in vivo* strategy has been inconsistently applied due to avoidance of sexual activity secondary to anxiety or fear.

3. Where the client does not have a partner and cannot engage in *in vivo* exercises.

4. Where preoccupation or ruminative thinking significantly interferes with or prohibits either partner's ability to relax and focus on specific sexual activities and sensations.

5. When specific attitudes or cognitive sets unrelated to fear (e.g., "Sex is immoral and not to be practiced." "I hate my partner and question our relationship's validity.") need to be altered to allow a commitment to treatment.

This list implies that covert behavioral techniques are most effectively used in conjunction with *in vivo* strategies in a multivariate approach to the treatment of sexual problems (e.g., Annon, 1974; LoPiccolo *et al.*, 1972; Snyder *et al.*, 1975; Sayner and Durrell, 1975).

One of the purposes of this chapter has been to describe those cognitive behavioral methods that have some research data to support their validity in the treatment of sexual difficulties. It is not this author's contention that other cognitive or quasi-cognitive techniques are invalid or unnecessary. In fact, as can be gleaned from the preceding review, many of the cognitive behavioral programs have drawn liberally from different areas of psychology in identifying methods that will maximize attitude change, positive cognitive sets, treatment expectancies, and placebo effects. Some of these more general strategies include:

1. Information dispersal—bibliotherapy, media presentation, sexual "de-mythification," disavowing irrational beliefs.

2. Permission-giving—professional sanctioning or sexual interaction.

3. Audio-visually aided attitude change—vicarious learning and acceptance of previously avoided sexual activities (e.g., films of masturbation or different intercourse positions).

4. Therapist-induced attitude change—positive expectations and cognitive sets toward sexuality role-played by the therapist. This is not intended as an exhaustive catalog, but suggests the important relationship between various cognitive and behavioral factors in developing an effective sexual-treatment strategy. In conclusion, while evidence is yet preliminary, research findings converge from *in vivo* behavioral and cognitive intervention studies to posit a multivariate approach as the most efficacious in facilitating rapid and permanent changes in the treatment of sexual problems (e.g., Annon, 1974; Geisinger, 1969; LoPiccolo and Miller, 1975; Rehm and Rosensky, 1974). Cognitive behavioral strategies, in particular, appear to be effective and necessary when treating those sexual dif-

ficulties moderated by anxiety, fear, self-doubt, ruminative thought
processes, relationship concerns, and dysfunctional cognitive conditioning patterns.

REFERENCES

Annon, J. *The behavioral treatment of sexual problems. Vol. 1. Brief therapy.* Honolulu:
  Enabling Systems, Inc., 1974.
Annon, J. *The behavioral treatment of sexual problems. Vol. 2. Intensive therapy.* Hono-
  lulu: Enabling Systems, Inc., 1975.
Ard, B. *Treating psychosexual dysfunction.* New York: Jason Aronson, 1974.
August, R.V. Libido altered with the aid of hypnosis: A case report. *American Journal
  of Clinical Hypnosis,* 1959, *2,* 88.
Baily, H. Studies in depression, II: Treatment of the depressed, frigid woman. *The
  Medical Journal of Australia,* 1973, *1,* 834–837.
Bandura, A. *Principles of behavior modification.* New York: Holt, Rinehart and Win-
  ston, 1969.
Barbach, L. Group treatment of preorgasmic women. *Journal of Sex and Marital Ther-
  apy,* 1974, *1,* 139–145.
Beck, A. Cognitive therapy: Nature and relation to behavior therapy. *Behavior Ther-
  apy,* 1970, *1,* 184–200.
Bindrim, P. A report on a nude marathon: The effect of physical nudity on the prac-
  tice of interaction in marathon groups. *Psychotherapy: Theory, Research, and
  Practice,* 1968, *5,* 180–188.
Bindrim, P. Nudity as a quick grab for intimacy in group therapy. *Psychology Today,*
  1969, June, 24–28.
Brady, J. Brevital—relaxation treatment of frigidity. *Behavior Research and Therapy,*
  1966, *4,* 71–77.
Callahan, E., and Leitenberg, H. Aversion therapy for sexual deviation: Contingent
  shock and covert sensitization. *Journal of Abnormal Psychology,* 1973, *81,* 60–73.
Cautela, J.R. Covert sensitization. *Psychological Reports,* 1967, *20,* 459–468.
Cautela, J.R. Covert reinforcement. *Behavior Therapy,* 1970, *1,* 33–50.
Cautela, J., Walsh, K., and Wish, P. The use of covert reinforcement in the modifica-
  tion of attitudes toward the retarded. *Journal of Psychology,* 1971, *77,* 257–260.
Coulton, D. Hypnotherapy in gynecological problems. *American Journal of Clinical
  Hypnosis,* 1960, *3,* 95–100.
Curtis, R., and Presly, A. The extinction of homosexual behavior by covert sensitiza-
  tion: A case study. *Behavior Research and Therapy,* 1972, *10,* 81–83.
Davison, G. Systematic desensitization as a counterconditioning process. *Journal of
  Abnormal Psychology,* 1968, *73,* 91–99.
Deutsch, R. *The key to feminine response in marriage.* New York: Random House, 1968.
Ellis, A. *Reason and emotion in psychotherapy.* New York: Lyle Stuart, 1962.
Ellis, A. The treatment of frigidity and impotence. In H. Greenwald (Ed.), *Active psy-
  chotherapy.* New York: Atherton Press, 1967, 328–336.
Ellis, A. The treatment of sex and love problems in women. In V. Frank and V. Burtle
  (Eds.), *Women in therapy.* New York: Brunner/Mazel, 1974, 284–306.

Ellis, A. An informal history of sex therapy. *The Counseling Psychologist*, 1975a, 5, 9–13.

Ellis, A. The rational-emotive approach to sex therapy. *The Counseling Psychologist*, 1975b, 5, 14–21.

Eysenck, H., and Rachman, S. *The causes and cures of neuroses.* San Diego: Robert A. Knapp, 1965.

Flowers, J. Imagination training in the treatment of sexual dysfunction. *The Counseling Psychologist*, 1975, 5, 50–51.

Franks, C. Pavlovian conditioning approaches. In D. Levis (Ed.), *Learning approaches to therapeutic behavior change.* Chicago: Aldine, 1970, 108–143.

Freud, S. *The basic writings of Sigmund Freud.* A. Brill (Ed. and Translator), New York: Modern Library, 1938.

Friedman, D. The treatment of impotence by brietal relaxation therapy. *Behavior Research and Therapy*, 1968, 6, 257–261.

Friedman, D. An interpersonal aspect of psychogenic impotence. *American Journal of Psychotherapy*, 1973, 17, 421–429.

Geisinger, D. Controlling sexual interpersonal anxieties. In J. Krumboltz and C. Thoreson (Eds.), *Behavioral counseling: Cases and techniques.* New York: Holt, Rinehart and Winston, 1969, 454–469.

Gunther, B. Sensory awakening and sensuality. In H. Otto (Ed.), *The new sexuality.* Palo Alto, Calif.: Science and Behavior Books, 1971.

Hartman, W., and Fithian, M. Desert retreat. In J. and J. Robbins (Eds.), *An analysis of human sexual inadequacy.* New York: Signet, 1970.

Haslam, M. The treatment of psychogenic dyspareunia by reciprocal inhibition. *British Journal of Psychiatry*, 1965, 111, 280–282.

Hogan, R. Implosively oriented behavior modification: Therapy considerations. *Behavior Research and Therapy*, 1969, 7, 177–183.

Hussain, A. Behavior therapy using hypnosis. In J. Wolpe, A. Salter, and L. Reyna (Eds.), *The conditioning therapies: The challenge in psychotherapy.* New York: Holt, Rinehart and Winston, 1964, 54–61.

Husted, J. Desensitization procedures in dealing with female sexual dysfunction. *The Counseling Psychologist*, 1975, 5, 30–37.

James, B. Case of homosexuality treated by aversion therapy. *British Medical Journal*, 1962, 1, 768–770.

Kanfer, F. Self-regulation: Research issues and speculation. In C. Neuringer and J. Michael (Eds.), *Behavior modification in clinical psychology.* New York: Appleton-Century-Crofts, 1970, 178–220.

Kanfer, F. and Saslow, G. Behavioral diagnosis. In C. Franks (Ed.), *Behavior therapy: Appraisal and status.* New York: McGraw-Hill, 1969, 417–444.

Kaplan, H. *The new sex therapy.* New York: Brunner/Mazel, 1974.

Kaufman, J. Organic and psychological factors in the genesis of impotence and premature ejaculation. In C. Wahl (Ed.), *Sexual problems: Diagnosis and treatment in medical practice.* New York: The Free Press, 1967, 133–148.

Kazdin, A. Covert modeling and the reduction of avoidance behavior. *Journal of Abnormal Behavior*, 1973, 81, 87–95.

Kegel, A. Sexual functions of the pubococcygens muscle. *Western Journal of Surgical and Obstetrical Gynecology*, 1952, 60, 521.

Kelly, G. Impotence. In A. Ellis and A. Abarbanel (Eds.), *The encyclopedia of sexual behavior* (Vol. 1). New York: Hawthorn Books, 1961, 515–527.

Kendrick, S., and McCullough, J. Sequential phases of covert reinforcement and covert sensitization in the treatment of homosexuality. *Journal of Behavior Therapy and Experiemental Psychiatry*, 1973, 3, 229–231.

Klein, M., Dittman, A., Parloff, M., and Gill, M. Behavior therapy: Observations and reflections. *Journal of Consulting and Clinical Psychology*, 1963, 33, 259–266.

Knight, R. Functional disturbance in the sexual life of women: Frigidity and related disorders. *Bulletin of the Menninger Clinic*, 1943, 7, 25–35.

Kraft, T., and Al-Issa, I. The use of methohexitone sodium in the systematic desensitization of premature ejaculation. *British Journal of Psychiatry*, 1968, 114, 351–352.

Kroger, W. Comprehensive approach to ecclesiogenic neuroses. *Journal of Sex Research*, 1969, 5, 2–11.

Lazarus, A. The treatment of chronic frigidity by systematic desensitization. *Journal of Nervous and Mental Disease*, 1963, 136, 272–278.

Lazarus, A. In support of technical eclecticism. *Psychological Reports*, 1967, 21, 415–416.

Lazarus, A. Learning theory and the treatment of depression. *Behavior Research and Therapy*, 1968, 6, 83–89.

Lazarus, A. (Ed.) *Clinical behavior therapy*. New York: Brunner/Mazel, 1972.

Lazarus, A., and Rachman, C. The use of systematic desensitization in psychotherapy. In H.J. Eysenck (Ed.), *Behavior therapy and the neuroses*. New York: pergamon, 1960, 181.

Lobitz, W., and LoPiccolo, J. The role of masturbation in the treatment of sexual dysfunction. Paper presented at the joint Oregon Psychological Association and Washington State Psychological Association, Gleneden Beach, Oregon, 1971.

Lobitz, W., and LoPiccolo, J. New methods in the behavioral treatment of sexual dysfunction. *Journal of Behavior Therapy and Experimental Psychiatry*, 1972, 3, 265–271.

LoPiccolo, J. A behavioral approach to sexual dysfunction: Sexual dissatisfaction groups. Workshop presented at the annual meeting of the American Association of Behavior Therapy, Miami, December, 1973.

LoPiccolo, J., and Lobitz, W. The role of masturbation in the treatment of orgasmic dysfunction. *Archives of Sexual Behavior*, 1972, 2, 163–171.

LoPiccolo, J., and Lobitz, W. Behavior therapy of sexual dysfunction. In L. Hammerlynck, L. Handy, and E. Mash (Eds.), *Behavior change: Methodology, concepts, and practice*. Champaign, Ill.: Research Press, 1973.

LoPiccolo, J., and Miller, V. A program for enhancing the sexual relationship of normal couples. *The Couseling Psychologist*, 1975, 5, 41–45.

LoPiccolo, J., Stewart, R., and Watkins, B. Case study: Treatment of erectile failure and ejaculatory incompetence in a case with homosexual etiology. *Journal of Behavior Therapy and Experimental Psychiatry*, 1972, 3, 233–236.

Marquis, J.M. Orgasmic reconditioning: Changing sexual object choice through controlling masturbatory fantasies. *Journal of Behavior Therapy and Experimental Psychiatry*, 1970, 1, 263–271.

Masters, W., and Johnson, V. *Human sexual inadequacy*. Boston: Little, Brown, and Company, 1970.

Maultsby, M. *Rational counseling handbook*. Lexington, Ky.: Univ. of Kentucky Press, 1971.

Maultsby, M., and Ellis, A. *Techniques for using rational-emotive imagery (REI)*. New York: Institute for Rational Living, 1974.

Max, L. Breaking up a homosexual fixation by the conditioned reaction technique: A case study. *Psychological Bulletin*, 1935, *32*, 734.

McGovern, K., Stewart, R., and LoPiccolo, J. Secondary orgasmic dysfunction: 1. Analysis and strategies for treatment. *Archives of Sexual Behavior*, 1975, *4*, 265–275.

Meichenbaum, D. Cognitive modification of test anxious college students. *Journal of Consulting and Clinical Psychology*, 1972, *39*, 370–380.

Meichenbaum, D. The clinical potential of modifying what clients say to themselves. *Psychotherapy: Theory, Research, and Practice*, 1974, *11*, 103–117.

Mirowitz, J. Utilization of hypnosis in psychic impotence. *British Journal of Medical Hypnotism*, 1966, *17*, 25–32.

O'Connor, J., and Stern, L. Results of treatment in functional sexual disorders. *New York State Journal of Medicine*, 1972, *72*, 1927–1934.

Ovesey, L., and Meyers, H. Retarded ejaculation: Psychodynamics and psychotherapy. *American Journal of Psychotherapy*, 1968, *22*, 185–201.

Rehm, L., and Rosensky, R. Multiple behavior therapy techniques with a homosexual client: A case study. *Journal of Behavior Therapy and Experimental Psychiatry*, 1974, *5*, 53–57.

Richardson, R. Hypnotherapy in frigidity. *The American Journal of Clinical Hypnosis*, 1963, *5*, 194–199.

Rimm, D., and Masters, J. *Behavior therapy*. New York: Academic Press, 1974.

Rubin, I. *Sexual life after sixty*. New York: New American Library (Signet edition), 1965.

Sarason, I. Test anxiety and cognition. *Journal of Personaity and Social Psychology*, 1973, *28*, 58–61.

Sayner, R., and Durrell, D. Multiple behavior therapy techniques in the treatment of sexual dysfunction. *The Counseling Psychologist*, 1975, *5*, 38–41.

Semans, J. Premature ejaculation: A new approach. *Southern Medical Journal*, 1956, *49*, 353–362.

Singh, H. Therapeutic use of thioridizine in premature ejaculation. *American Journal of Psychiatry*, 1963, *119*, 891–898.

Snyder, A., LoPiccolo, J., and LoPiccolo, L. Secondary orgasmic dysfunction. II. Case study. *Archives of Sexual Behavior*, 1975, *4*, 277–283.

Staats, A. Social behaviorism, human motivation, and the conditioning therapies. In. B. Maher (Ed.), *Progress in experimental personality research* (Vol. 5). New York: Academic Press, 1970, 111–168.

Stampfl, T., and Levis, D. Essentials of implosive therapy. *Journal of Abnormal Psychology*, 1967, *72*, 496–503.

Stone, A., and Levine, L. Group therapy in sexual maladjustment. *American Journal of Psychiatry*, 1950, *107*, 195–202.

Tinling, D. Auto-desensitization to phobic fears with an audio-visual instructional aid. In R. Rubin and C. Franks (Eds.), *Advances in behavior therapy, 1968*. New York: Academic Press, 1969, 11–15.

Ullmann, L., and Krasner, L. *Case studies in behavior modification*. New York: Holt, Rinehart and Winston, 1965.

Willy, A., Vander, I., and Fisher, O. *The illustrated encyclopedia of sex* (Rev. ed.) New York: Cadillac Publishing, 1967.

Wilson, G. Innovations in the modification of phobic behaviors in two clinical cases. *Behavior Therapy*, 1973, *4*, 426–430.

Wish, P. The use of imagery-based techniques in the treatment of sexual dysfunction. *The Counseling Psychologist*, 1975, *5*, 52–55.

Wittels, F. *The sex habits of American women*. New York: Eton, 1951.

Wolpe, J. *Psychotherapy by reciprocal inhibition*. Stanford, Calif.: Stanford University Press, 1958.

Wolpe, J. *The practice of behavior therapy*. New York: Pergamon, 1969.

Wolpe, J., and Lazarus, A. *Behavior therapy techniques: A guide to the treatment of neuroses*. New York: Pergamon, 1966.

Wolpin, M. Guided imagining to reduce avoidance behavior. *Psychotherapy: Theory, Research, and Practice*, 1969, *6*, 122–124.

4

Cognitive Behavior Modification of Mood Disorders

DAVID D. BURNS AND AARON T. BECK

Depression is a disorder of the entire psychobiologic system including the emotions, thoughts, behaviors, and somatic functions. The
emotional component is characterized by a blue mood involving
feelings of sadness, anhedonia, guilt, irritability, and despair. The
somatic symptoms include hypochrondriasis, insomnia or hyper-
somnia, weight gain or loss, constipation or diarrhea, fatigue, and
decreased libido. The behavioral changes are characterized by passivity, lethargy, inactivity, social isolation, withdrawal from work,
and avoidance of pleasurable activities.

In some patients there is an associated anxiety component that
consists of fear, apprehension, and a sense of impending doom.
Frank panic attacks may be accompanied by somatic sensations
such as a jumpy stomach, tingling fingers, rapid breathing, and
light-headedness.

For every dysphoric emotional state there is a corresponding
mental set that consists of the ideas and beliefs occurring at the

DAVID D. BURNS AND AARON T. BECK • Department of Psychiatry, University
of Pennsylvania, Philadelphia, Pennsylvania 19104.

time the negative affect is experienced. Such cognitions in depressed patients tend to revolve around themes such as worthlessness, hopelessness, and suicide. For example, the patient who feels despair might believe: "I'm a total failure in life. Nothing I've done is worthwhile." The patient who feels guilty typically ruminates about the past and present: "I shouldn't have cheated on that exam when I was in college. I shouldn't have snapped at my daughter. This proves how worthless I really am. I've ruined my life and I'm ruining my family's life." Such an individual sees his life as a series of shoulds and musts that underscore how he never measures up. The patient who feels hopeless and suicidal might be thinking, "My case is worse than anybody else's. I'm certain there is no treatment that will help me, and I know I can't help myself. My problems are real and there is no solution. This suffering is unbearable and will never stop. I'd be better off dead." The cognitions of anxious patients are characterized by a sense of danger and imminent catastrophe. The patient may believe he is about to lose control and is on the verge of an irreversible collapse. He may believe he is losing his mind and his ability to think and function in a normal manner.

The thoughts, feelings, and behaviors of depressed or anxious individuals typically interact in a predictable manner. Because the patient takes his cognitions seriously and places a high degree of belief in his thoughts, he tends to experience many adverse emotions. He then takes these emotions as confirmatory evidence that his beliefs are in fact correct. In other words, he reasons, "Because I feel bad, I must be a bad human being." He doesn't see that he is involved in circular reasoning, and that he has actually created his adverse feelings with his negative internal dialogue. His difficulty is then confounded when he begins to modify his behavior consistent with his beliefs and feelings. For example, the patient who believes that he is worthless and undesirable may begin to avoid associates and friends, and to spend prolonged periods of time alone so as to avoid the inevitable rejection he anticipates. Then, having avoided people, he begins to notice that no one is interacting with him and concludes, "It must really be the case that I am obnoxious since I'm alone most of the time."

Thus, the patient's behavior and the consequences of his behavior reinforce the cognitions that initiated the problem. To make matters worse, he may lose his appetite and sexual drive and become preoccupied with somatic aches and pains, and conclude from these somatic symptoms that his body is worn out and degenerating, and even that he is dying. The patient does not realize he is involved in a self-perpetuating closed system. He goes round and round, deeper into the spiral of depression. Some patients have described this experience as being sucked into a whirlpool. His negative beliefs and feelings as well as his disturbed bodily functions and maladaptive behaviors continue to reinforce one another, and lead him to believe that his life is empty and useless.

This process may evolve slowly and insidiously, over a period of months, or may develop suddenly. One young patient with recurrent depressions described the experience: "It is as if I am suddenly hit with a cosmic jolt. I realize that everything I've ever done or tried to do is worthless. Even my successes appear meaningless. I become convinced that this misery will never end. Suicide appears as the only meaningful alternative."

The patient does not realize that the thoughts that continually flow through his or her mind in response to external events or daydreams play a central and causal role in the development of the dysphoric emotions. The negative cognitions have an automatic quality and the individual typically accepts his interpretations of reality at face value. He feels convinced that his "automatic thoughts" are accurate and reasonable. It rarely occurs to the patient to evaluate his internal dialogue critically and logically. He doesn't realize that the upsetting thoughts are usually exaggerated, illogical misinterpretations of external and internal events. This is surprising when you consider the fact that many depressed individuals are bright, successful people who are capable of assessing the problems and difficulties of others with a high degree of empathy and accuracy. But, when thinking about his own life, the patient's evaluations are frequently harsh, critical, and distorted.

We find that the distortions involved in the cognition of depressed and anxious patients are accessible to intervention with a variety of techniques that will be described below. We have found that the resulting corrections in the patient's illogical cognitions have a profound effect on the emotional and behavioral components of the syndrome, and result in significant and rapid improvement.

If you suspect that your patient has been suffering from a clinically significant mood disorder, the first step is to confirm the presence of depressive illness and to measure its intensity. The Beck Depression Inventory (BDI) (Table I) provides a rapid and convenient screening tool. The patient is instructed to read each item carefully on this multiple-choice questionnaire and to circle the number next to the answer that best reflects how he has been feeling during the past week. If the patient cannot decide between two answers, he is instructed to circle the higher number. This form takes only a few minutes for the patient to complete. It is worthwhile to have the patient fill this form out just prior to all subsequent visits. The information obtained from the BDI will provide a major guide to treatment.

Scoring the BDI consists of adding up the encircled numbers. The higher the score, the more severe the depression. The score is evaluated according to the following classification system: 0–9, no depression or minimal depression; 10–14, borderline depression; 15–20, mild depression; 21–30, moderate depression; 31–40, severe depression; 41–63, very severe depression.

In scoring the BDI it is important to pay special attention to item 9, which asks the patient to assess his suicidal tendencies. If it is at all relevant ask the patient directly, "Are you feeling suicidal?" The question will rarely, if ever, upset the patient. Most patients who had such thoughts will find relief in discussing the matter. Such discussions are for some patients a major deterrent to suicide. If the patient acknowledges the presence of suicidal fantasies, ask him whether he has any serious intentions actually to make the suicide attempt. Inquire whether there are any special reasons for him to reject the idea of suicide, such as family responsibilities, religious belief, the hope of recovery, or any other deterrent. If no specific deterrent exists and if the patient feels totally hopeless, he is at risk. If the patient is impulsive and appears to have a high probability of suicide, it is of crucial importance to intervene immediately and to to focus all therapeutic efforts on reversing suicidal impulses. Even suicidal attempts that do not reflect serious intent can miscarry. Thus, any suicidal thought or action should be taken seriously by the therapist. Many so-called gestures are followed later by successful suicides. Some cognitive approaches to suicide intervention will be discussed subsequently.

TABLE I. BECK INVENTORY

1. 0 I do not feel sad.
   1 I feel sad.
   2 I am sad all the time and I can't snap out of it.
   3 I am so sad or unhappy that I can't stand it.
2. 0 I am not particularly discouraged about the future.
   1 I feel discouraged about the future.
   2 I feel I have nothing to look forward to.
   3 I feel that the future is hopeless and that things cannot improve.
3. 0 I do not feel like a failure.
   1 I feel I have failed more than the average person.
   2 As I look back on my life, all I can see is a lot of failures.
   3 I feel I am a complete failure as a person.
4. 0 I get as much satisfaction out of things as I used to.
   1 I don't enjoy things the way I used to.
   2 I don't get real satisfaction out of anything anymore.
   3 I am dissatisfied or bored with everything.
5. 0 I don't feel particularly guilty.
   1 I feel guilty a good part of the time.
   2 I feel quite guilty most of the time.
   3 I feel guilty all of the time.
6. 0 I don't feel I am being punished.
   1 I feel I may be punished.
   2 I expect to be punished.
   3 I feel I am being punished.
7. 0 I don't feel disappointed in myself.
   1 I am disappointed in myself.
   2 I am disgusted with myself.
   3 I hate myself.
8. 0 I don't feel I am any worse than anybody else.
   1 I am critical of myself for my weaknesses or mistakes.
   2 I blame myself all the time for my faults.
   3 I blame myself for everything bad that happens.
9. 0 I don't have any thoughts of killing myself.
   1 I have thoughts of killing myself, but I would not carry them out.
   2 I would like to kill myself.
   3 I would kill myself if I had the chance.
10. 0 I don't cry any more than usual.
   1 I cry more now than I used to.
   2 I cry all the time now.
   3 I used to be able to cry, but now I can't cry even though I want to.
11. 0 I am no more irritated now than I ever am.
   1 I get annoyed or irritated more easily than I used to.
   2 I feel irritated all the time now.
   3 I don't get irritated at all by the things that used to irritate me.
12. 0 I have not lost interest in other people.
   1 I am less interested in other people than I used to be.
   2 I have lost most of my interest in other people.
   3 I have lost all of my interest in other people.

(continued)

TABLE I. BECK INVENTORY *(continued)*

13.   0   I make decisions about as well as I ever could.
     1   I put off making decisions more than I used to.
     2   I have greater difficulty in making decisions than before.
     3   I can't make decisions at all anymore.
14.   0   I don't feel I look any worse than I used to.
     1   I am worried that I am looking old or unattractive.
     2   I feel that there are permanent changes in my appearance that make me look unattractive.
     3   I believe that I look ugly.
15.   0   I can work about as well as before.
     1   It takes an extra effort to get started at doing something.
     2   I have to push myself very hard to do anything.
     3   I can't do any work at all.
16.   0   I can sleep as well as usual.
     1   I don't sleep as well as I used to.
     2   I wake up 1–2 hours earlier than usual and find it hard to get back to sleep.
     3   I wake up several hours earlier than I used to and cannot get back to sleep.
17.   0   I don't get more tired than usual.
     1   I get tired more easily than I used to.
     2   I get tired from doing almost anything.
     3   I am too tired to do anything.
18.   0   My appetite is no worse than usual.
     1   My appetite is not as good as it used to be.
     2   My appetite is much worse now.
     3   I have no appetite at all anymore.
19.   0   I haven't lost much weight, if any, lately.
     1   I have lost more than 5 pounds.
     2   I have lost more than 10 pounds.
     3   I have lost more than 15 pounds.
      I am purposely trying to lose weight by eating less. Yes ____ No ____
20.   0   I am no more worried about my health than usual.
     1   I am worried about physical problems such as aches and pains; or upset stomach; or constipation.
     2   I am very worried about physical problems and it's hard to think of much else.
     3   I am so worried about my physical problems, that I cannot think about anything else.
21.   0   I have not noticed any recent change in my interest in sex.
     1   I am less interested in sex than I used to be.
     2   I am much less interested in sex now.
     3   I have lost interest in sex completely.

CHARACTERISTICS OF COGNITIVE BEHAVIOR THERAPY

Cognitive therapy differs from conventional forms of psychotherapy both in the types of problems that are discussed in the therapy sessions as well as in the manner in which the therapist and patient interact. In contrast with the "nondirective therapies" (such as psychoanalysis or client-centered therapy), the cognitive therapist helps to structure the therapy session and actively interacts with the patient. Because the depressed or anxious patient feels lost, confused, and disorganized, the therapist helps him restructure his thinking and behavior in a systematic manner.

The main content of the session is focused on the here-and-now and less attention is paid to childhood material. This is not to say that we feel the past is not important or that discussions of how past experiences may have contributed to distorted thinking are excluded. However, the major thrust is clarifying the patient's thinking and feelings during the therapy sessions and between therapy sessions.

The therapist and the patient work together as a collaborative team. The therapist trains the patient in a number of self-help exercises that are done on a daily basis as homework assignments to be completed between therapy sessions. The successful completion of these assignments is stressed as a major mechanism in the therapeutic process. The homework assignments are designed to facilitate a restructuring of the patient's maladaptive thoughts and behaviors.

Whereas the focus of classical behavior therapy is modification of the patient's overt behavior through reinforcement techniques, the primary goal of cognitive therapy involves a transformation of distorted thinking patterns. Thus, the data of greatest importance to the therapist involve the patient's inner experiences, including his feelings, thoughts, daydreams, and attitudes. The therapist demonstrates that the patient's behavior is a consequence of his mental set. Behavior-modification techniques are then used to demonstrate to the patient the irrationality of his beliefs. When the patient assumes more adaptive behavior patterns, he usually begins to change his attitudes and feelings about himself. The therapist and patient design and carry out behavioral experiments that demonstrate to the patient that his intensely negative self-concept and world view are incorrect. The patient carries out the experiment between sessions and gathers data about the outcome. As the patient begins to behave more normally, he views himself as normal.

The second type of homework assignment utilizes predominantly verbal techniques. The patient is trained to record the "automatic thoughts" that flow through his mind in response to various upsetting events. He learns to correlate these thoughts with his emotional responses. He then applies a number of tests to determine whether these attitudes are reasonable, logical, and valid. As he learns to analyze these erroneous cognitions, he is taught to restructure his thoughts in a more realistic, reasonable manner.

The overall strategy of the behavioral/verbal approach is to uncover the patient's distortions and to train the patient to assess the degree of his belief in these distortions. The therapist and patient then design specific experiences or logical demonstrations that reveal the fallacies and traps in the patient's automatic thoughts. They then substitute more correct appraisals and interpretations of the patient's experience, as well as more appropriate behavioral responses. The following sections will contain examples of therapeutic strategies that are used to counteract the cognitive distortions of depressed and anxious patients.[1]

Cognitive Distortions in Depressed Patients

Depression has traditionally been viewed primarily as an affective disorder and any thinking abnormalities have been regarded as a result of the affective disturbance. In recent years, however, there are increasing amounts of data that indicate that there is a thinking disorder in depression and that this thinking disorder may be more central than was previously believed (Beck, 1976). For example, recent studies of the performance of depressed patients on a proverb-interpretation test indicate that such individuals have a loss of abstract thinking just as schizophrenics do, although the degree of difficulty was not as profound in the depressed group (Braff and Beck, 1974). In contrast to the highly generalized and bizarre thinking of schizophrenics, the thought disorder in depression tends to be more focalized and discrete and less bizarre (Braff and Beck, 1974).

---

[1] Individuals wishing to obtain a more detailed therapist's manual for cognitive behavior modification may do so by writing to Aaron T. Beck, M.D., 204 Piersol Building Gl, Hospital of the University of Pennsylvania, Philadelphia, Pennsylvania 19104.

In addition to thinking in an overly concrete manner, depressives view the world in an "all-or-nothing" manner. They see things as either black or white (dichotomous thinking). Other thinking errors include overgeneralization and selective abstraction. For example, depressives may typically focus on the negative in the environment and overlook or discount the positive, thus concluding that the whole of reality is negative. This distorted thinking can reach delusional proportions in individuals with a severe degree of depression. A number of correlational studies have confirmed a predominance of negative thinking in the dreams, projective test responses, self-concepts, and attitudes of depressed patients (Beck, 1976; Beck and Shaw, 1977).

The therapy we use is directed at the "eye of the storm," not at the patient's emotional turbulence but at the way the patient sees himself and his world. This depressive vision can best be characterized by a negative view of the self and the world, as well as the past, present, and future.

Negative View of the Self. A negative self-concept is common among depressed patients. The frequency of this symptom appears to correlate with the severity of the disorder, with over 80% of severely depressed patients expressing self-dislike and low self-evaluation (Beck, 1967). The patient typically views himself as deficient in those personal qualities he most highly regards: intelligence, achievement, popularity, attractiveness, health, strength, etc. This depressive self-image can be characterized by the four D's: the patient feels Defeated, Defensive, Diseased, and Deprived (Beck, 1967).

Psychiatrists for many years have had a tendency to "buy into" the patient's depressive self-evaluation system without asking for checks as to the validity of what the patient is saying about himself. The patient is frequently so persuasive and persistent in his maladaptive thinking that the therapist may get led down the path and agree that the patient's negative self-concept is indeed valid. This is illustrated by the writings of such a keen observer as Freud in his treatise, "Mourning and Melancholia":

> The patient represents his ego to us as worthless, incapable of any achievement and morally despicable; he reproaches himself, vilifies himself and expects to be cast out and punished. . . . It would be

equally fruitless from a scientific and therapeutic point of view to contradict a patient who brings these accusations against his ego. He must *surely be right in some way* [italics ours] and be describing something that is as it seems to him to be. Indeed, we must at once confirm some of his statements without reservation. He *really is as lacking in interest and as incapable of love and achievement as he says* [italics ours]. . . . He also seems to us justified in certain other self-accusations; *it is merely that he has a keener eye for the truth than other people who are not melancholic* [italics ours]. When in his heightened self-criticism he describes himself as petty, egoistic, dishonest, lacking in independence, one whose sole aim has been to hide the weaknesses of his own nature, it may be so far as we know, *that he has come pretty near to understanding himself* [italics ours]; we only wonder why a man has to be ill before he can be accessible to truth of this kind. (Freud, 1917, pp. 155–156)

This negative self-concept is illustrated by a young woman referred for treatment from New York, where she had been unsuccessfully treated with analytic therapy for several years since the onset of severe, unremitting depression in her early teen years. She had numerous wrist-slashing episodes in addition to at least one serious suicide attempt involving pill overdosage. She had been hospitalized many times, including closed-ward confinement. The referring psychiatrist recommended a minimum of three years of additional hospitalization, and appeared to agree with the patient that the prognosis was not positive, and that her dream of a professional career was unrealistic. At the time of the initial consultation with this patient, the testing indicated severe depression and a high degree of hopelessness, and the patient expressed the desire to kill herself. The family history indicated that several relatives had attempted suicide, two of them successfully. When the therapist inquired as to the reasons the patient wanted to kill herself, she responded that she was basically a lazy human being. She explained that because she was lazy and worthless she deserved to die.

The therapist used cognitive techniques to demonstrate to the patient the illogic of her position. In the first place, the patient owned up that even if she really were lazy, she was only one of millions of lazy people in the United States. Because she agreed that they would not deserve to die because of their laziness, she concluded that she too would not deserve to die because of laziness. She acknowledged she had been using a double standard in evaluating her own performance, and admitted she would never be so harsh in her judgments of other people. She expressed considerable relief when the therapist proposed that she use a single reasonable standard for judging herself and others.

In addition to this, the therapist pointed out to the patient that inactivity and a lack of interest in life were symptoms of depression. He suggested to her that in our society people are not condemned to death because of symptoms of an illness. Like many depressives the patient had made the mistake of confusing symptoms of depression with ingrained permanent characteristics of her own personality, and concluded she was a lazy and worthless person. She had forgotten that depression is a disease of time-limited duration and had overlooked the fact that during periods when she was not depressed she had been ambitious and hardworking.

Depressed individuals often confuse the symptoms of their illness with their own identity. They reason that their feeling of weakness and fatigability and their performance difficulties indicate that they are inadequate. As a result, they will often discount any disconfirming evidence that indicates that they are not actually lazy and inadequate, or when they do succeed, or when previous successes are pointed out to them, they will frequently reply that his disconfirming evidence is just a "fluke."

For example, after a six-week hospitalization in Philadelphia, the young woman's depressive illness was resolved enough to the point where she could be discharged. She became a part-time university student. Prior to enrolling she predicted she would be unable to sit through a single class. When she finally received an "A" at the completion of the course, she discounted this evidence of her own competence and initiative by saying that she was basically not capable of making it as a full-time university student: "The only reason I received an "A" was because the class was too easy. I already knew the material and so the grade really didn't count." When she went on to receive all "A's" her first semester as a full-time student, she again concluded that the evidence didn't count: "I'm a lazy and incompetent person. I will never be able to keep it up. It had to be an accident of some sort."

For such individuals, an ongoing series of successful experiences over a period of time will usually result in a lessening of the belief in their worthlessness and inadequacy. However, the tendency of some depressives to maintain such beliefs despite considerable evidence to the contrary is quite impressive.

Many depressives, like the young woman, tend to evaluate their worth as human beings in terms of their performance in career-related tasks. In evaluating her performance, she concentrated on negatives and overlooked evidence that she could perform successfully. She evaluated her performance in terms of perfectionistic all-or-nothing standards. If she had received a high examination grade, she would think almost exclusively of the questions she missed, and conclude that she was a total failure as a human being.

As a result of such attitudes, she developed depressive reactions whenever she perceived her performance as being less than perfect. The blue mood and panic she then experienced seemed to convince her that it was, in fact, terrible to be imperfect because she felt terrible. When the depressive symptoms evolved, she experienced increasing lethargy and inactivity and began to withdraw from normal activities. Then she would interpret her decreased productivity as further evidence of her inadequacy and worthlessness. Thus, the vicious cycle of depressive thoughts, feelings, and behaviors would continue to feed itself.

Negative View of the World. In addition to a negative view of the self, many depressives develop a negative view of the external world. The patient construes his experiences negatively, and interprets his interactions with his environment as representing defeat, deprivation, or disparagement. He sees life as a series of burdens, obstacles, and traumas (Beck, 1967). His negative beliefs regarding the world have an *a priori* quality. The patient is convinced about the validity of his pessimism, regardless of any disconfirming data.

This negative world-view seems to result from the distorted manner in which the depressed individual processes information. Positive and neutral experiences are ignored—or screened out—so that predominantly negative events dominate the patient's conscious awareness.

For example, when the young woman discussed above became a university student, she reported to her therapist after several days of living in the dormitory that she had some data that proved to her that the world was no good. She explained that she had heard some premedical students in the dormitory talking. They were making fun of a young woman named Joan who appeared to be upset. One student had said to another, "If you're looking for Joan, you can probably find her in her dormitory room sitting on the ledge of the window." The patient concluded from overhearing this conversation that people are "insensitive and no good . . . whenever people are polite or kind to one another, they are just being insincere and covering up the meanness and badness that is at their core. Just pick up the paper and you'll see the many reports of rapes, murders, and violence, and you will know what reality is made of. The universe is no good."

Like many intelligent depressed individuals, she made a rather convincing case for her point of view. Nevertheless, her thinking was unrealistic because she focused on certain negative events in her environment and expanded these to her full phenomenal field. While it is true that there are many negative events in the world, it is also true that there are many neutral events as well as many good events. This young woman was overlooking the fact that people had not been cruel, mean, or disrespectful to her. Thus, she was making the thinking error of overgeneralization, or selective abstraction. She was focusing on those negative events in the environment, overlooking or discounting the positive, and then concluding that the whole of reality is negative.

Negative View of the Past and Future. Many depressed patients report they cannot remember ever having been happy even though friends and relatives will confirm that aside from episodic periods of depression they did appear to be happy individuals. However, the depressed patient frequently distorts his memories of the past and concludes that he always has been and always will be depressed. If the therapist points out a period of time when the patient acknowledged being happy, he will typically respond, "Well, that period of time doesn't count. Happiness is an illusion of some kind. The real me is depressed and inadequate. I was just fooling myself then. The cards are stacked against me and always will be."

As the patient projects this negative view into the future, he becomes convinced he is hopeless. He anticipates that his current problems and suffering will continue indefinitely. As he looks ahead, he can envision only endless pain and deprivation (Beck, 1967). He feels certain that he will never get better and that any improvement will be transient and insignificant. He is convinced he will continue to relapse back into depression all of his life. To back up this point of view, many patients can document years and years of chronic illness that has not responded to antidepressant medications, psychotherapy, or shock treatment. Many of those who have recovered have gone on to experience relapse after relapse. Frequently, each episode is more severe and accompanied by greater disillusionment and frustration.

It is of interest that the degree of hopelessness in depressed patients is often higher and more severe than the hopelessness seen in terminal malignancy patients. A depressed young man recently told his therapist: "At night I pray, hoping to develop a malignancy. Then I wouldn't be expected to try, and I could just wait to die." The hopelessness in depressed patients is highly correlated with suicide impulses (Beck, Kovacs, and Weissman, 1975). It is crucial to expose the illogic behind the patient's hopelessness early in the treatment process so as to prevent an actual suicide attempt.

A fifty-year-old auto-parts dealer was referred by a psychoanalyst for cognitive therapy of a depression of 10 years duration. The patient had received intensive therapy from three psychiatrists during this time, including treatment with antidepressants, phenothiazines, electroshock therapy, and insight-oriented psychotherapy. He had received no benefit from any of these treatments and had exhausted his financial reserves, having spent over eighty thousand dollars in his efforts to overcome his depression. In addition to typical depressive symptoms, he complained of severe aches and pains in his head and back, which he attributed to a "popping of my brain cells and a tearing to shreds of the tendons and fibers in my spinal cord." He was convinced that he had undergone irreversible brain damage and had lost all powers to concentrate, to function effectively, or to enjoy life.

At the beginning of the first therapy session he expressed considerable resentment and hopelessness, and handed the therapist a suicide note he had prepared for his daughter to read after his death. He stated emphatically that he was convinced he could never get better, and he would defer suicide and consent to treatment only if he were given a money-back guarantee: "You get me better—then I'll pay . . . I say this only because I know you have nothing to offer and I'd just as soon settle the issue now . . . I've been conned enough by doctors. I'd be better off dead and you know it . . . I'll pay for today's session, but not one more cent until I'm better . . . I'm a fighter and I've struggled for 10 years. But now it's time to give up."

The initial score was 44 on the Beck Depression Inventory, consistent with a very severe depression. The therapist's assessment of the suicidal potential was high, as the patient acknowledged no deterrent to suicide and expressed explicit intentions to commit suicide. The patient refused to make any additional appointments, but agreed to a phone call from the therapist after his proposal had been considered.

The authors of this paper consulted following the session in an attempt to develop a therapeutic strategy that would undercut the patient's hopelessness. A decision was made to consent to the patient's demand for a "money-back guarantee," despite the obvious difficulty with the case, so as to determine whether such an unusual approach might be useful in exceptional situations. It was decided that therapy would proceed on a month-to-month basis. Each month, the aim would be to reduce the depression score by a predetermined amount, mutually agreed upon by patient and therapist. If the patient did not achieve the goal for the month, he would not be billed for that month's psychotherapy.

When the therapist called he explained to the patient that he understood his frustration, but emphasized that the lack of response to treatments in the past does not prove he will fail to respond to treatment in the future. Medical science moves on, and new discoveries in treatment are made on an ongoing basis. It was important for the patient to understand that he had not been treated by an approach similar to cognitive therapy, and that many individuals with depression as severe as his had experienced a satisfactory response to treatment. The therapist explained that the patient's hopelessness was simply a symptom of depression and not a description of reality. Thus, the hopelessness was a reason for treatment, not for suicide. To emphasize this, the therapist explained he would gladly accept the patient's financial terms, and outlined the details of the proposal.

In response to this information, the patient burst into tears and said, "Doctor, this is the stuff miracles are made of." He immediately experienced some emotional relief, and at the second session three days later, the depression score had dropped to 34, well below the patient's aim for the first month of treatment. The therapist received payment that month and every subsequent month until the depression scores were in the normal range (below 10).

The therapist's initial response—while somewhat unusual— communicated a sense of commitment, compassion, and flexibility that undercut the patient's cynicism and fostered a sense of therapeutic rapport in an angry patient understandably disillusioned with therapists. The therapist indicated that he would not "buy into" the patient's hopelessness, but had a conviction that the patient could and would receive help if he made the effort. The intervention also contained the element of surprise, suggesting to the patient that he was being treated with an approach that was at least fresh and different. Finally, the therapist exposed the illogic in the patient's statement that he would be a cognitive-therapy nonresponder. Although the patient was an expert in the symptoms of depression, he was not an expert in the treatment of depression, and had no way to foretell the future or adequately assess his prognosis.

Like most depressive thinking, suicidal hopelessness is usually the product of distorted thinking. The patient sees himself caught in a trap from which there is no exit. Because he experiences his suffering as unbearable, he concludes that suicide is the only reasonable solution to his problems.

For example, a thirty-five-year-old wholesale frozen-food distributor had experienced chronic depression since his divorce six years earlier. He had been raising his two daughters and did not know the whereabouts of his wife and only son. A tragic historical event was the suicide of his father when he was fifteen years old. His father died in his arms.

In the past year the patient's depression had intensified and he found it increasingly difficult to go to work or to call on customers. He would spend his time doing errands around the house saying,

"Tomorrow I must get started calling on customers." He felt in danger of being fired, and each day of avoidance made it more difficult for him to go to work and face his boss. The avoidance led to shame. He was convinced that he was not suffering from depression but from laziness. He shared with his therapist his conviction that it would be preferable for him to commit suicide as this was his only "realistic solution." The therapist inquired what problems he had that would be realistically solved by suicide. "First, I have lost face with my boss. He pays me a salary and I haven't made any sales or calls on customers for over a month. I couldn't stand to face him or any of my clients. I'm sure I've lost my job and all self-respect. Second, in the absence of commissions, I'm not making enough money to support my daughters adequately. One of these days they'll want to go to college and I won't have any money. Third, I'm constantly depressed, and I'm not the kind of father I ought to be. Lately, they've been asking me, 'Daddy, why are you acting differently?' "

The therapist pointed out the illogic of his position. First, he had no real evidence that he had lost his job or had lost face. In order to find out, he would have to contact his employer, explain his situation frankly, and get some information. And if he had lost the employer's respect and/or job—which seemed unlikely in light of the fact that the employer had suggested and helped to underwrite the therapy—suicide would not correct the situation. Nor would suicide help his daughters go to college or obtain good fathering. Suicide would, in fact, add further to their burden by removing the only parent who had been willing to raise them following the divorce.

It was helpful to this patient to realize that suicide simply involved further avoidance of his problems, but did not represent a solution. He had no real evidence that his problems were in any way insoluble, since he had not attempted any solutions. He had overlooked the fact that prior to his depression he had been an energetic successful salesman and was not, in fact, lazy or incompetent.

Although not entirely convinced by the therapist's appraisal, he did agree to call his boss and to call on one customer. The employer expressed support and empathy and assured him that his job was not in danger. When he called on the customer, he did receive some ribbing about "being on vacation" for the past six weeks, but also landed a small order. He later reported with surprise that the discomfort from being teased was actually quite small in comparison with the intense depression he experienced every day at home avoiding work. This discovery gave him courage to call on other customers, and over a two-week period he built back up to a normal working schedule and began making plans for the future. As he began to see the future, the past, and the present more objectively and learned to view himself and his external environment with more perspective, there was a corresponding improvement in the rest of his symptomatology.

COGNITIVE DISTORTIONS IN ANXIOUS PATIENTS

The cognitions of anxious patients have a different theme from those of depressed patients, although anxiety and depression often coexist in the same individual. The depressed patient typically believes that a tragedy has already occurred and that his problems are inherently hopeless and insoluble. In contrast, the anxious patient feels as if he is on the edge of the cliff ready to fall. He believes that some tragedy is about to occur.

During an anxiety attack, there are at least two kinds of cognitive phenomena occurring. First, there is often a mental visual image that preciptates the anxiety attack. For example, a therapist moved out of Philadelphia and referred one of his patients to one of the authors. Prior to the first visit, the patient called saying that her heart was pounding and she was dizzy, sick, and frightened and unable to come for the visit. The therapist asked her, "Did you have any visual images or fantasies about what would happen if you did come to see me?" She replied that she had a frightening daydream of passing out on the train. This is a typical visual image of an anxious patient and is characterized by a sense of danger and loss of control.

The cognitive approach involves training the patient to identify these visual images or daydreams that precipitate the anxiety and then to evaluate whether or not such images are indeed as realistic and catastrophic as the patient imagines them to be. For example, the therapist asked the prospective new patient on the phone: "Suppose you did in fact faint on the train—what then?" She replied that in all likelihood she would wake up in a minute and discover several concerned passengers trying to arouse her. She acknowledged that such an experience might be somewhat embarrassing or uncomfortable but was in no way catastrophic or terrible. She also admitted she had, in fact, never actually fainted, although she had often feared loss of control during periods of anxiety. She experienced considerable relief when she realized that her anxiety symptoms had been actually produced by her high degree of belief in her visual fantasy, and that the actual probability of a fainting spell was actually quite low, based on her past experience.

The therapist proposed that prior to the next scheduled session she look for upsetting visual images and frightening thoughts and make notes about these on the train, including a numerical count of the number of such images as well as the content of the fantasies. This paradoxical maneuver of instructing the patient to look for, analyze, and write down these thoughts and fantasies undercut the patient's fear and avoidance of such anxiety reactions. She appeared in person at the next therapy session and reported that there had been no cognitive or emotional upset since the telephone call, although she had been diligently looking for one!

Once the patient experiences the initial symptoms of anxiety due to this upsetting visual image, he characteristically transforms the symptoms of anxiety into a full-blown attack. At this point, the cognitions are usually remarkably similar from patient to patient. For example, the patient might think, "I'll never get out of this," or "I'm going crazy," and "I'm losing my mind," or "I'm going to lose control." These thoughts create more anxiety and the subsequent uncomfortable somatic symptoms seem to confirm the patient's belief that something terrible is indeed happening to him.

The patient may withdraw from his usual activities due to these symptoms. For example, a university student experienced panic while studying for an important exam. He began to think, "I can't concentrate. I'm losing my mind. I'll blow the exam." These thoughts intensified his panic. He therefore stopped studying, refused to take the exam, and received an incomplete in the course. Since he was a conscientious student with a 3.5 grade average and had never before withdrawn from an exam, he concluded, "I must really be going downhill." This added further to his anxiety and depression and so he dropped out of school entirely. He then began to think, "I'm just a dropout now. That proves that there must be something wrong with my mind." After he dropped out of school, he experienced a frank panic attack while smoking marijuana on a date. Because his friends appeared to enjoy marijuana, he took his reaction as further evidence that something was wrong with him.

He then avoided his friends and experienced a sense of shame and the feeling that he had lost face. After several months of relative isolation he began to think, "I must really be insane. I'm a social reject as well as an academic failure." He went to an analytically oriented therapist for two years and found it difficult to talk during the therapy sessions because of the analyst's silence and his own mounting anxiety. During each session he was preoccupied with thoughts such as "If I can't even talk to a psychiatrist, there must be something terribly wrong with me." The therapist's silence added further to his panic and sense of paralysis. He frequently experienced anxiety in response to images in which he saw himself locked up in a mental hospital, being scorned by former friends, etc. Essentially, this patient was giving himself frequent danger signals in the form of upsetting thoughts and images and erroneous interpretations of the symptoms of anxiety. Because of the therapist's inactivity, the patient was highly vulnerable to internal stimulation—much like a sensory-deprivation experiment.

The strategy of the cognitive therapist involved training the patient to monitor and evaluate realistically his automatic thoughts by using the Daily Record of Dysfunctional Thoughts. This is a form that patients fill out on a daily basis between therapy sessions and record their uncomfortable emotions (including sadness, anxiety, or anger), as well as their negative thoughts. They then are to write down a rational response to the negative thought and monitor the degree of emotional relief they experience. The patient was taught to design and carry out behavioral experiments involving risk-taking exercises that would provide additional data for evaluating and modifying his beliefs.

For example, whenever he contemplated participating in any social interaction with peers, he became frozen with anxiety and self-doubt, and invariably avoided the interaction. When he was invited to a party by a former friend (the situation provoking the dysphoria), he recorded his emotional reaction as "anxiety, 80%." He then recorded a number of "automatic thoughts" that flowed through his mind immediately following the invitation and he assessed his degree of belief in these thoughts (between 0 and 100%). These included: (1) They will smoke pot at the party (90%). (2) If they smoke pot, they will put pressure on everyone to smoke pot (80%). (3) If I don't smoke pot, I will be ostracized (100%). (4) Because I will be anxious, I will not be able to think of anything to say (100%). (5) If I am quiet, they will conclude I'm peculiar (100%). (6) If I talk and they find out how upset I've been, they will look down on me and realize what a jerk I am (100%). (7) If others look down on me, this will mean that I'm a worthless human being (90%).

After recording these automatic thoughts, he then generated the following "rational responses" to each of the "automatic thoughts," and assessed his degree of belief in each of these: (1 and 2) They may not smoke pot, and if they do they may not insist that everyone do so. I have the right to say I don't care for pot (100%). (3) There are probably many people who don't smoke pot and who are accepted by others. Since they are not ostracized, there is no reason to think I will be (90%). (4) Even though I am anxious, I can talk to some people if I choose. Anxiety makes me uncomfortable but doesn't make it impossible to speak (80%). (5) Quiet people are not necessarily peculiar. Some people look up to people who are quiet (80%). (6) If they find out I've been lonely and upset they may express concern rather than rejection (95%). (7) If others look down on me it doesn't prove I am worthless, since others are not in a position to sit in judgment on me. If I respect myself, the opinions of others will be less important. It is impossible to please everybody, and it is also very unlikely that every single person will look down on me (100%).

After recording these data, he was able to see the incompatibility between the "automatic thoughts" and the "rational responses." The effect was to create a cognitive dissonance, such that he was forced to choose whether the automatic thoughts or rational responses were more realistic. He correspondingly reduced his degree of belief in each of his automatic thoughts. At this point, he

experienced partial emotional relief, and his anxiety levels—
although not eliminated—fell to the 30–40% level.

The therapist proposed that since many of his upsetting cognitions involved actual predictions about the behavior and attitudes
of others, he would have to perform an experiment in order to
become more convinced about the truth of the matter. The therapist
suggested that although it would require some courage, it would be
to his advantage if he actually attended the party. This would allow
him to gather considerable data concerning his beliefs. In order to
reduce his anxiety levels somewhat, prior to leaving for the event
he was to read the "automatic thoughts" and "rational responses."

Because depressed and anxious patients have the capacity for
transforming neutral or even positive events into negative experiences, it is important that such behavioral experiments be set up in
such a way that a successful outcome is virtually assured. Therefore,
the therapist suggested that the patient develop a list of behavioral
aims with regard to the party. The therapist suggested he give himself a reward if he could accomplish any goals regardless of whether
or not he enjoyed the party. Simply going to the party constituted
one goal. The other goals included: attempt to carry on a conversation with at least one other person; learn as much about that person
as possible, so as to be able to write a brief biographical
sketch about that individual and bring this write-up to the
therapist; politely but assertively decline any invitation to smoke
marijuana; if you do decline marijuna, ask the host whether your
nonparticipation in this creates any discomfort for others; obtain
information relative to as many of the other automatic thoughts as
possible; if any emotional discomfort arises during the party, attempt to identify the automatic thoughts and write them down
later; prior to leaving for the party, write down a prediction regarding how pleasurable it will be (from 0 to 100%); after the party write
down the amount of pleasure actually experienced (from 0 to 100%);
and after the party, count the number of goals that were actually
achieved.

The development of discrete, easily attainable personal behavioral goals counteracted the patient's expectation that he had to perform for others at the party. He could successfully accomplish many
of these goals regardless of the amount of pleasure or interpersonal
success he experienced at the party. The goals were designed to in-

volve the patient in the process of being at the party so as to distract him from his obsessional concerns with the outcome of the experience.

It was not surprising that the patient's actual experience at the party was substantially divergent from his negative expectations. Although a few individuals did smoke pot, they were in the minority. He became engaged in a lengthy conversation with the wife of the host and learned that she, too, had at times experienced anxiety and depression. He actually enjoyed himself, and was one of the last guests to leave.

While a single successful experience does not entirely reverse a pattern of chronic catastrophizing, self-doubt, and avoidance, it contributed significantly in this case to a reversal of the patient's sense of hopelessness and worthlessness. He experienced substantial emotional relief, and was able to initiate a systematic program of coping with his fears in collaboration with the therapist.

As with depression, the anxiety syndrome begins with characteristic upsetting thoughts and images. Catastrophic themes involving loss of control, mental deterioration, and rejection are frequently involved. The dysphoric emotional states and maladaptive behavior patterns then seem to reinforce the patient's belief system resulting in a self-perpetuating closed system.

The therapist attempts to "open up" this system at the cognitive level by training the patient to identify and correct the frightening thoughts that produce the symptoms. We assure the patient that although he experiences unpleasant reactions that mean to him that he is going insane, he is in point of fact *not* going insane despite his intense discomfort. We teach the patient to think more realistically and to modify his behavior in small steps until a normal emotional and behavioral pattern has again been established. The aim is to create a "self-esteem cycle" in which realistic attitudes, feelings, and behavior patterns become mutually reinforcing.

Comparative Efficacy of Cognitive Behavior Modification versus Antidepressant Drug Therapy in the Treatment of Depressed and Anxious Patients

We have recently been conducting a series of studies testing the efficacy of short-term structured cognitive behavior modification for chronically or intermittently depressed outpatients. To date we have treated several hundred depressed individuals with cognitive psychotherapy. The therapy involves training patients to identify distorted thinking and to modify this thinking as well as maladaptive behavior patterns as described previously.

Our present systematic study (Rush, Beck, Kovacs, and Hollon, 1977), which involved the treatment of 41 unipolar depressed outpatients during the past two and a half years, was designed as a controlled comparison of cognitive psychotherapy with an antidepressant drug of proven efficacy (imipramine). The subjects were moderately to severely depressed outpatients with a mean period of 8.8 years since the onset of the first depressive episode. Seventy-five percent were suicidal. A number of these individuals had symptoms of anxiety in addition to depression.

Patients were randomly assigned to the drug therapy ($n = 22$) or the cognitive-therapy group ($n = 19$). The patients in the cognitive-therapy group were seen initially twice a week for a maximum of 20 visits in 12 weeks. Frequency of visits tapered off so that the mean was 1.5 sessions per week, or 15.2 interviews for the course of treatment. Patients in the drug group were seen weekly. Imipramine was given in increasing doses to a maximum of 250 mg per day for a maximum of 12 weeks. In addition to chemotherapy, these patients received approximately 15 minutes of supportive psychotherapy at each visit.

Analysis of the data revealed several interesting findings: (1) Although both the chemotherapy and cognitive therapy groups showed almost identical mean depression scores at the beginning of treatment (30 in both groups) on the Beck Depression Inventory—and similar rates of improvement for the first eight weeks—the cognitive-therapy group improved more rapidly in the initial phase of treatment. (2) The dropout rate (due to patients' intolerance of drug side effects or lack of improvement) was substantially higher in the chemotherapy group (8 versus 1). (3) When the dropouts are included in the computations, the mean end of treatment score on the BDI was significantly better in the cognitive-therapy group (7.3 versus 17.4; one-way analysis of covariance revealed $p < 0.01$). When dropouts were excluded from the computations, the mean BDI score was still significantly better in the cognitive-therapy group (5.9) than in the pharmacotherapy group (13.0); one-way analysis of covariance indicated $p < 0.05$. (4) Seventy-nine percent of the cognitive-therapy group showed marked or complete remission of symptoms as compared to 23% of the pharmacotherapy patients. (5) Significant reductions in Hamilton Anxiety scores were observed in both the cognitive-therapy and pharmacotherapy groups. Between-groups comparison did not show a significant difference in favor of one treatment over the other, although the trend toward lower anxiety scores seemed to favor the cognitive-therapy group ($p < 0.15$) when dropouts were excluded from analysis. (6) Follow-up studies at three and six months on 38 patients indicated substantially fewer relapses in the cognitive-therapy group as compared with the drug-therapy group (Rush *et al.*, 1977). When completers plus dropouts were included in the analysis, the cognitive-therapy group had significantly lower BDI scores at three months ($p < 0.01$) than the pharmacotherapy group and showed a nonsignificant trend at six months ($p < 0.11$). Similar results were obtained when dropouts were excluded from analysis.

The significance of these studies lies in the fact that for the first time we have been able to demonstrate in a controlled study that psychological techniques are effective in treating moderately to severely depressed suicidal outpatients. The second significant feature is that this new approach works much faster than traditional methods of psychotherapy. Most of the patients started to improve in the first week, particularly in terms of suicidal ideation. If our findings are substantiated, the patient who receives the newer type of psychotherapy can look forward to relatively prompt relief rather than the many weeks of suffering and flirting with suicide that we observe in patients receiving traditional therapy. Third, this approach provides an alternative to chemotherapy as a short-term treatment of depression. It is especially indicated for those patients who cannot or will not take antidepressant drugs, who prematurely discontinue drug treatment, or have not responded to drug treatment by previous therapists. Finally, the encouraging preliminary results from the follow-up evaluations indicate that the patients treated for depression with cognitive techniques tend to have more lasting results than those treated with antidepressant drug therapy. This is of particular importance because of the relapsing nature of depressive illness. The findings may indicate that the patients treated with cognitive therapy show greater gains in terms of their ability to cope with life's difficulties on an ongoing basis.

This study was designed to evaluate cognitive therapy alone versus antidepressant drug therapy so as to determine whether the therapy does have value in the treatment of severe mood disorders. Further studies are now in progress to determine whether the combination of the two treatment modalities has an additive effect, as compared with either treatment alone.

REFERENCES

Beck, A.T. *Depression: Clinical, experimental, and theoretical aspects.* New York: Hoeber, 1967. (Republished as *Depression: Causes and treatment.* Philadelphia: University of Pennsylvania Press, 1972).

Beck, A.T. *Cognitive therapy and the emotional disorders.* New York: International Universities Press, 1976.

Beck, A.T., Kovacs, M., and Weissman, A. Hopelessness and suicidal behavior: An overview. *Journal of the American Medical Association,* 1975, *234,* 1136–1139.

Beck, A.T., and Shaw, B.F. Cognitive approaches to depression. In A. Ellis and R. Grieger (Eds.), *Handbook of rational emotive theory and practice.* New York: Springer, 1977.

Braff, D.L., and Beck, A.T. Thinking disorder in depression. *Archives of General Psychiatry,* 1974, *33,* 456–459.

Freud, S. *Collected Papers, 1917.* (Translated Joan Riviere, Vol. IV, Chapters 8, Mourning and Melancholia, pp. 155–156). London: Hogarth Press Ltd., 1952.

Rush, A.J., Beck, A.T., Kovacs, M., and Hollon, S. Comparative efficacy of cognitive therapy and pharmacotherapy in the treatment of depressed outpatients. *Cognitive Therapy and Research,* 1977, *1,* 17–37.

5

Anger and Coping with Stress

COGNITIVE BEHAVIORAL INTERVENTIONS

RAYMOND W. NOVACO

Howard Beale, veteran anchorman of the Universal Broadcasting Company, became the mad prophet of the movie, *Network*, as he implored television audiences across the nation:

> So, I know you've been bugged. You've got to get mad. You've got to say, "I'm a human being, damn it! My life has value!" So, I want you to get up now. I want all of you to get up out of your chairs. I want you to get up right now and go to the window, open it, and stick your head out and yell, "I'm as mad as hell, and I'm not going to take this anymore!" Things have got to change, but first, you've got to get mad.

It seems that Howard Beale has touched a nerve when he enjoins us to revolt against the adversities of everyday living.

Anger is one of the most talked-about but least studied of human emotions. Poets, playwrights, and composers have portrayed anger in artistic form; philosophers have examined its meaning. Yet, surprisingly, anger has eluded the attention of experimentally minded psychologists. This probably has been a function of behavioristic traditions that favored the study of aggressive be-

RAYMOND W. NOVACO • Program of Social Ecology, University of California, Irvine, California 92717.

havior over that of anger. Although anger inductions have been an integral part of the prolific research on aggression, experimental and theoretical interest in anger has been incidental to the study of harm-doing behaviors. More than three quarters of a century ago, G. Stanley Hall stated, "Psychological literature contains no comprehensive memoir on this very important and interesting subject" (Hall, 1899, p. 516). That remark echoes here.

The cognitive trend in contemporary psychology, particularly among clinical psychologists, has in part sprung from disenchantment with the strict behavioristic formulations. The interrelationships between thoughts, feelings, and actions are now receiving deserved attention. Mahoney (1977) presents a succinct analysis of these developments, as well as the problems and issues confronting those with a cognitive-learning orientation. However, despite this surge of interest in cognitive and affective intrapersonal processes, anger and its cognitive correlates remain neglected phenomena, when compared to the extent of study that has been given to other emotions such as anxiety, depression, and pain. Notwithstanding the involvement of anger in the problem constellations of clinical populations, no existing theory of psychotherapy articulates a coherent view of anger disorders or the means by which they might be remedied.

This chapter will delineate a cognitive behavioral approach to the treatment of anger problems. This therapeutic approach, which involves cognitive regulation and skills training for the management of anger, has been evaluated experimentally and has been shown to be successful in the treatment of severe anger problems (Novaco, 1975, 1976b, 1977). The treatment model is called *stress inoculation*, and it has been applied to problems of anxiety and pain, as well as anger (Meichenbaum and Cameron, 1973; Meichenbaum, 1975b; Meichenbaum and Novaco, 1978; Turk, 1974). The concepts of stress and anger will be developed as they pertain to this treatment approach to anger disorders.

HUMAN STRESS

Stress can be understood as a state of imbalance between environmental demands and the response capabilities of the person or system to cope with these demands. The topic of human stress has emerged as a rubric under which a wide variety of adaptation-related phenomena has been investigated. At times, this heterogeneity has prompted the suggestion that usage of the concept of stress be discontinued in favor of subordinate concepts that are more restricted in scope, such as threat, arousal, conflict, or anxiety.

As a brief justification for using the term "stress," as opposed to restricting the theoretical language to the more specific term of anger, it can be said that the routine exposure to stressors in the absence of commensurate resources to cope has a cumulative adverse effect over time. With regard to anger, it is asserted that persons who are prone to provocation and are without the psychological resources for coping are thereby susceptible to health impairments (e.g., cardiovascular disorders), to diminished work efficiency, and to disruption of personal relationships. The point is that chronic anger can have extensive consequences that go considerably beyond the simple experience of an unpleasant emotional state.

The term stress has been borrowed from engineering, where its usage refers to an external force applied to a physical structure that produces a strain on the structure. The resultant strain is a function of the magnitude of the stress and of the properties of the structure. The psychological meaning of stress, which refers to a condition of the organism, parallels the engineering concept of strain. In a behavioral view, the term "stressor" denotes the external forces experienced by the organism, and their stress effects are determined by the characteristics of the structures on which they impact (Lazarus, 1966; Selye, 1976). The failure to distinguish the terms "stressor" and "stress" has led at times to an equivocal usage of the concept of stress as referring to both an agent and to a result. Stress is construed most clearly as a hypothetical state that is induced by environmental forces and manifested by reactions at various physiological, behavioral, and social levels. This analysis thus distinguishes *stressors* as aversive events that exert demands for adaptation, *stress* as a hypothetical state denoting a condition of imbalance between demands and resources for coping, and *stress reactions* as the adverse health and behavioral consequences of exposure to environmental demands.

The study of stress is concerned with the adaption of the organism to various environmental fields. Environmental fields are domains of elements that are described at particular levels of analysis, such as the biological, psychological, social, and physical levels. Stressors are elements in the environmental fields that disturb the organism's equilibrium, interfere with its performance, or even threaten its survival.[1] The rapidly expanding body of research on human stress[2] supports Wohlwill's (1970) view that the environment not only elicits responses but can also constrain human functioning and can have a lasting imprint on health and behavior over time.

The above remarks are intended to clarify the context in which the terms "stress" and "stress inoculation" are used. The present cognitive behavior therapy model is applied to human stress and adaptation at a particular level of analysis, namely, the psychological, and the reader should be mindful of this boundary condition. That is, there are many sources of stress in the various environmental fields to which we are exposed, and for a number of these stress-inducing conditions (such as exposure to excessive noise, economic fluctuations, traffic congestion, or population density) the appropriate stress-ameliorating intervention may not be a clinical, psychotherapy procedure.[3] In terms of value premises, it is not the

[1] Stressors do not necessarily arise in the environment independent of the person's actions. Many stressors (e.g., life-change events or various forms of provocation) are a result of the person's prior activity.

[2] The interested reader is referred to the seminal works of Selye (1976), Lazarus (1966), Glass and Singer (1972), and Dohrenwend and Dohrenwend (1974). Compilations of theory and research pertaining to human stress across disciplinary perspectives can be found in Insel and Moos (1974, Levine and Scotch (1970), and Monat and Lazarus (1977).

[3] Clinical interventions generally aim to mitigate stress effects by increasing the person's (psychological) resources for coping with environmental demands. Ecological or community approaches place greater emphasis on modifying the environmental demands or risk factors. Recent research in the behavioral sciences has demonstrated that the prevalence of physical illnesses, mental disorders, depressed mood, and social disorganization are in part a function of identifiable variations in the physical and social environment (cf. earlier footnoted references on stress). Although the knowledge base is far from adequate for interventions at the level of public or organizational policy, it ultimately may be more efficacious in reducing the nonspecific effects of stress to pursue change efforts at environmental levels rather than to focus on the individual. An excellent review and conceptualization of pertinent research in the field of environmental psychology can be found in Stokols (1978).

assumption of the present analysis that the locus for change regarding human stress necessarily or primarily resides within the individual.

The stress interventions to be described herein are formulated at the psychological level of analysis. The most extensively developed and influential formulation of psychological stress is that of Lazarus (1966, 1967). The theoretical model of stress developed by Lazarus consists of an integration of the concepts of threat, appraisal, and coping. Threat is defined not only in terms of a stimulus configuration that could be categorized as noxious or harmful, but also with regard to the individual's appraisal of the threat circumstances. The judgment or perception of the significance of the stressor is called *primary appraisal*. Coping refers to the activation of behavior designed to deal with threat. The form of coping that is initiated is determined by *secondary appraisal*, which involves the individual's judgment of the consequences of available coping strategies. In the Lazarus model, cognitive processes are central to an understanding of stress.

Psychological formulations of stress, in addition to that of Lazarus (Appley and Trumbull, 1967; Arnold, 1967; Cofer and Appley, 1964; and McGrath, 1970), emphasize the role of the *perceived* environmental situation. Particular stressors are not viewed as having uniform effects across individuals, and particular individuals may be more vulnerable to exposure to certain environmental events. Thus, it is the perceived environmental demands and the individual's perception of threat that must be determined in order to calibrate potential adverse effects. In sum, psychological approaches to stress give considerable attention to mediational processes and are *interaction focused*. That is, they are concerned with the interchange between person and environment and concentrate on the intervening factors that mediate the relationship between stressors and stress outcomes.

ANGER AND ITS DETERMINANTS

Anger is an affective stress reaction to aversive events that are called provocations. Anger, as a subjective affect, consists of a combination of arousal, identifiable by autonomic nervous system (Ax,

1953; Funkenstein, King, and Drolette, 1954, 1957; Schachter, 1957) and central nervous system (Moyer, 1971, 1973) indices, and a cognitive labeling of that arousal as anger (Konečni, 1975b). Consistent with psychological views of stress, anger is determined by one's cognitive structuring of the situation. In purely cognitive terms, anger can be viewed as an attempt to extort a validation of one personal constructs (Kelly, 1954) in an effort to control an aversive situation.

Historically, the psychological study of anger has a dotted record. In an impressive early work, Hall (1899) provides a linguistic and conceptual analysis of anger based on a questionnaire survey. His report presents 313 written responses to the questionnaire on anger, for which he had received over 2,000 returns from around the country. These questionnaire responses address the causes of anger, manifestations of anger, objects of anger expression, aftereffects of arousal, mechanisms of control, and treatment principles. Hall's material is a rich source of hypotheses about anger and its cognitive correlates. Other early analyses of anger that merit attention are the research reports of Richardson (1918), who used methods of introspection, and of Gates (1926), who studied the anger of female students through their self-ratings of daily events. The earliest clinical account that I have located on anger was reported by Witmer (1908) regarding an eleven-year-old boy who "was subject to outbursts of uncontrollable and unreasoning anger" (p. 157).

The appearance of the classic monograph by Dollard, Doob, Miller, Mowrer, and Sears (1939) on frustration and aggression might have generated more research on anger than it did were it not for the values of behaviorism and for the perceived association of anger arousal with drive-reduction concepts in the study of aggressive behavior. Research on physiological processes by Ax (1953), Funkenstein et al. (1954, 1957), and Schachter (1957) that was concerned with the autonomic-system changes associated with anger was conducted in medical settings and has interfaced with mainstream psychological research for the most part only in experimentation on aggression catharsis (e.g., Gentry, 1970; Hokanson and Burgess, 1962a, 1962b; Hokanson, Willers, and Koropsak, 1968;

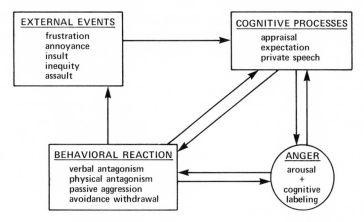

Figure 1. Determinants of anger arousal.

Kahn, 1966). Recent trends in aggression research, notably the work of Konečni (Konečni, 1975a, 1975b; Konečni, Crozier, and Doob, 1976; Konečni and Ebbesen, 1976), may redirect experimental interest to the study of the emotion of anger and its cognitive determinants.

In the therapeutic model to be presented, anger is construed as being determined by *external events*, *internal processes*, and *behavioral reactions*. To put it simply, anger can be examined in terms of aversive events, how these events are appraised or interpreted, and the behaviors that are enacted in response to these events. These three sets of determinants have mutually influenced relationships as depicted in Figure 1. Anger is viewed as a combination of physiological arousal and a cognitive labeling of that arousal as a function of internal and external cues and of one's own overt and covert behavior in the situation (Konečni, 1975a and 1975b; Lazarus, 1967; Schachter and Singer, 1962).

Cognitive processes occupy a central role in the experience of anger arousal within this model. Aversive events have no direct relationship upon anger except as mediated by appraisal, expectations, and private speech. These factors and their operations will be elaborated below. Aversive events function as provocations, because of the way they are construed.[4] Anger arousal, in turn, has a reciprocal relationship to the mediating cognitions in that the experience of anger determines subsequent cognitions about the situation.

Similarly, mutually influenced relationships exist between anger arousal and behavioral reactions, especially aggression. Konečni (1975a, 1975b) proposed that a bidirectional causal relationship exists between anger and aggression, and he has supported this thesis with exceptionally performed experiments. Although there may be some disagreement concerning the aggression→anger relationships, it has been generally established that the arousal of anger does facilitate aggressive behavior (Rule and Nesdale, 1976), and, when anger has been induced, aggressive behavior does lower anger arousal.

Antagonistic behavior in response to aversive events results in defining one's emotional state as anger. Anger is inferred from our behavior, as well as from other internal and external cues. This follows from the James-Lange theory of emotion, according to which we derive knowledge about our emotion from observations of our own behavior in particular contexts (e.g., I am angry because my fists are clenched, and I have been insulted). Furthermore, aggressive behavior is likely to incite others to behave aversively, which then increases the probability for anger in the subject. Provocation experiences between police and assaultive criminals have been shown by Toch (1969) to escalate sequentially in a series of antagonistic counter-responses.

COGNITIVE MEDIATORS OF ANGER AROUSAL

Cognitive theorists have been fond of quoting the Stoic philosopher, Epictetus, who once said, "Men are disturbed not by things,

---

[4] Proneness to provocation may also result from dispositional states of the organism. Somatic-affective conditions, such as tension, fatigue, or hunger, may prime anger reactions to aversive events. For example, Gates (1926) found that a higher frequency of anger incidents occurred in time periods just preceding dinner. The mechanisms by which somatic states increase the probability of anger is an important question for research. Biochemical factors may play a pivotal role in lowering the threshold of aversiveness at which an event elicits anger or, in cognitive terms, in expanding the range of events that are appraised as provocations.

but by the view which they take of them." Similarly, the prescriptions of Buddhism's "Four Noble Truths" teach that the malaise of human existence originates in ignorant cravings, all which can be remedied by Buddha's "Eightfold Path," which in our own language consists largely of cognitive self-control prescriptions (cf. Allen, 1959; Rahula, 1959). The emphasis placed on cognitive determinants in the present approach reflects the influence of the personality theories of George Kelly (1955) and Julian Rotter (1954), as well as the more recent clinical views of Albert Ellis (1962, 1973), Aaron Beck (1976), and especially Donald Meichenbaum (1977).

Provocation experiences are mediated by the appraisal of the aversive event. Appraisal has been a prominent concept in the literature on psychological stress (Arnold, 1967; Averill, 1973; Lazarus, 1966). Appraisal is used here to refer to cognitive evaluations of past and present events, as well as to judgments about one's behavior in response to these events. Considerable evidence in the literature on aggression has shown that appraisal of provocation influences aggressive behavior. Pastore (1952) found that the arbitrariness of frustration was a significant determinant of aggressive responses, as more aggression was reported in response to thwartings that were without justification. The justification for aggression has been shown to increase the magnitude of aggressive responses in several studies (Berkowitz and Rawlings, 1963; Brock and Buss, 1964; Meyer, 1972). Importantly, the perceived aggressive intent of one's opponent has been found to elevate aggressive responding (Epstein and Taylor, 1967; Taylor, 1967).

While justification for aggression and perceived intentionality of antagonism serve to heighten aggressive acts, other appraisal processes have been shown to reduce aggressive behavior. Cognitive reinterpretation of the provoking experience was found to lower aggression by several investigators (Green and Murray, 1975; Kaufmann and Feshbach, 1963; Mallick and McCandless, 1966). Evaluations of one's own anger reactions can also reduce aggression, when based on the perceived values of observers (Borden, 1975) or on the judgment that one's anger level is inappropriately high (Berkowitz, Lepinski, and Angulo, 1969).

Expectations refer to the subjective probabilities that a person has concerning future events. Expectations are based on appraisal processes. They may be specific to a particular situation or generalized across a set of functionally related situations (Rotter, 1954). When one's experience is discrepant from expectations, arousal occurs, as equilibrium is disturbed and the person seeks to adjust to the demands of the situations. The arousal will be labeled as anger when situational cues are present that have a learned connection with anger and particularly when one is inclined to behave aggressively.

Expectations as mediators of anger and aggression can be illustrated with reference to sex roles. Sex-role expectation has been offered as an explanation for the observed differences in the expression of aggression toward males and females. The majority of research investigations that have varied the sex of instigator/target of aggression have found that both men and women behave less aggressively toward women than toward men (Frodi, Macaulay, and Thome, 1977). The review of sex differences in aggression by Frodi et al. (1977) concluded that "sex role expectations, in interaction with the behavior encountered, play a significant part in determining men's and women's aggressiveness" (p. 643). In addition, observed increases in female aggression toward aggressive male instigators have been thought to result from a violation of social expectations (Taylor and Epstein, 1967).

Expectations influence anger in several ways: (1) high expectations for desirable consequences that do not result can make an undesired outcome more aversive; (2) high expectations that someone will behave aversively can reduce one's provocation threshold so that anger and antagonistic reactions have a higher probability of occurrence; and (3) low expectations that one can effectively manage a conflict situation can lead to anger and aggression in an attempt to achieve control over the aversive experience.

Private speech is the internal dialogue that expresses appraisals and expectations in language form. Private speech can act as a self-arousal mechanism and can steer one's course of action. Antagonistic self-statements may inflame anger by focusing attention on aversive characteristics of persons and situations and by revivifing provocation incidents. Ruminations about aversive experiences can prolong anger beyond the point that it would otherwise have dissipated. Self-arousal processes have been implicated in the occurrence of aggressive behavior (Bandura, 1973; Konečni, 1975a). However, the relationship between private speech and provocation is hypothetical at present.

Early learning-theory formulations (Dollard and Miller, 1950) emphasized the role of thought and language as cue-producing responses that affect emotional arousal. The effects of self-statements on emotional state have just begun to be explored. No research has been reported on the relationship between private speech and provocation. However, a number of studies have appeared that have found that arousal or anxiety states are influenced by self-verbalization. Rimm and Litvak (1969) sought to test several RET propositions, one of which states that implicit verbalization is linked to emotional arousal. These authors found that affectively loaded sentences increased respiration rate and depth. Schwartz (1971) found that affectively loaded words increase heart rate, and, using a similar procedure, May and Johnson (1973) demonstrated that internally elicited thoughts to stimulus words having stressful content influence heart rate, respiration, and, to some extent, skin conductance. Galvanic skin response effects were obtained by Russell and Brandsma (1974) for anxiety-arousing sentences, but no effects resulted for respiration. Rogers and Craighead (1977) failed to replicate the Russell and Brandsma (1974) results but did find that the degree of discrepancy from belief about oneself did mediate the physiological effects of the self-statements. In sum, these studies have shown that private speech has measurable autonomic system effects and can be considered to be implicated in emotional arousal.

Basis for a Cognitive Therapy for Anger

The anger-management procedures are based on the conviction that emotional arousal and the course of action that such arousal instigates are determined by one's cognitive structuring of the situation. The therapeutic procedures involve interventions at the cognitive, affective, and behavioral levels, but the cognitive control components are relatively new to behavior-therapy methods. Nevertheless, there is good reason to believe that cognitive procedures can be usefully applied to problems of anger and aggression.

Mythologies and intellectual prejudices have long induced us to view emotions as being associated with the baser qualities of humans. Averill (1974) has argued that prior to the eighteenth century it was common to speak of emotions as "passions" by which the individual was "gripped," "seized," or "torn." Various forms of symbolism extrinsic to a scientific analysis had linked emotional arousal to irrational and noncognitive activities. However, the classic experiment by Schachter and Singer (1962) and a comparable procedure by Conn and Crowne (1964) found that the cognitive aspects of a situation influence how people label their emotional arousal and the degree to which they will be observed to exhibit anger. Pertinent to the stress-inoculation model of therapy to be described, theories of psychological stress emphasize cognitive mediators (Arnold, 1967; Appley and Trumbull, 1967; Lazarus, 1966).

With respect to the cognitive mediation of anger, there is considerable evidence that cognitive factors influence the occurrence of aggressive behavior. Attention to the role of cognition began with the authors of the frustration–aggression monograph (Dollard, Doob, Miller, Mowrer, and Sears, 1939) who often alluded to cognitive processes as mediators of the occurrence, inhibition, and displacement of aggression. The current theories of Berkowitz (1970, 1973, and 1974), Bandura (1973), and Feshbach (1970) stipulate that the stimulus control of aggressive behavior is a cognitively mediated process. As discussed above in regard to the appraisal of provocation, the amplification and attenuation of aggression has been found to be influenced by cognitive factors.

In theories of psychotherapy, the influence of thought on emotion is most emphasized by Beck (1976), Kelly (1955), and Ellis (1973). Much of the recent impetus among clinical psychologists for cognitive approaches to behavior change is due to Ellis, whose rational-emotive therapy is predicated on a concept of maladjustment stipulating that it is not events themselves that cause distress but rather one's interpretations and internal sentences about those events. Ellis (1977) has recently extended RET specifically to the management of anger. Outstanding work on cognitive change methods has been performed by Goldfried (Goldfried, 1971; Goldfried and Goldfried, 1975; D'Zurilla and Goldfried, 1971), Kanfer (1975), Mahoney (1974), and Meichenbaum (1974, 1977). Mahoney and Arnkoff (1977) provide a thorough review of the varieties of cognitive and self-control therapies, and the recent book by Beck (1976) offers a refreshing synthesis of cognitive approaches to emotional disorders.

THE STRESS-INOCULATION MODEL

The stress-inoculation procedures are a coping-skills therapy. That is, they are concerned with developing the client's competence to adapt to stressful events in such a way that stress is reduced and personal goals are achieved. The term "inoculation" is a medical metaphor. The therapeutic process works by exposing the client to manageable doses of a stressor that arouse, but do not overwhelm, his/her defenses. The client thereby learns to cope with the stressful events that have a high probability of occurrence.

The anger-management procedures intervene at the cognitive, somatic, and behavioral levels to promote adaptive coping with provocation. The stress-inoculation approach involves three basic steps or phases: cognitive preparation, skill acquisition, and application practice.

Cognitive Preparation. The cognitive preparation phase is designed to educate clients about the functions of anger and about their personal anger patterns, to provide a shared language system between client and therapist, and to introduce the rationale of treatment. An instructional manual for clients is used to facilitate these tasks (Novaco, 1976c). Clients are asked to keep a diary, which serves as a data base for discussion of the treatment concepts.

The beneficial effect of cognitive preparation for impending stress has been demonstrated by studies of hospitalized patients with regard to surgical trauma (Andrew, 1970; Cassell, 1965; Egbert, Battit, Welch, and Bartlett, 1964; Janis, 1958). These studies have shown that cognitive interventions for the distress of surgery have led to better adjustment during surgery, shorter time to discharge, and reduction in the use of medication. Personality variables, such as repression-sensitization, do, however, mediate the intervention effects (Andrew, 1970). In a recent study, Langer, Janis, and Wolfer (1975) demonstrated that a cognitive intervention consisting of reappraisal, calming self-talk, and selective attention effectively reduced both pre- and postoperative stress.

The anger-control components of the cognitive preparation phase consist of (1) identifying the persons and situations that trigger anger, (2) distinguishing anger from aggression, (3) discriminating justified from less justified anger, (4) understanding the determinants of anger, (5) understanding anger in terms of interaction sequences, and (6) introducing the anger-management techniques as coping strategies to handle conflict and stress. As a cognitive self-control therapy, this approach to the treatment of anger assumes that personal knowledge about one's anger patterns facilitates the capacity to regulate anger arousal. Effective self-management is dependent on awareness of the external contingencies that elicit anger, as well as the internal and behavioral concomitants of this emotional state.

Skill Acquisition. Corresponding to the analysis of anger determinants, the client is provided with cognitive and behavioral coping skills. At the cognitive level, the client is taught to alternatively view provocation events (Kelly, 1955) and to modify the exaggerated importance often attached to events (Ellis, 1973). A basic goal is to promote flexibility in one's cognitive structuring of situations. The appraisal of aversive events as personal affronts or ego threats is challenged by the therapist and alternative appraisals are suggested. In this regard, the ability to "not take things personally" is viewed as a fundamental skill. Therapeutically, this involves shifting from an ego orientation to a task orientation with respect to provocation. A task orientation consists of focusing on desired outcomes and implementing a behavioral strategy to produce those outcomes. In addition, the client is encouraged to maintain a sense of humor. Humor has been found to reduce aggression-related arousal (Singer, 1968), and its use in the present procedure refers to not taking oneself and one's predicaments too seriously.

The most important cognitive intervention consists of the use of self-instructions (Meichenbaum, 1974). The cognitive control of anger by means of private speech is accomplished by first dissecting a provocation experience into a sequence of stages: (1) preparing for a provocation; (2) impact and confrontation; (3) coping with arousal; and (4) subsequent reflection (a) conflict unresolved, (b) conflict resolved. Stages three and four provide for the possible failure of self-regulation and for the mitigation of additional self-arousal by ruminations. The self-regulated private speech functions as an instructional cue that guides the client's thoughts, feelings, and behavior in the direction of effective coping.

In the case study reported by Witmer (1908) of the eleven-year-old boy who had been subject to "outbursts of uncontrollable and unreasoning anger" and to "mean moods," there appears a delightful account of anger control by self-statements. Witmer, who adopted an educational approach to therapy in his treatment of children, described an incident near the end of the boy's treatment, where the boy protested about having to wash his hands at mealtime and threatened to not return to the table. He did return, and later said to the clinician present, "I nearly got mad, but I just said to myself, 'I will control my temper' " (p. 178). Examples of coping self-statements used in the stress-inoculation approach are contained in Table I. These can be offered to clients as examples, but the client should be encouraged to generate his/her own self-statement package as applied to the specific anger situations used in the application phase (see below).

A variety of behavioral skills are imparted to the client to facilitate anger regulation and the management of provocation events. The general goals of the behavioral interventions are to provide skills for responses that are incompatible with anger, for increased competence in interpersonal communication, and for problem-solving. Emphasis is placed on maximizing the adaptive functions of anger and minimizing its maladaptive functions. That is, the capacity of anger as an emotional state to energize behavior, to potentiate a sense of personal control, to serve as a discriminative cue for coping, and to facilitate expression of negative sentiments in an acceptable form can be valuable to human functioning and should be facilitated. In contrast, the extent to which anger arousal is disruptive to performance, is an unnecessary defensive reaction, instigates aggressive behavior, or becomes an undiscriminating means of impression management, it has less desirable consequences and should be attenuated (cf. Novaco, 1976a).

A basic behavioral component to the treatment procedure is relaxation training. The Jacobsen (1938) procedures of systematically tensing and relaxing sets of muscles are used, as they enable the client to identify internal cues associated with tension and to learn

Table I. Examples of Anger Management Self-Statements Rehearsed in Stress-Inoculation Training

---

Preparing for a provocation
    This could be a rough situation, but I know how to deal with it. I can work out a plan to handle this. Easy does it. Remember, stick to the issues and don't take it personally. There won't be any need for an argument. I know what to do.

Impact and confrontation
    As long as I keep my cool, I'm in control of the situation. You don't need to prove yourself. Don't make more out of this than you have to. There is no point in getting mad. Think of what you have to do. Look for the positives and don't jump to conclusions.

Coping with arousal
    Muscles are getting tight. Relax and slow things down. Time to take a deep breath. Let's take the issue point by point. My anger is a signal of what I need to do. Time for problem-solving. He probably wants me to get angry, but I'm going to deal with it constructively.

Subsequent reflection
    a. Conflict unresolved
        Forget about the aggravation. Thinking about it only makes you upset. Try to shake it off. Don't let it interfere with your job. Remember relaxation. It's a lot better than anger. Don't take it personally. It's probably not so serious.
    b. Conflict resolved
        I handled that one pretty well. That's doing a good job. I could have gotten more upset than it was worth. My pride can get me into trouble, but I'm doing better at this all the time.
        I actually got through that without getting angry.

---

relaxation as an alternative response. The relaxation techniques are used in a counterconditioning procedure for anger-eliciting situations. Following Goldfried (1971), these techniques are viewed as self-control methods, whereby the person develops competence in mastering troublesome internal states. Emphasis is placed on mental as well as physical relaxation.

Through self-monitoring of anger patterns, the client is taught to recognize anger from both internal and external cues. The therapeutic model stipulates that anger is an emotional response to stressful demands that signals that problem-solving strategies need to be implemented. In this regard, the client must learn to focus on issues and objectives and to engage in behaviors instrumental to achieving desired outcomes. This process is facilitated by es-

tablishing a task-oriented response set that interposes thought between impulse and action, thus preventing aggression over-reac-
tions and the accumulation of anger by self-stimulation. Training in
verbal communication and assertiveness augment the problem-
solving methods.

APPLICATION PRACTICE

The value of application practice has been emphasized by a variety of skills-training approaches (D'Zurilla and Goldfried, 1971;
Meichenbaum, 1975a; Suinn and Richardson, 1971). The anger-
management procedures emphasize personal competence, and
therefore involve testing the client's capability to manage provocative situations. While the skill acquisition phase involves the introduction, modeling, and rehearsal of coping techniques, the practice phase allows clients to test their proficiency by applying the
anger-control methods to anger situations as regulated by the therapist.

The practice is conducted by means of imaginal and role-playing inductions of anger. The content of these provocation simula-
tions is presented sequentially in hierarchical form. That is, a hierarchy of anger situations that the client is likely to encounter in real
life is constructed with the client, and the coping skills that have
been rehearsed with the therapist then are applied to these scenarios beginning with the mildest and progressing to the most
anger-arousing. This process continues throughout the course of
treatment and enables both client and therapist to gauge the degree
of improvement.

A full account of the treatment procedures and the assessment
scheme with which they are integrated is contained in the author's
therapist manual (Novaco, 1976d). The procedural portions of this
manual are contained in an appendix to this chapter, which provides a session-by-session description of the clinical techniques
and an elaboration of the therapy approach.

EXPERIMENTAL EVALUATION

Prior to the author's research on the treatment of anger (Novaco, 1975, 1976b, 1977), no work of an experimental nature existed

with regard to cognitive interventions for anger problems. However, desensitization methods had been shown to be effective in reducing anger by Rimm, deGroot, Boord, Reiman, and Dillow (1971) for persons who experienced anger in automobile-driving situations and by Herrell (1971) for a young soldier who became excessively angry when given orders. Kaufman and Wagner (1972) also had proposed a behavior technology called "the barb" for the treatment of temper-control problems and discussed its application to a male adolescent. There are a number of other reports of psychoanalytic and behavior-modification approaches to aggressive behavior. Recently, assertion training has been proposed in the behavioral literature as a method of treatment.

What distinguishes the present approach from other behavioral alternatives is the emphasis on cognitive factors and the attempt to provide an integrated theoretical framework. That is, the treatment model is intended to be more than a technology. The model is based on an articulated conception of anger and the factors that determine its manifestation and expression. The present state of development is far from a theory in the scientific sense, but the model specifies a number of testable propositions regarding anger arousal and anger regulation that hopefully will receive experimental attention. The treatment procedures themselves also specify a set of therapeutic stages and processes that lend themselves to experimental analysis.

In the initial treatment project (Novaco, 1975, 1976b), the comparative effectiveness of cognitive coping and relaxation training were examined separately and in combination. The project examined the extent to which cognitive processes and relaxation techniques could be therapeutically used to regulate the experience and expression of anger for 34 persons who were both self-identified and assessed as having serious anger-control problems. The treatment program consisted of an experimental combination of cognitive self-control and relaxation procedures aimed at increasing personal competence in managing provocations and regulating the arousal of anger. Component treatments were incorporated into the experimental design to permit a comparative evaluation.

The substance of the treatment program was derived from a functional analysis of the role of anger in human behavior and from a set of hypothetical principles for anger management derived from the research literature on aggression and behavior therapy. The propositions served as heuristic statements of conditions that would hypothetically facilitate the management of anger. The propositions were integrated with a functional analysis of anger and involved the therapeutic arrangement of variables affecting competence in the regulation of anger and the constructive response to provocations. From this formulation of factors and strategies for anger control, four treatment conditions were constructed: (1) the primary treatment, which combined cognitive and relaxation controls; (2) a cognitive-treatment condition; (3) a relaxation-training condition; and (4) an attention-control condition. Each was conducted over a period of six sessions.

The experimental treatments were evaluated in a pre- and posttreatment design by an anger-inventory assessment, by laboratory provocations an imaginal, role-play, and direct-experience modes using self-report and physiological indices, and by anger diary ratings. The anger inventory was a self-report instrument developed by the author and has since been refined. It consists of 80 descriptions of provocation incidents for which the respondent rates anger that he/she would experience on a five-point scale. The laboratory provocation procedures were also constructed for this project and consisted of two provocation instances for both the imaginal and role-play modes and for both the pre- and posttreatment procedures. A direct-encounter provocation was also used in the posttreatment series. The dependent variables consisted of self-report ratings of anger, changes in systolic and diastolic blood pressure, the number of galvanic skin responses, and ratings of coping behaviors for the provocation incidents. Throughout the treatment phase, participants kept a diary of their real-life anger experiences and rated their personal anger incidents on a seven-point scale. The series of assessments and treatment involved 12 visits of approximately 45 minutes each.

It was predicted that: (1) the combined treatment condition would result in the greatest improvement on all dependent variables when compared to all other treatment groups; (2) all three treatment conditions would each differ significantly from the attention-control condition; (3) the cognitive treatment alone would be

TABLE II. TREATMENT GROUP CHANGE SCORES [a] FOR SELF-REPORT OF ANGER
AND BLOOD PRESSURE

	Treatment conditions			
Dependent measure	Combined	Cognitive	Relaxation	Control
Inventory	−60.00	−49.67	−24.25	−7.50
Self-rating of anger				
Imaginal provocations	− 2.25	− 1.88	− 1.65	− .50
Role-play provocations	− 1.88	− 1.19	− 1.00	− .37
Systolic blood pressure				
Imaginal provocations	− 1.57	− 2.69	+ .57	+2.07
Role-play provocations	− 8.50	− 3.94	− .63	− .25
Diastolic blood pressure				
Imaginal provocations	− 5.82	− 2.33	− 3.50	+1.57
Role-play provocations	− 5.75	− 2.06	+ 1.21	−1.38

[a] Change scores were computed by subtracting the pretreatment mean from the posttreatment mean. A minus value indicates therapeutic change.

superior to relaxation training alone in the reduction of anger for the inventory and for the role-play and direct-provocation conditions; (4) relaxation training alone would result in a greater reduction in anger than the cognitive treatment for the imaginal-provocation condition.

A portion of the results of this investigation are illustrated in Table II, which contains mean change scores (posttreatment minus pretreatment) for self-report of anger, as well as for the anger inventory. Analyses were not performed on these means, since a repeated measures design was used, and they are presented here only to illustrate the treatment effects. It can be seen that the greatest degree of change occurred for the combined-treatment group, followed by the cognitive-treatment condition.

Across the multiple indices and procedures used in the project, it was found that the combined-treatment condition had a very significant and generalized effect in reducing anger and increasing anger management when compared to the attention-control condition. The effects of the combined treatment were significantly different from the attention-control condition for the anger inventory, all measures except two for both the imaginal and the direct-provocation procedures, and for five measures in the role-play mode. The means for the anger-diary ratings reflected the differential improvement hypothesized for the treatment groups, but this measure was not judged to be rigorous enough to justify further analysis.

Although less effective than the combined treatment, the cognitive-treatment condition showed significant improvement over the controls. There were significant differences in favor of the cognitive group for the inventory and for nearly half of the anger measures across provocation modes. It was therefore concluded that the cognitive treatment resulted in a definite and generalized improvement in anger management. Compared to the combined treatment, the cognitive-treatment condition was most often not statistically different, as only six contrasts reached significance. However, the combined treatment was consistently the more improved group on the basis of the magnitude of the means.

The relaxation-training condition differed from controls across anger measures for the imaginal provocations but not for the inventory or the other provocation modes. The results for the imaginal provocations thus demonstrated a good transfer of training for the relaxation group, but the effects were limited in their generalizability. The comparison of relaxation training with the combined treatment found only one dependent-variable contrast in the imaginal condition where the combined-treatment group was more improved. However, there was a sizeable significant difference in favor of the combined treatment for the inventory, and nearly half of the anger measures in the role-play and direct provocation modes resulted in significant contrasts, thus indicating the combined treatment to be superior.

There were surprisingly few significant differences between the cognitive and the relaxation group, although the magnitude of the means was often in favor of the cognitive condition. Since the relaxation-treatment group differed more often from the combined treatment in the less improved direction and less often from controls in the more improved direction than did the cognitive-treatment group, it was concluded that the cognitive treatment alone resulted in greater improvement than did the relaxation treatment alone.

Following this encouraging beginning, the treatment approach to anger was reconceptualized in terms of the stress-inoculation model that was initially proposed by Meichenbaum and Cameron (1973). The stress-inoculation approach for anger problems was first applied in a community psychology intervention regarding the training of law-enforcement officers who routinely must manage an assortment of provocation and conflict situations (Novaco, 1977b).

The revised approach was then evaluated clinically in a case study of a hospitalized patient with severe anger problems (Novaco, 1977a). This patient was seen in therapy three times per week for three and a half weeks in the hospital, during which time staff ratings of his behavior showed progressive improvement on anger dimensions, and convergent evidence was obtained on self-monitored ratings of his behavior on weekend leaves from the hospital. Following discharge, he was seen biweekly for a two-month period, and in this interval, the frequency of anger reactions and his ability to manage provocative incidents showed continued improvement. In a follow-up on this case one year after discharge, the patient reported to be doing well and being "98% normal."

An experimental evaluation of the therapist-training procedure has been conducted recently in a consultation project with experienced probation officers. A group of participants were trained in the treatment method over a period of 10 sessions and compared to an untrained control group. The project participants each has at least four years of experience in probation counseling, and the groups were matched on educational and professional background. Half of each group had masters degrees in counseling or social work. The weekly training sessions were evaluated by the project participants, who in these weekly ratings expressed a high degree of satisfaction with the training experience. After the training procedure was completed, the experimental group and control groups were given a case history to analyze and for which they were to plan a course of treatment. Two months after the completion of training, the groups were compared for their performance on a role-play test intake interview for an adolescent with anger problems. The case-history material has not as yet been analyzed, but results for the interview performance showed significant differences between groups, as the trained counselors were significantly superior on ratings of interviewer poise, effectiveness in reaching an understanding of the problem, and rapport with the client. The ratings were obtained from the interviewee and from an independent rater of the taped recording, both of whom were blind to the fact that half of the counselors were untrained in the treatment method. An experimental report on this project is in preparation.

Given the prevalence of anger-related clinical disorders among the populations that are being served and can be served by mental-health practitioners, it is hoped that the treatment methods developed by the author will receive additional clinical trials and experimental research. The stress-inoculation model provides a useful format for the cognitively oriented therapist, and its various stages and components are amenable to experimental analysis.

REFERENCES

Allen, G.F. *The Buddha's philosophy*. London: Unwin Press, 1959.

Andrew, J.M. Recovery from surgery, with and without preparatory instruction for three coping styles. *Journal of Personality and Social Psychology*, 1970,0 *15*, 223–226.

Appley, M., and Trumbull, R. *Psychological stress*. New York: Appleton-Century-Crofts, 1967.

Arnold, M. Stress and emotion. In M.H. Appley and R. Trumbull (Eds.), *Psychological stress*. New York: Appleton-Century-Crofts, 1967, 123–140.

Averill, J.R. Personal control over aversive stimuli and its relationship to stress. *Psychological Bulletin*, 1973, *80*, 286–303.

Averill, J.R. An analysis of psychophysical symbolism and its influences on theories of emotion. *Journal for the Theory of Social Behavior*, 1974, *4*, 147–190.

Ax, A.F. The physiological differentiation between fear and anger in humans. *Psychosomatic Medicine*, 1953, *15*, 433–442.

Bandura, A. *Aggression: A social learning analysis*. Englewood Cliffs: Prentice-Hall, 1973.

Beck, A. *Cognitive therapy and the emotional disorders*. International Universities Press, 1976.

Berkowitz, L. The contagion of violence: An S-R mediational analysis of some effects of observed aggression. In W.J. Arnold and M.M. Page (Eds.), *Nebraska Symposium on Motivation*, 1970. Lincoln: University of Nebraska Press, 1970, 95–135.

Berkowitz, L. Words and symbols as stimuli to aggressive response. In J. Knutson (Ed.), *The control of aggression*. Chicago: Aldine-Atherton, 1973.

Berkowitz, L. Some determinants of impulsive aggression: Role of mediated associations with reinforcements for aggression. *Psychological Review*, 1974, *81*, 165–176.

Berkowitz, L., Lepenski, J., and Angulo, E.J. Awareness of our anger level and subsequent aggression. *Journal of Personality and Social Psychology*, 1969, *11*, 293–300.

Berkowitz, L., and Rawlings, E. Effects of film violence on inhibitions against subsequent aggression. *Journal of Abnormal and Social Psychology*, 1963, *66*, 405–412.

Borden, R.J. Witnessed aggression: Influence of and observer's sex and values on aggressive responding. *Journal of Personality and Social Psychology*, 1975, *31*, 567–573.

Brock, T.C., and Buss, A. Effects of justification for aggression and communication with the victim on post-aggression dissonance. *Journal of Abnormal and Social Psychology*, 1964, *68*, 403–412.

Cassell, S. Effect of brief puppet therapy upon the emotional responses of children undergoing cardiac catheterization. *Journal of Counseling Psychology*, 1965, *29*, 1–8.

Cofer, C.M., and Appley, M.H. *Motivation: Theory and research*. New York: Wiley, 1964.

Conn, L., and Crowne, D.P. Instigation to aggression, emotional arousal, and defensive emulation. *Journal of Personality*, 1964, *32*, 163–179.

Craig, K.D. Physiological arousal as a function of imagined, vicarious, and direct stress experiences. *Journal of Abnormal Psychology*, 1968, *73*, 513–520.

Dohrenwend, B.S., and Dohrenwend, B.P. (Eds.) *Stressful life events: Their nature and effects*. New York: Wiley, 1974.

Dollard, J., Doob, L., Miller, N., Mowrer, D.H., and Sears, R.R. *Frustration and aggression*. New Haven: Yale University Press, 1939.

Dollard, J., and Miller, N.E. *Personality and psychotherapy: An analysis in terms of learning, thinking, and culture*. New York: McGraw-Hill, 1950.

D'Zurilla, T., and Goldfried, M. Problem solving and behavior modification. *Journal of Abnormal Psychology*, 1971, *78*, 107–126.

Egbert, L.D., Battit, G.E., Welch, C.E., and Bartlett, M.K. Reduction of postoperative pain by encouragement and instruction of patients. *New England Journal of Medicine*, 1964, *270*, 825–827.

Ellis, A. *Reason and emotion in psychotherapy*. New York: Lyle Stuart, Inc., 1962.

Ellis, A. *Humanistic psychology: The rational-emotive approach*. New York: Julian Press, 1973.

Ellis, A. *How to live with and without anger*. New York: Reader's Digest Press, 1977.

Epstein, S. and Taylor, S.P. Instigation to aggression as a function of degree of defeat and perceived aggressive intent of opponent. *Journal of Personality*, 1967, *35*, 265–289.

Feshbach, S. Aggression. In P. Mussen (Ed.), *Carmichael's manual of child psychology*. New York: John Wiley, 1970, 159–260.

Frodi, A., Macaulay, J., and Thome, P.R. Are women always less aggressive than men? A review of the experimental literature. *Psychological Bulletin*, 1977, *84*, 634–660.

Funkenstein, D.H., King, S.H., and Drolette, M. The direction of anger during a laboratory stress-inducing situation. *Psychosomatic Medicine*, 1954, *16*, 404–413.

Funkenstein, D.H., King, S.H., and Drolette, M. *Mastery of stress*. Cambridge, Mass.: Harvard, 1957.

Gates, G.S. An observational study of anger. *Journal of Experimental Psychology*, 1926, *9*, 325–336.

Gentry, W.D. Effects of frustration, attack, and prior aggressive training on overt aggression and vascular processes. *Journal of Personality and Social Personality*, 1970, *16*, 718–725.

Glass, D., and Singer, J. *Urban stress: Experiments on noise and social stressors*. New York: Academic Press, 1972.

Goldfried, M. Systematic desensitization as training in self-control. *Journal of Consulting and Clinical Psychology,* 1971, *37,* 228–235.

Goldfried, M., and Goldfried, A.P. Cognitive change methods. In F.H. Kanfer and A.P. Goldstein (Eds.), *Helping people change.* New York: Pergamon Press, 1975.

Green, R., and Murray, E. Expression of feeling and cognitive reinterpretation in the reduction of hostile aggression. *Journal of Consulting and Clinical Psychology,* 1975, *43,* 375–383.

Hall, G.S. A study of anger. *American Journal of Psychology,* 1899, *10,* 516–591.

Herrell, J.M. Use of systematic desensitization to eliminate inappropriate anger. Proceedings of the 79th Annual Convention of the American Psychological Association. Washington, D.C.: *American Psychological Association,* 1971, 431–432.

Hokanson, J.E., and Burgess, M. The effects of three types of aggression on vascular processes. *Journal of Abnormal and Social Psychology,* 1962a, *64,* 445–449.

Hokanson, J.E., and Burgess, M. The effects of status, type of frustration, and aggression on vascular processes. *Journal of Abnormal and Social Psychology,* 1962b, *65,* 232–237.

Hokanson, J.E., Willers, K.R., and Koropsak, E. The modification of autonomic responses during aggressive interchange. *Journal of Personality,* 1968, *36,* 386–404.

Insel, P., and Moos, R. (Eds.) *Health and the social environment.* Lexington, Mass.: D.C. Heath, 1974.

Janis, I.L. *Psychological stress: Psychoanalytic and behavioral studies of surgical patients.* New York: Wiley, 1958.

Kahn, M. The physiology of catharsis. *Journal of Personality and Social Psychology,* 1966, *3,* 278–286.

Kanfer, F. Self-management methods. In F. Kanfer and A. Goldstein (Eds.) *Helping people change.* New York: Pergamon Press, 1975, 309–355.

Kaufman, L.M., and Wagner, B.R. Barb: A systematic treatment technology for temper control disorders. *Behavior Therapy,* 1972, *3,* 84–90.

Kaufmann, H., and Feshbach, S. The influence of anti-aggressive communications upon the response to provocation. *Journal of Personality,* 1963, *31,* 428–444.

Kelly, G. *The psychology of personal constructs* (Vols. 1 and 2). New York: Norton, 1955.

Konečni, V.J. Annoyance, type and duration of post-annoyance activity, and aggression: "The cathartic effect," *Journal of Experimental Psychology: General,* 1975a, *104,* 76–102.

Konečni, V.J. The mediation of aggressive behavior: Arousal level versus anger and cognitive labeling. *Journal of Personality and Social Psychology,* 1975b, *32,* 706–712.

Konečni, V.J., Crozier, J.B., and Doob, A.N. Anger and expression of aggression: Effects on aesthetic preference. *Scientific Aesthetics,* 1976, *1,* 47–55.

Konečni, V.J., and Ebbesen, E. Disinhibition versus the cathartic effect: Artifact and substance. *Journal of Personality and Social Psychology,* 1976, *34,* 352–365.

Langer, E.L., Janis, I.L., and Wolfer, J.A. Reproduction of psychological stress in surgical patients. *Journal of Experimental Social Psychology,* 1975, *11,* 155–165.

Lazarus, R. *Psychological stress and the coping process.* New York: McGraw-Hill, 1966.

Lazarus, R. Cognitive and personality factors underlying threat and coping. In M.H. Appley and R. Trumbull (Eds.), *Psychology stress.* New York: Appleton-Century-Crofts, 1967.

Lefcourt, H. The functions and illusions of control and freedom. *American Psychologist,* 1973, *28,* 417–425.

Levine, S., and Scotch, N.A. (Eds.) *Social stress*. Chicago: Aldine Publishing Company, 1970.

Mahoney, M.J. *Cognition and behavior modification*. Cambridge, Mass.: Ballinger, 1974.

Mahoney, M.J. Reflections on the cognitive-learning trend in psychotherapy. *American Psychologist*, 1977, *32*, 5–13.

Mahoney, M., and Arnkoff, D. Cognitive and self-control therapies. In S.L. Garfield and A.E. Bergin (Eds.), *Handbook of psychotherapy and behavior change* (2nd Ed.). New York: Wiley, 1977.

Mallick, S.K., and McCandless, B.R. A study of catharsis of aggression. *Journal of Personality and Social Psychology*, 1966, *4*, 591–596.

May, J.R., and Johnson, H.J. Physiological activity to internally elicited arousal and inhibitory thoughts. *Journal of Abnormal Psychology*, 1973, *82*, 239–245.

McGrath, J.C. *Social and psychological factors in stress*. New York: Holt, Rinehart, and Winston, 1970.

Meichenbaum, D. *Cognitive behavior modification*. Morristown, N.J.: General Learning Press, 1974.

Meichenbaum, D. Self-instructional methods. In F.H. Kanfer and A.P. Goldstein (Eds.), *Helping people change*. New York: Pergamon Press, 1975a.

Meichenbaum, D. A self-instructional approach to stress management: A proposal for stress inoculation training. In C. Spielberger and I. Sarason (Eds.), *Stress and anxiety* (Vol. 2). New York: Wiley, 1975b.

Meichenbaum, D. *Cognitive behavior modification*. New York: Plenum Press, 1977.

Meichenbaum, D., and Cameron, R. Stress inoculation: A skills training approach to anxiety management. Unpublished manuscript, University of Waterloo, Ontario, Canada, 1973.

Meichenbaum, D., and Novaco, R.W. Stress inoculation: A preventive approach. In C. Spielberger and I. Sarason (Eds.), *Stress and anxiety* (Vol. 5). New York: Halstead Press, 1978.

Meyer, T. Effects of viewing justified and unjustified real film violence on aggressive behavior. *Journal of Personality and Social Psychology*, 1972, *22*, 21–29.

Monat, A., and Lazarus, R.S. (Eds.) *Stress and coping: An anthology*. New York: Columbia University Press, 1977.

Moyer, K.E. The physiology of aggression and the implications for aggression control. In J.L. Singer (Ed.), *The control of aggression and violence*. New York: Academic Press, 1971.

Moyer, K.E. The physiological inhibition of hostile behavior. In J.F. Knutson (Ed.), *The control of aggression*. Chicago: Aldine, 1973.

Novaco, R.W. Anger and coping with provocation: An instructional manual. University of California, Irvine, 1976c.

Novaco, R.W. Therapist manual for stress inoculation training: Clinical interventions for anger problems. University of California, Irvine, 1976d.

Novaco, R.W. *Anger control: The development and evaluation of an experimental treatment*. Lexington, Mass.: D.C. Heath, Lexington Books, 1975.

Novaco, R.W. The functions and regulation of the arousal of anger. American *Journal of Psychiatry*, 1976a, *133*, 1124–1128.

Novaco, R.W. Treatment of chronic anger through cognitive and relaxation controls. *Journal of Consulting and Clinical Psychology*, 1976b, *44*, 681.

Novaco, R.W. Stress inoculation: A cognitive therapy for anger and its application to a case of depression. *Journal of Consulting and Clinical Psychology*, 1977a, *45*, 600–608.

Novaco, R.W. A stress inoculation approach to anger management in the training of law enforcement officers. *American Journal of Community Psychology*, 1977b, *5*, 327–346.

Pastore, N. The role of arbitrariness in the frustration-aggression hypothesis. *Journal of Abnormal and Social Psychology*, 1952, *47*, 728–731.

Rahula, W.S. *What the Buddha taught*. London: Gordon Frazer, 1959.

Richardson, R.F. *The psychology and pedagogy of anger*. Baltimore: Warwick and York, Inc., 1918.

Rimm, D.C., de Groot, J.C., Boord, P., Reiman, J., and Dillow, P.V. Systematic desensitization of an anger response. *Behavior Research and Therapy*, 1971, *9*, 273–280.

Rimm, D.C., and Litvak, S.B. Self-verbalization and emotional arousal. *Journal of Abnormal Psychology*, 1969, *74*, 181–187.

Rogers, T., and Craighead, W.E. Physiological responses to self-statements: The effects of statement valence and discrepancy. *Cognitive Therapy and Research*, 1977, *1*, 99–120.

Rotter, J.B. *Social learning and clinical psychology*. Englewood Cliffs, N.J.: Prentice-Hall, 1954.

Rule, B., and Nesdale, A. Emotional arousal and aggressive behavior. *Psychological Bulletin*, 1976, *83*, 851–863.

Russell, P.L., and Brandsma, J.M. A theoretical and empirical integration of the rational-emotive and classical conditioning theories. *Journal of Consulting and Clinical Psychology*, 1974, *42*, 389–397.

Schachter, J. Pain, fear, and anger in hypertensives and normotensives: A psychophysiological study. *Psychosomatic Medicine*, 1957, *29*, 17–29.

Schachter, S., and Singer, J.E. Cognitive, social, and physiological determinants of emotional state. *Psychological Review*, 1962, *69*, 379–399.

Schwartz, G.E. Cardiac responses to self-induced thoughts. *Psychophysiology*, 1971, *8*, 462–467.

Selye, H. *The stress of life* (2nd Ed.) New York: McGraw-Hill, 1976.

Singer, D.L. Aggression arousal, hostile humor, and catharsis. *Journal of Personality and Social Psychology Monograph Supplement*, 1968, *8*, No. 1, Part 2.

Stern, R.M., and Anschel, C. Deep inspirations as stimuli for responses of the autonomic nervous system. *Psychophysiology*, 1968, *5*, 132–141.

Stokols, D. Environmental psychology. *Annual Review of Psychology*, 1978, *29*, 253–295.

Suinn, R., and Richardson, F. Anxiety management training: A non-specific behavior therapy program for anxiety control. *Behavior Therapy*, 1971, *2*, 498–510.

Taylor, S.P. Aggressive behavior and physiological arousal as a function of provocation and the tendency to inhibit aggression. *Journal of Personality*, 1967, *35*, 297–310.

Taylor, S.P., and Epstein, S. Aggression as a function of the interaction of the sex of the aggressor and the sex of the victim. *Journal of Personality*, 1967, *35*, 474–486.

Toch, H. *Violent men*. Chicago: Aldine Publishing Co., 1969.

Turk, D. Cognitive control of pain: A skills-training approach. Unpublished manuscript, University of Waterloo, Ontario, Canada, 1974.

Witmer, L. The treatment and cure of a case of mental and moral deficiency. *The Psychological Clinic*, 1908, *2*, 153–179.

Wohlwill, J. The emerging discipline of environmental psychology. *American Psychologist*, 1970, *25*, 303–312.

Wolpe, J., and Lazarus, A. *Behavior therapy techniques*. Oxford: Pergamon Press, 1966.

Appendix
Therapeutic Interventions
for Anger Problems

The material in this appendix is intended to supplement the conceptual presentation of the stress-inoculation approach to anger management that is given in the author's chapter in this book. The descriptions of the assessment and treatment procedures given here have been part of the therapist manual that was developed for training purposes.

While explicit information concerning assessment and therapy procedures is provided herein, it is essential that these procedures be used with a prior understanding of the theoretical ideas on which they are based. Only through a sound grasp of the conceptual framework can the therapeutic methods be properly implemented.

ASSESSMENT OF ANGER PROBLEMS

There presently does not exist a theory or systematic conception of anger arousal that specifies the parameters of anger disorders. Assessment and therapy should be interrelated, and they also should follow from an articulated conceptual system. In the absence of this ideal, a few concepts are offered here that may serve as a scaffolding for understanding anger problems.

At the outset it is proposed that anger not be construed solely as a negative emotion. Anger has a variety of adaptive and maladaptive functions in affecting behavior (cf. Novaco, 1976). Whether or not a person's anger patterns constitute a problem must be determined on the basis of criteria that relate to personal health, work performance, interpersonal relationships, or societal standards.

Dimensions of Anger. Anger reactions to provocation events can be examined with respect to several parameters: (a) frequency, (b) intensity, (c) duration, (d) mode of expression, (e) effect on performance, (f) effect on relationships, (g) effect on health. Information on these parameters can be obtained in a clinical interview, but a self-report rating scale (Dimensions of Anger Reactions) can be used to assess these parameters of anger reactions.

These parameters should then be examined with respect to the various behavior settings within which the client functions and to the persons in those settings with whom the client interacts. Clients with chronic anger problems seem to have a predictable set of social contacts that result in anger. Information in this regard is important for at least two reasons: (1) the therapeutic procedures are self-control methods, which require that the person become an astute observer of one's own behavior; and (2) the stress-inoculation procedures include a method whereby the person learns to prepare for a provocation experience and uses self-instructions to guide his cognitive appraisal and behavior in responding to aversive events.

The assessment task is to determine the settings and persons with which anger has problem manifestations, according to the various dimensions of anger reactions outlined above. In order to determine the range of situations in which a client's anger is aroused, the type of situation most likely to arouse anger, and the overall magnitude of a respondent's proneness to provocation, an inventory of provocation circumstances, the Novaco Anger Scale, has been developed. An early version of this scale was reported in Novaco (1975). The current instrument consists of 80 items for which the respondent rates the degree of anger on a five-point scale. A copy of the scale and its descriptive statistics can be obtained from the author.

The client's ratings across the range of items on self-report scales provide an avenue of inquiry into the anger problem. A structured interview on anger patterns can be conducted by reviewing those items or factors on which the client scores high. In fact, respondents can discover common denominators of their anger reactions when their responses to the scale are reviewed. For example, clients have commented, "I found that I am mostly bothered by things people say to me," or "It seems that I get upset most when I'm not treated fairly," or "It's all these little annoyances that shouldn't really bother me."

Determinants of Anger. An anger problem is not an anger problem. That is to say, the kinds of psychological deficits that result in the inability to manage anger are not homogeneous across individuals or clinical populations. The anger-related deficits of hypertensives, child-abusing parents, time-urgent corporate executives, hospitalized depressives, juvenile delinquents, paranoids, and impulsive youngsters are likely to be quite different. Nor should these category labels be understood to imply homogeneity with respect to anger determinants.

Clients' anger experiences can be examined in terms of the events that happen in their lives, how they interpret and experience those events, and how they behave when and after these events occur. The factors, referred to as *external events, internal processes,* and *behavioral reactions,* have been delineated in the author's chapter.

External events. These are the circumstances in which the client's anger is aroused with greatest frequency. The anger scale facilitates their identification. The cluster of events that routinely provoke anger for the client may be similar in nature (frustrations, annoyances, insults, inequities, etc.) or they may vary widely. To be sure, events are not provocative in themselves, nor do particular provocations have universal meaning or effect. The impact of an aversive event will depend on a number of factors internal to the client.

Internal processes. Anger arousal is mediated by appraisal and expectation. External events are provocative because they are construed in a particular way or because they are at variance with expectations. The meaning of the aversive event to the individual must be determined, and expectations regarding self and others should be identified as facilitators of anger.

Antagonistic self-statements inflame anger. Ruminations about aversive experiences can prolong anger beyond the point that it would otherwise have dissipated and can reinstigate the provocation. The content of the client's private speech thus should be examined for its anger-instigative qualities, and it will provide information about the client's cognitive structuring of the situations of provocation.

Somatic and affective factors also influence the occurrence of anger. Tension and agitation can prime anger reactions. High tension levels reflect a lowered inability of the person to cope with external demands. Consequently, provocation experiences have a magnified impact, and composed, conciliatory reactions are less likely to be available. Temperament or prevailing mood also influences anger. A person whose affective tone is characterized by ill-humor is emotionally inclined to become angry or annoyed. In addition, anger can result from a failure to understand and appreciate the feelings of others. Lack of empathy has thwarted the resolution of many conflicts.

Behavioral reactions. Antagonistic responses to aversive events result in the definition of one's emotional state as anger. Anger is inferred from our behavior, as well as from other internal and external cues. Furthermore, aggressive behavior in an interpersonal context is likely to incite others to behave aversively, which increases the probability for anger in the subject.

For some clients, avoidance is the predominant response mode for provocation incidents. Here the anger is kept inside, perhaps to smolder and result in displaced aggression toward another target. The avoidance, withdrawal, or denial strategy may be adopted in particular behavior settings (e.g., at the office), but in another setting where inhibitory influences are absent (e.g., at home), the accumulated anger erupts. Such avoidance response styles are likely to prolong physiological arousal (e.g., a longer recovery time for blood pressure to return to resting levels) and engender hostile attitudes since the instigation to anger is left unchanged.

Treatment Procedure

The anger-management procedures intervene at the cognitive and behavioral levels to promote adaptive coping with provocation. The stress-inoculation approach involves three basic steps or phases: cognitive preparation, skill acquisition, and application practice. The theoretical developments of these phases of the treatment method can be found in Chapter 5 in this book.

The procedural sequence described here is intended to be flexible Individual differences of clients and of therapists will require modifications in timing and emphasis. In addition, the therapeutic mode, whether individual or group, will necessitate adjustments in procedure. In general, the sessions are designed to be one hour in length for individual therapy and one and a half hours if conducted in groups.

Session 1. The first session follows the completion of pretreatment tests, such as the anger scales or other behavioral measures (cf. Novaco, 1975). Test performance is reviewed with the client, using the high anger responses as points for discussion. Following a brief review of these test materials, the client's problem with anger is assessed more fully through an interview process. The interview analysis should follow these steps:

1. Obtain a statement by the client regarding (a) the degree to which he believes he has a problem with anger; (b) the greatest concern he has about his anger; and (c) how working on this problem will make his life different.

2. Conduct a "situation × person × mode of expression" analysis of the anger problem. That is, examine the range of settings in which the person functions (i.e., home, work, school, commerce, recreational, driving), the persons involved in those settings (i.e., parents, mate, siblings, friends, fellow workers, strangers), and how anger is expressed when aroused under these various circumstances (i.e., verbal antagonism, physical antagonism, passive aggression, avoidance, self-derogation, constructive action).

3. Try to assess the client's deficits in anger control by examining the determinants of anger arousal. That is, examine the external events, internal processes, and behavioral reactions that are predominantly involved for this client.

   a. *External events* (frustration, annoyance, insult, inequity, abuse, etc.). What particular aspects of situations trigger anger arousal? Are there any particular forms of provocation that are most often encountered and that easily arouse anger? How reasonable is it to be angry when these events occur?

b. *Internal factors.* (1) *Cognitive* (appraisals, expectations, self-statements). Try to help the client to become aware of the many ways in which his thoughts influence his feelings. What do these provocation events mean to the person? How does he interpret the behavior of others? Does his anger come from how he expects others to behave? Are these expectations unreasonable? What kinds of things does he say to himself when provocations occur? This can all be facilitated by having the person close his eyes and "run a movie" of the anger experience to relive his thoughts and feelings. (2) *Affective* (tension, temperament, empathy). Is the person tense or agitated? Look for nonverbal cues as indicators. Does he feel "on edge," "wound up," "uptight"? Any problems with sleeping? Any physical problems related to tension such as headache, chest pains, nervous stomach, high blood pressure? How capable is he at laughing at himself or seeing the less serious side of life? Is he sensitive to the feelings of others?

c. *Behavioral factors* (antagonism, hostility, avoidance). How does the person customarily respond when provoked in a given situation? How does his behavior influence how he feels? How do others respond to his reactions? How capable is he at communicating his feelings to others? Are there any signs of positive assertiveness?

4. The rationale for treatment should be presented to the client in accord with the material in the instruction manual. That is, clients should be given an overview of what will be done and the theory behind the procedure.

Note: Assessment is a process that is not completed in a single session, and it is inevitable that what is presented above as material for session 1 will carry over to session 2. Remember, these are guidelines.

Homework. At the end of the first session, the client is asked to maintain a diary of anger experiences. The diary should provide three pieces of information: (1) the frequency of anger experiences (obtained by an account of each incident); (2) the degree of anger experienced, as rated by the client for each incident; and (3) the degree of proficiency demonstrated by the client in managing anger in that situation, also as rated by the client (cf. Novaco, 1975).

Clients are given a set of index cards on which to record hierarchy incidents. They should be instructed to write down a set of anger experiences that they have had and are likely to experience again, ranging from minor annoyances to infuriating events. They will invariably need help with this task in the next session.

Following from the cognitive analysis, instruct the clients to "listen to yourself with a third ear" so as to tune in to anger-instigating private speech. Have them try to notice the kinds of self-statements they emit when anger is experienced.

Session 2. The second session begins with a review of homework assignments from the initial session. These consist of (1) anger-diary ratings, (2) index cards for hierarchy scenarios, (3) report on internal dialogue ("listening to yourself with a third ear").

1. Using the client's diary statements about recent anger experiences, continue to obtain assessment of the anger problem. That is, get a more refined view of the situations, persons, and mode of expression involved with anger arousal.

2. Establish the hierarchy. Order the index cards containing the anger scenarios so that a graduated series of seven situations are produced. Set these aside until the end of the session when the lowest anger situation will be used.

3. Introduce relaxation training. Begin by doing deep-breathing exercises and emphasize the importance of breathing control in achieving relaxation. Go through the full set of muscle exercises. Pay particular attention to breathing rate and to any part of the body that the client has difficulty relaxing.

The Jacobsen (1938) procedure of alternative tensing and relaxing muscles is recommended, since angry people are inclined to tense their muscles and this procedure tells them to do what they are already doing, thus minimizing resistance to relaxation induction.

4. While the client is still relaxing have him imagine a quiet, mellow, tranquil scene. After he imagines that scene for 30 seconds, present the first anger-hierarchy scene, which should be a mild annoyance:

"Just continue relaxing like that. Now I want you to imagine the following scene: (Present the scene as described on the card.) See it as clearly and as vividly as you can. If you feel the least bit angry as you imagine it, signal me by raising the index finger of your right hand."

If the client does not signal anger for 15 seconds, then instruct him to "shut it off and just continue to relax. You are doing very well." If the anger is signaled, instruct him as follows:

You have signaled anger, now see yourself coping with the situation. See yourself staying composed, relaxing, settling down. Continue to imagine the scene but see yourself handling it effectively. (15 seconds)

Bring the client back to the tranquil scene for another 30 seconds of imagination and continued relaxation. Then have the client take a deep breath before opening his eyes.

5. Review how the procedure went. Obtain information on how the anger scene was experienced. Explain the strategy of successive approximations to the top of the hierarchy. Instruct the client to practice the relaxation exercises at home and to continue to "listen to oneself with a third ear," to tune in to anger-eliciting private speech.

Session 3. At this point the client has hopefully begun to tune in to our view of the anger process and share in our language system. This is not a small matter. Like looking through a special lens, it helps to sharpen one's observations and gives clients a new handle on the things that trouble them.

This session will introduce the important staging strategy and continue work on the hierarchy using both cognitive and relaxation coping.

1. Review the diary and continue to refine your assessment of the client's problem. Examine the timing and impact of anger-facilitating self-statements using a diary example. Try to specify at this point what is the client's predominant style of coping. Praise him for working on homework tasks. Check on the accuracy and usefulness of the hierarchy.

2. Begin the cognitive interventions by first explaining that our feelings are caused not by events themselves but by our thoughts or beliefs about those events. How we think determines how we feel.

Mention the Ellis concept of A-B-C in further making this point. Then,

a. Select example provocations from persons' lives and identify the Antecedent events, Beliefs, and Consequent behaviors.

b. Make an attempt to alter B. That is, try to help clients alternatively view the situation. Modify their appraisal of its significance, the intentions of others, etc., or alter any maladaptive expectations of the behavior of others, themselves, or the consequences of the situation.

Determine how they construed the situation (preconceptions of the event, interpretations of other's behavior, justifications of their own actions) and give particular attention to the internal dialogue before, during, and after the incident.

3. Using information from the diary, have clients sort out the situations for which anger is "justified" versus those for which it is less justified or even counterproductive. Mention the varied functions of anger and state that our objective is to maximize the positive functions and minimize the negative. As they become better at recognizing when it is okay to be angry and when it is not okay, they will be more able to use anger in positive ways.

4. Induce relaxation. Follow the same steps as the last session. This time, add some relaxing imagery.

5. Present the next hierarchy scene. First have them imagine being in a tranquil, peaceful place. Then have them see themselves in the provocation situation. In addition to the relaxation in coping with the anger experience, suggest that they cope cognitively with the provocation.

6. Review the experience of the relaxation and cognitive coping process. Remind the clients to practice the relaxation at home.

Session 4

1. Review the anger diary and ask if any progress has been made on the hierarchy situations in real life. That is, inquire how the person has done on those situations that you have practiced under relaxation. Check again the appropriateness of the hierarchy.

2. Select an example incident. Try to modify thoughts about the anger situation such as intolerance for mistakes, unreasonable

expectations of self and others, impatience, or the felt necessity for retaliation. Try to sharpen the person's discrimination of when anger is justified.

3. Arrive at a sharp understanding of the person's feelings of anger in this situation to as complete an extent as possible. Try to make him become fully aware of the signs of anger physiologically and behaviorally. Have him tune in to the bodily cues of anger and the effects it has on behavior.

4. Help the client to understand the feelings of others in that situation. What's it like to be the other guy? Role-play will usually help with this. Have the client take the role of the other person and you take his part. Encourage empathy for the other person's point of view.

5. Introduce the staging idea of breaking down an anger experience into chunks. Indicate that trying to handle something all at once is difficult, so we will instead attack it part by part. Use an example to illustrate the various stages:

   a. *Preparing* for a provocation (when possible)
   b. *Impact* and confrontation
   c. *Coping* with arousal and agitation
   d. *Reflecting* or thinking back when conflict is unresolved or conflict is resolved.

This will require that you model explicitly how to view an anger experience and cope with it using these stages. Therefore, you will have to "think out loud" how to handle the situation cognitively. Use self-statements as the means to express constructive appraisals and expectations. Give client the handout describing the examples of self-statements for the various stages. Emphasize the personal-control aspects.

6. Rehearsal of these strategies by clients is now conducted. Have them try out the steps in the coping sequence for the same incident. Ask them to "say out loud" how they are thinking their way through the situation. Have them generate a set of self-statements that is suitable for this situation.

7. Induce relaxation and work on the next two hierarchy items. Remember to use relaxation imagery and instruct them to see themselves coping cognitively.

Sessions 5–10

1. Review the diary incidents and evaluate the progress on treatment objectives. Sharpen assessment of particular difficulties in managing anger. Be sure to praise the clients for any accomplishments.

2. Emphasize how anger can be used as a *signal* to cue us in to what to do in a situation. State that to use anger in positive ways, arousal must be kept at moderate levels. This leads to *impulse control* or thinking before acting. Once again, review the material on staging and self-statements for managing provocation.

3. Begin the behavioral interventions. This is intended to gear the clients to a problem-solving approach to conflict. These can be made in three important areas:

a. *Communication of feelings.* Effective provocation management requires that the person knows what to say. Take an example and in role-play demonstrate or model how to express anger constructively. Have the clients rehearse the recognition and expression of anger in role-play.

b. *Assertion.* Help the clients understand that confrontation does not mean hostility. One way to accomplish this is by setting up a role-play in which you instruct them to be as hostile as they can, then examine their behavior and search for more constructive forms of expression. This is particularly effective if you first have them play a very passive, submissive role. In coaching assertive behavior, have them become more proficient in being direct, firm, and explicit in making requests for change in another person's behavior.

c. *Staying task-oriented.* Help them stay focused on the desired outcomes of anger situations. This means not taking things personally, knowing what one wants to get out of a situation, and working toward that goal. Anger situations should be seen as problems that need a solution. Help them discover strategies that will achieve constructive resolution.

4. Work on the next hierarchy item, first imaginally, then in role-play. Use abbreviated relaxation procedures prior to the imaginal presentation. Emphasize the task-oriented concept in role-play.

References

Jacobsen, E. *Progressive relaxation*. Chicago: University of Chicago Press, 1938.

Novaco, R.W. *Anger control: The development and evaluation of an experimental treatment*. Lexington, Mass.: D.C. Heath, Lexington Books, 1975.

Novaco, R.W. The functions and regulation of the arousal of anger. *American Journal of Psychology*, 1976, *133*, 1124–1128.

6

Cognitive Treatment of Somatic Disorders

W. DOYLE GENTRY

The use of cognition-based behavior therapies in the treatment of mental or psychiatric disorders has been well documented (Mahoney, 1974; Meichenbaum, 1974). However, the extension of such therapies into the field of physical or somatic disorders has only just begun. The reasons for this are two-fold: (1) very little attention has been given to the behavioral treatment of somatic disorders in general (Gentry, 1975a, 1975b; Katz and Zlutnick, 1975; Williams and Gentry, 1977); and (2) the majority of studies that have dealt with the behavioral treatment of somatic disorders to date have either utilized an operant approach, which is basically concerned with the consequences of illness behavior as the focus of therapy, or have emphasized the physiological (tension) basis of bodily dysfunction as the primary target of behavioral intervention. Thus, a "black-box" behavior modifier who is attempting to decrease spastic behavior in a patient with cerebral palsy (Sachs and Mayhall, 1971) by punishing such behavior with painful electric shocks is unconcerned about what the patient thinks, what his attitudes are regarding his spasms, and so forth; in short, the patient's cognitions are

W. DOYLE GENTRY • Department of Psychiatry, Duke University Medical Center, Durham, North Carolina 27710.

irrelevant to successful treatment. Similarly, investigators who use EMG biofeedback to reduce headache intensity in patients suffering from tension headaches (Budzynski, Stoyva, and Adler, 1970) are only concerned with the patient's cognitions if they in any way interfere with or enhance the patient's ability to process the biofeedback information and subsequently to change bodily function in the desired direction, e.g., to relax and thus decrease the EMG activity in scalp and neck muscles. Some reviewers of operant conditioning of autonomic nervous-system responses, and their ultimate application to somatic disorders in humans, have indicated the importance of cognitive mediation (Katkin and Murray, 1968); while others (Crider, Schwartz, and Shnidman, 1969) have questioned the necessity of a cognitive mediation hypothesis for biofeedback and other behavioral strategies of altering somatic behavior, concluding that "it is currently a debatable question that cognitive activity *per se* produces any marked autonomic effect at all" (p. 458).

The purpose of the present chapter is to describe those studies that have utilized cognition-based behavior therapies in the treatment of somatic disorders (e.g., asthma, ulcers, tension and migraine headaches, epilepsy); to suggest other areas of illness and/or illness-related behavior (e.g., chronic pain, compliance with medical regimen) where cognitive therapy might legitimately be applied; to discuss the possible role of cognitions in corrective biofeedback treatment; and finally, to present a model of cognitive behavior modification (CAB model) that may serve as an alternative to the more popular ABC model of operant conditioning frequently employed in the treatment of physical disorders.

LITERATURE REVIEW

By far, the most frequent use of cognitions in the behavioral treatment of somatic disorders has involved the technique of systematic desensitization. This particular behavior therapy strategy involves the pairing of covert events (thoughts, images) with an overt, behavioral act by the patient, namely, relaxation. To the extent that a patient can produce anxiety-evoking cognitive stimuli in the presence of a suppression of anxiety, then the subsequent ability of these stimuli (cognitions) to elicit anxiety and anxiety-based behavior(s) is weakened. This process is referred to both as counterconditioning and reciprocal inhibition.

Some examples of the use of systematic desensitization in treating somatic disorders are as follow. Hedberg (1973) reported a case in which he used this technique to treat a patient with a twenty-two-year history of chronic diarrhea. When treatment began, the patient was averaging 10 bowel movements a day and 3 "accidents" a week. She could maintain bowel control for only up to 30 seconds and was in a constant state of anxiety about having accidents in public places (grocery stores, dining rooms). As a result, she had stopped all of her community activities, as well as many personal relationships. Treatment consisted of pairing muscle relaxation, which she practiced daily at home, with three stimulus hierarchies all dealing with interpersonal anxiety and one additional hierarchy in which proximity to a bathroom was the primary variable. The patient received 12 sessions of desensitization over a six-week period, as well as booster sessions at posttreatment intervals of two months and two years. After only 3 sessions, the patient noted significant reduction in subjective anxiety associated with her diarrhea, and after 8 sessions had achieved satisfactory bowel control. At this point, she reported an increase in both social and physical activity, and more satisfaction in her roles as wife and mother. Her improved bowel control remained during follow-up and two years later "the patient was defecating once daily and able to control her bowels for hours if it was not convenient to go to the bathroom" (p. 68).

Gray, England, and Mohoney (1965) employed desensitization in treating benign vocal nodules in a twenty-nine-year-old woman, who had experienced hoarseness for six months prior to therapy, which had resulted in total voice loss. The patient learned to imagine three different types of interpersonal situations, which had previously elicited anxiety reactions, while in a state of deep muscle relaxation. These included: (a) the disciplining of her children, (b) her relationship with her husband, and (c) her relationship with another man with whom she was emotionally involved. After a total of 15 sessions over a period of three weeks, she was symptom-free.

In fact, "a laryngeal examination by the laryngologist revealed that the vocal folds had cleared, with only slight vestiges of former swelling" (p. 192).

Moore (1965) found that while relaxation training, suggestion, and systematic desensitization were all equally effective in altering the subjective reports of asthmatic patients regarding the number of asthma attacks they had each week, only the desensitization technique produced objective improvement in respiratory function. With desensitization, a steady reduction in the number of attacks took place, dropping from an average of 3.0 per week to 0.5 per week after only 8 sessions. The magnitude of improvement in respiratory function for this condition was approximately 50%, i.e., change in maximum peak flow. A similar improvement was noted by Cooper (1964) for a twenty-four-year-old woman suffering from intractable bronchial asthma.

Taylor (1972) used desensitization in the treatment of a fifteen-year-old female patient with pollakiuria, i.e., excessive number of urinations per day. The patient reported intermittent episodes of excessive urination over a period of nine years with an acute exacerbation of this condition during the school year just prior to seeking therapy. Three desensitization hierarchies were devised that involved the patient's riding to school, being in school, and participating in classroom activities. While Taylor failed to report actual data on the change in frequency of urinations resulting from treatment, he noted that they were normal at the end of three months of treatment and again at a four-month follow-up.

Other examples of the use of systematic desensitization with physical disorders include: spasmodic torticollis (Meares, 1973), epilepsy (Parrino, 1971), hives (Daniels, 1973), neurodermatitis (Wolpe, 1959), migraine headaches (Mitchell and Mitchell, 1971), insomnia (Geer and Katkin, 1966), vomiting (Lang, 1965), and chronic muscle spasms in the neck (Butler and Salamy, 1975).

A second behavioral technique used in treating somatic disorders is thought-stopping. In using this technique, the therapist directly attacks the disruptive or anxiety-evoking cognition (thought, image) by shouting, "Stop!" whenever the patient produces same, either spontaneously or upon command. The patient is then told to say, "Stop!" subvocally whenever such thoughts occur, which if not disrupted will lead to anxiety and somatic symptomatology. Daniels (1973), for example, used thought-stopping, along with systematic desensitization, in treating a twenty-three-year-old female suffering from urticaria (hives). The patient's major complaint involved facial swelling and itching over her entire body, which occurred daily and was directly related to strong feelings of anxiety and hostility toward members of her husband's family, toward her husband whenever he indicated approval or understanding of his family's behavior, and toward various other individuals she interacted with both as a graduate student and junior high school teacher. As part of treatment, she was told to say, "Stop!" whenever she encountered individuals or situations that aroused large amounts of tension, e.g., her father-in-law, sister-in-law, supervisor, and the pupils she taught in school. Having disrupted the negative cognitions, she was then instructed to say subvocally, "Relax," and to follow this with another subvocal statement (cognition) that was positive, e.g., "He's only trying to be helpful," in referring to her father-in-law (p. 349). The patient's hives terminated completely after 12 weeks of therapy and had not reappeared 23 months later at follow-up.

Suinn (1977) reported using thought-stopping in his treatment of coronary heart disease (CHD) patients characterized by a Type-A behavior pattern. He notes that certain types of negative thoughts (cognitions) compete with relaxation, which is the goal of his stress-management training program, and in fact build up tension in the Type-A individual; these include thoughts about succeeding, worries about having insufficient time, thoughts about being overcommitted, and so forth. Such thoughts, if left unchecked, lead to increased feelings of stress, a sense of "loss of control," and ultimately to the manifestation of a behavior pattern that has been shown to be highly associated with CHD. If the Type-A patient cannot successfully disrupt these thoughts with the thought-stopping procedure, Suinn offers another possible way of lessening their impact on the person, namely, to have them deliberately engage in such cognitions, but only in specific, time-limited circumstances (e.g., in a specific room, while sitting in a specific chair, or only at a specific time of the day).

A third technique for competing with disruptive cognitions in patients with somatic disorders is positive imagery. Chappell and Stevenson (1936) used this technique in treating patients with peptic ulcers. The patients were trained in a group setting to select some thought(s) or image(s) of a pleasant time of life, which they could focus on whenever they began to worry or feel anxious. Training sessions occurred daily over a period of six weeks and treated patients were compared with ulcer patients who were not exposed to positive imagery. The results were indeed impressive. The treated group of patients (n=32), with one exception, were free from subjective symptoms at the end of three weeks of training. While training continued, these patients were encouraged to expand their diet to "eating about anything they desired, for the first time in many years." All but two of the treated patients were able to tolerate the expanded diet without any recurrence of ulcer symptoms. The control group of patients, on the other hand, who were also symptom-free at the end of a month of medication and special diet had a 90% relapse rate when they began the expanded diet program. At the end of a three-year follow-up, the results were even more pronounced. The patients treated with positive-imagery training were still relatively healthy and symptom-free, with the exception of two individuals (6%) who had evidenced a recurrence of ulcer disease as serious as before treatment three years earlier.

A fourth type of cognitive treatment for somatic disorders was proposed by Efron (1957) in work with epileptic-seizure patients. Using a classical conditioning procedure, Efron was able to teach patients with epilepsy to abort seizures by focusing their attention on a bracelet, which during conditioning had been paired with the odor of concentrated jasmine, a substance known to arrest seizure activity in humans. He also found quite accidentally, however, that a patient could abort seizures merely by thinking about (or visualizing) the bracelet, which in turn produced the olfactory hallucination of jasmine. The patient he reported on, who had evidenced continuous seizure episodes for the previous 26 years, was able to go for 14 months without any seizure activity at all simply by thinking about the bracelet whenever she felt a seizure coming on (aura). While the seizure took slightly longer to subside when the patient only thought about the bracelet, as compared to when she actually took it from her purse and looked at it, the overall therapeutic effect was the same. Mahoney (1974) refers to this procedure as "covertly mediated conditioned inhibition."

Finally, Wilson (1973) employed what Mahoney refers to as "a contiguous pairing procedure utilizing imaginary stimuli" (1974, p. 81) in the treatment of a chronic urination disorder. The patient he was treating, a twenty-one-year-old male college student, would not urinate if anyone else were in the bathroom or was likely to enter; neither would he defecate under such circumstances. Wilson had the client continue to attempt urination/defecation only under "safe" conditions, but also to imagine someone entering the bathroom at the point where urination was inevitable. This "shifting of stimulus control by the method of fading" was successful and in only two weeks the young man was able to initiate and complete urination while imagining another man standing next to him. He was subsequently able to urinate without difficulty in public rest rooms no matter how crowded they happened to be. Interestingly, there was no improvement in the defecation disorder, suggesting to Wilson the "efficacy of the specific technique rather than a general placebo effect" (p. 429).

OTHER AREAS OF APPLICATION

With respect to other areas of illness or illness-related behavior that might be amenable to cognitive therapy, two such areas come to mind: chronic pain and compliance with medical regimen.

Meichenbaum and Turk (1976) have recently reviewed the "long history but . . . short past" of using cognitive strategies to cope with acute and chronic pain and the laboratory studies that suggest that *stress-inoculation training* can effectively increase pain tolerance in individuals subjected to experimentally induced pain. Stress-inoculation training involves three types of training (sensory-discriminative, motivational-affective, cognitive-evaluative), which are provided through the medium of imagery-rehearsal and role-playing, both widely used behavioral techniques. In *sensory-discriminative* training, subjects are taught to mediate the sensory input of pain by such means as mental and physical relaxation and by attending to slow, deep breathing. In the *motivational-affective* training, they are offered strategies for dealing with "feelings of helplessness" and "absence of control," which often accompany the experience of chronic pain. These strategies include: (1) *attention-diversion* (mental arithmetic), (2) *somatization* (focusing on bodily sensations), and (3) *imagery manipulations* (which include imaginative inattention, imaginative transformation of pain in fantasy, and imaginative transformation of the context in which pain is experienced). These cognitive strategies are presented to the subject in "cafeteria style," as some are more useful to certain individuals than others, and the subjects are encouraged to use the techniques at "critical moments" when the pain is most unbearable and when the person is most likely to "give up" and passively accept the pain experience. Finally, in the *cognitive-evaluative* phase of training, the subjects are asked to generate self-statements, e.g., "One step at a time; you can handle the situation" and "Don't think about the pain, just what you have to do" that can be employed as needed in preparing for the pain experience, in confronting and coping with the pain especially at "critical moments," and for use as self-reinforcement, a self-generated consequence to successfully handling the pain situation. In the training program, subjects are asked to imagine themselves in painful situations, are asked to imagine how and when they would utilize the variety of cognitive coping strategies in dealing with the pain, and they eventually become proficient in dealing with the pain totally on a subvocal (cognitive) level. Laboratory data on subjects undergoing experimentally induced pain (Turk, 1975) indicate that this type of training was instrumental in increasing the pain tolerance of subjects by 88% (from a mean of 17 minutes to a mean of 32 minutes), whereas a control group not receiving this training was only able to enhance pain tolerance by 6% (from a mean of 18 minutes to a mean of 19 minutes). These authors noted the promising application of this technique to a patient with a long-standing history of migraine headaches, as well as to other types of chronic pain syndromes.

Only one attempt has been made to define the problems of patient compliance with medical regimen using a behavioral framework (Zifferblatt, 1975). It has been suggested that compliance is primarily a function of the environmental events that immediately precede (antecedent cues) and follow (consequences) it, i.e., an operant analysis. However, it was also pointed out that compliance may equally as well be a function of patient expectations (which can be defined in terms of subvocal self-statements such as "This medicine is going to make me well!" or "I know this stuff really won't help me!") and thus cognitive behavior modification might legitimately be employed (Gentry, 1977). Cognitions could come into play even using the operant analysis in that, as Gentry (1977, p. 207) noted:

> Many of the antecedent cues and covert consequences of compliance or noncompliance could be internalized. The patient could learn to tell himself "It's time for your medicine." in association with meal times and to follow up the medication intake with a self-statement such as "Good, there you feel better now that you've taken your medicine on time."

Finally, it is conceivable that any and all somatic disorders that can be viewed as involving the "urge" to do something, e.g., the urge to cough, the urge to scratch, the urge to vomit, the urge to urinate/defecate more or less frequently, could be dealt with via cognitive behavior therapies. Urges can be defined as subvocal (cognitive) self-statements (I have to . . .), which in turn lead to specific somatic behavior, independent of an affective response, which could be dealt with directly by means of systematic desensitization, thought-stopping, and other similar techniques.

ROLE OF COGNITIONS IN BIOFEEDBACK

The role of cognitions in biofeedback therapy is at the same time unknown and controversial. As was noted earlier, some investigators have suggested that cognitive mediation (some type of processing of information by the brain) is central to an understanding of the subject's ability to change autonomic nervous-system activity with the aid of external feedback. Others, on the other hand, feel that the connection between thoughts, self-statements, etc., and changes in autonomic responses has not been sufficiently studied, at least to the extent that one can say that cognitive mediation is central to our appreciation of the mechanisms by which biofeedback is effective. One study of biofeedback with cardiac patients (Weiss and Engel, 1971) actually describes how individuals can and do use cognitions as a means of altering a maladaptive somatic response pattern, in this case premature ventricular contractions (PVCs). In this study, the investigators attempted to train eight patients hospitalized with PVCs to control their heart rate. Each patient was taught to increase and decrease his/her heart rate according to visual cues; a green light signaled heart-rate speeding and a red light indicated heart-rate slowing. If the patient responded correctly, a yellow light indicated successful performance (reward). Patients were thus able to monitor their heart rate continuously. Five of the eight patients (63%) learned to systematically control their rate with biofeedback and subsequently showed a significant decrease in PVC activity. In four of the five patients who learned heart-rate control, the benefits of training lasted for up to 21 months of follow-up. For several of the patients, it was clear that they were able to speed or slow their heart rate via cognitions (imagery). For example, one patient reported that he could speed up his heart rate if he "thought about bouncing a rubber ball" (p. 314); another patient stated that "she thought about arguments with her children and about running through a dark street during the speeding sessions" (p. 309) and that she could slow her heart rate if "she thought about swinging back and forth in a swing (p. 309)." Weiss and Engel noted, however, that the use of imagery in controlling heart rate, and thus PVCs, is idiosyncratic with no consistent pattern evident across patients.

In another study of operant conditioning of heart rate in subjects without cardiac disease, Engel and Hansen (1966) noted that heart-rate slowing could be achieved via biofeedback in some cases when the subject concentrated on objects in the room (e.g., aligning holes in acoustical tiles), a technique similar to that used by Meichenbaum and Turk in stress-inoculation training with pain subjects, which they refer to as *attention-diversion* (they in fact use the example of counting ceiling tiles).

Clearly, more work needs to be done in this area before any definite conclusion can be reached concerning the actual or potential role of cognitive mediation in biofeedback treatment.

The CAB versus the ABC Model

Most of the work dealing with the behavioral treatment of somatic disorders done thus far has been carried out using the traditional operant approach, which stresses the relationship between a behavior (B) and the environmental events that immediately precede (antecedents-A) and immediately follow (consequences-C) it. Using this model (Gentry, 1975a), successful treatment of disorders such as asthma, heart-rate dysfunction, headaches, spasms in cerebral-palsied adults, chronic orthopedic pain syndromes, spasmodic torticollis (wry neck), epilepsy, vomiting, diarrhea and incontinence, enuresis, and neurodermatitis has been achieved. However, it seems equally probable that an alternative model (CAB) that proposes a relationship between cognitions (C), affect (A) or emotion, and behavior (B) can be applied successfully to physical disorders. The above review of studies that utilize techniques such as systematic desensitization, thought-stopping, positive imagery, and corrective biofeedback represent therapeutic interventions based on this model. The focus here is on the internal world of the patient, his thoughts and feelings, which in part may be an internalization of reinforcement relationships that initially fit the other ABC model, e.g., with respect to self-statements that are self-reinforcing, to self-generated cues (antecedents) that in turn occasion certain behaviors that are rewarded in some fashion, and so forth. Using certain strategies, one directly attacks the cognitions of the patient (negative self-statements); using other strategies, the bond between cognition and affect is weakened; in still others, the relationship between cognitions (attitudes, expectations, fears) and behavior is disrupted without necessarily considering the affective state of the individual. Common to all these strategies, however, is an attempt by the therapist to, as Meichenbaum suggests (1974), "influence the nature of the client's internal dialogue," in other words, cognitive behavior modification.

References

Budzynski, T., Stoyva, J. and Adler, C. Feedback-induced muscle relaxation: application to tension headaches. *Journal of Behavior Therapy and Experimental Psychiatry*, 1970, 1, 205–211.

Butler, P.E., and Salamy, A. Eliminating a conditioned muscle spasm by external inhibition by an electric vibrator. *Journal of Behavior Therapy and Experimental Psychiatry*, 1975, 6, 159–161.

Chappell, M., and Stevenson, T. Group psychological training in some organic conditions. *Mental Hygiene*, 1936, 20, 588–597.

Cooper, A.J. A case of bronchial asthma treated by behaviour therapy. *Behavior Research and Therapy*, 1964, 1, 351–356.

Crider, A., Schwartz, G.E., and Shnidman, S. On the criteria for instrumental conditioning: A reply to Katkin and Murray. *Psychological Bulletin*, 1969, *71*, 455–461.

Daniels, L.K. Treatment of urticaria and severe headache by behavior therapy. *Psychosomatics*, 1973, *14*, 347–351.

Efron, R. The conditioned inhibition of uncinate fits. *Brain*, 1957, *80*, 251–262.

Engel, B.T., and Hansen, S.P. Operant conditioning of heart rate slowing. *Psychophysiology*, 1966, *3*, 176–187.

Geer, J.H., and Katkin, E.S. Treatment of insomnia, using a variant of systematic desensitization: A case report. *Journal of Abnormal Psychology*, 1966, *71*, 161–164.

Gentry, W.D. Behavior modification of physical disorders. In W.D. Gentry (Ed.) *Applied behavior modification*. St. Louis: Mosby, 1975a, 130–147.

Gentry, W.D. *Behavioral treatment of somatic disorders*. Morristown, N.J.: General Learning Press, 1975b.

Gentry, W.D. Noncompliance to medical regimen. In R.B. Williams and W.D. Gentry (Eds.), *Behavioral approaches to medical treatment*. Cambridge, Mass.: Ballinger, 1977, 203–208.

Gray, B.B., England, G., and Mohoney, J.L. Treatment of benign vocal nodules by reciprocal inhibition. *Behavior Research and Therapy*, 1965, *3*, 187–193.

Hedberg, A.G. The treatment of chronic diarrhea by systematic desensitization: a case report. *Journal of Behavior Therapy and Experimental Psychiatry*, 1973, *4*, 67–68.

Katkin, E.S., and Murray, E.N. Instrumental conditioning of autonomically mediated behavior: theoretical and methodological issues. *Psychological Bulletin*, 1968, *70*, 52–68.

Katz, R.C., and Zlutnick, S. (Eds.), *Behavior therapy and health care: principles and applications*. Elmsford, N.Y.: Pergamon, 1975.

Lang, P.J. Behavior therapy with a case of nervous anorexia. In L.P. Ullmann and L. Krasner (Eds.), *Case studies in behavior modification*. New York: Holt, Rinehart, and Winston, 1965, 217–221.

Mahoney, M.J. *Cognition and behavior modification*. Cambridge, Mass.: Ballinger, 1974.

Meares, R.A. Behavior therapy and spasmodic torticollis. *Archives of General Psychiatry*, 1973, *28*, 104–107.

Meichenbaum, D. *Cognitive behavior modification*. Morristown, N.J.: General Learning Press, 1974.

Meichenbaum, D., and Turk, D. The cognitive-behavioral management of anxiety, anger, and pain. In P. Davidson (Ed.), *The behavioral management of anxiety, depression, and pain*. New York: Brunner/Mazel, 1976.

Mitchell, K.R., and Mitchell, D.M. Migraine: an exploratory treatment application of programmed behavior therapy techniques. *Journal of Psychosomatic Research*, 1971, *15*, 137–157.

Moore, K. Behavior therapy in bronchial asthma: a controlled study. *Journal of Psychosomatic Research*, 1965, *9*, 257–276.

Parrino, J. Reduction of seizures by desensitization. *Journal of Behavior Therapy and Experimental Psychiatry*, 1971, *2*, 215–218.

Sachs, D.A., and Mayhall, B. Behavioral control of spasms using aversive conditioning with a cerebral palsied adult. *Journal of Nervous and Mental Disease*, 1971, *152*, 362–363.

Suinn, R.M. Type A behavior pattern. In R.B. Williams and W.D. Gentry (Eds.), *Behavioral approaches to medical treatment*. Cambridge, Mass.: Ballinger, 1977, 55–65.

Taylor, D.W. Treatment of excessive frequency of urination by desensitization. *Journal of Behavior Therapy and Experimental Psychiatry*, 1972, *3*, 311–313.

Turk, D. Cognitive control of pain: a skills training approach. Unpublished manuscript, University of Waterloo, 1975.

Weiss, T., and Engel, B.T. Operant conditioning of heart rate in patients with premature ventricular contractions. *Psychosomatic Medicine*, 1971, *33*, 301–322.

Williams, R.B., and Gentry, W.D. (Eds.), *Behavioral approaches to medical treatment*. Cambridge, Mass.: Ballinger, 1977.

Wilson, G.T. Innovations in the modification of phobic behaviors in two clinical cases. *Behavior Therapy*, 1973, *4*, 426–430.

Wolpe, J. Psychotherapy based on the principles of reciprocal inhibition. In A. Burton (Ed.), *Case studies in counseling and psychotherapy*. New Jersey: Prentice Hall, 1959.

Zifferblatt, S.M. Increasing patient compliance through the applied analysis of behavior. *Preventive Medicine*, 1975, *4*, 173–182.

7

Countersensitization

AN AVERSIVE CONDITIONING MODEL FOR SELF-CONTROL OF EXCESSIVE PERFORMANCE STANDARDS

PATRICK H. DOYLE AND JOHN G. BRUHN

It is widely assumed that behavior problems arise in large measure from discrepancies between self-standards and actual performance. Hence a number of psychotherapies have as their focus the reduction of this discrepancy. However, the direct approach of using aversive conditioning to inhibit the excessive standards has been strangely absent from the literature. This paper discusses a specific type of covert sensitization as a means of reducing excessive performance standards and presents a case study illustrating its use.

Description of Covert Sensitization

Covert sensitization (Cautela, 1967) typically entails the client first imagining himself engaging in some undesirable behavior such as overeating and then mentally picturing himself experiencing vivid nausea. For example, an overeater imagines bringing a fork containing a piece of pie toward his mouth. As the pie comes

PATRICK H. DOYLE • Department of Psychology, University of Houston, Clear Lake City, Texas 77058. JOHN G. BRUHN • Community Affairs and Special Programs, University of Texas, Medical Branch, Galveston, Texas 78712.

closer to being ingested, his mental scenes increase in nausea going from queasiness to outright vomiting. The nausea is imagined to continue until the person desists his eating behavior, at which point he thinks of himself as very relaxed and relieved. The proposed outcome is that the client develops an aversion toward the undesirable behavior, thus resolving the problem. A review of the literature by Mahoney (1974) showed this method to have had some success in the treatment of sexual deviancy (e.g., Barlow, Leitenberg, and Agras, 1969). Prior to the application of covert sensitization in this case, though, a conditioning conceptualization of self-standards will be provided.

A Conditioning Conceptualization of Excessive Self-Standards

In the view of this paper, the person who feels the necessity of obtaining especially high performance levels has previously undergone trials where more moderate performance was paired with aversive consequences; for example, this could have resulted in part from a parent or sibling vividly depicting a child's lower performance in disagreeable terms. As an adult the person consequently feels uncomfortable or anxious with modest achievement levels.

Covert Sensitization of Excessive Self-Standards

This reversal of this maladaptive conditioning would be implemented through covert sensitization by substituting a vocal expression of the person's excessive self-standards for undesirable behavior. This would result in standards rather than some problematical behavior such as smoking being the focus of the procedure. For example, if a student experienced unmanageable stress in studying for an examination he might vocalize a statement similar to the following, "I *have* to obtain an 'A' on the examination." This would then be followed by him imagining an early stage of a highly nauseous state such as his stomach feeling queasy. In successive trials, the person would continue saying, "I have to obtain an 'A' on the examination," each time followed by a more advanced stage of a highly nauseous state. Thus, as the person repeated this statement, he would mentally progress from a queasy stomach to food inching up the esophagus to vomiting with considerable messiness and discomfort.

When the nausea progression had reached its apex, the person would then be requested to change his statement so as to reverse its meaning by the insertion of the word "don't" as in the following example: "I don't have to obtain an 'A' on the examination." The person would then begin repeating this revised version of his earlier statement, thus reversing his former extreme position on his personal standards. Similar to the earlier training, at each repetition of the statement he would be guided in imagining a change in the degree of nausea, but in this case it would be a step toward regaining comfort rather than intensifying the nausea. Typically, with each repetition of the revised statement, he would imagine the withdrawal of one of the previous steps in the buildup of the nausea. As an example, after the person says, "I *don't* have to obtain an 'A' on the examination," then the therapist would ask the person to imagine that the vomiting was diminishing; after another revised statement the person would think of the vomiting as almost completely stopped and so on toward complete relief. In the final stages, the revised statements would be paired with mild nausea and ultimately relaxation.

To summarize, in covert sensitization as described above the person's high level of performance standards is paired with nausea and then its repudiation is paired with increasing relief. This procedure is designed to inhibit the anxiety or stress normally associated with more moderate performances. In the case of the student studying for an examination, rather than being debilitated by the stress over excessive performance standards the student would be more able to study effectively.

COUNTERSENSITIZATION

As conceptualized in this paper, sensitization is used to counter the previous maladaptive sensitization that led to excessive standards; hence, it would seem useful to label this process *countersensitization*. One benefit of this term is that it communicates the nature of the approach. Another benefit is that the term "countersensitization" is logically related to desensitization. Both methods relate to allaying fears in a reciprocal inhibition paradigm. The former, however, proposes to do so by overcoming one sensitization with another (countersensitization) while the latter accomplishes this by removing the sensitization (*de*sensitization) in substituting relaxation.

Countersensitization would appear to be a fundamental category in the variety of approaches that could be utilized in modifying maladaptive conditioning; it is also a distinct conditioning method addressing the phenomenon of excessive self-standards that in the past has been largely ignored by behavioral psychologists.

A Modified Countersensitization Approach

As described previously, the procedure has relied on the development of a high degree of imagined nausea. However, the use of this method with its step-by-step buildup requires fairly large amounts of time. Consequently, it does not lend itself to self-administration since the client would be required to individually apply a fairly cumbersome treatment. Since self-administration is important, the procedure needs to be altered to facilitate its occurrence.

In altering the procedure the desired outcome would be a countersensitization method that was considerably abbreviated, contained mnemonic qualities to aid memory, and required little skill to apply. At the same time, however, it would require sufficient aversive content to be effective in inhibiting excessive self-standards. The direction taken in attempting to design such a procedure was based on an observation by Mahoney (1974); "While nauseous scenes have conventionally been used, little attention has been given to the promise of utilizing imagery or other forms of aversive experiences (e.g., physical injury . . .) (p. 103). The greater fear involved in physical injury, as against simply becoming quite nauseous, might be usable in the countersensitization procedure to achieve comparable inhibition results in fewer trials.

In addition, there is a highly credible relationship between excessive standards and physical disorders or injuries. The resulting stress apparently leads to peptic ulcers and cardiovascular disease as well as recklessness and automobile accidents. Thus, picturing a physical disorder in connection with stress-inducing self-standards would appear to be a logical relationship and, furthermore, one the client could understand would bear keeping in mind. Consequently, he would probably be able to feel a basic affinity for the procedure of using physical disorders to sensitize him to excessive self-standards. This would enhance the motivation of the client and possibly increase the effectiveness of the conditioning.

With this in mind, a countersensitization procedure that relied on physical disorder rather than nausea was devised. The procedure was also abbreviated, mnemonic, and self-administerable. In this method the person would, for example, say it was necessary to obtain an excessive grade on an examination and then imagine consequences such as being told he had contracted a certain disease. Such trials would presumably lead to an aversion of feeling that it was necessary to perform at such high levels. The exact form of this countersensitization procedure is illustrated in the context of the following case study.

CASE STUDY

The client was a thirty-two-year-old Caucasian male. He had held positions as a county deputy sheriff, police officer, and had served as a medic in the military. At the time treatment began he was carrying 12 credit hours of course work at the university and working as a building custodian. He seemed intelligent and articulate.

His presenting problem was a skin rash on both hands that had been diagnosed by a dermatologist as neurodermatitis secondary to anxiety. The patient had experienced a similar problem five years previously that continued for more than six months. His present episode had persisted for almost two years. At the time of the first visit the patient had been taking two and one half milligrams of Valium (q.i.d.) for a week and reported that he consistently observed the physician's regimen.

At the first session the patient reported little improvement in the dermatitis. It was located principally along the sides of the fingers, but the dyshydrosis was most severe between the forefinger and the thumb on the left hand. As the condition was soothed by scratching, there seemed to be a relationship between the ready access to this portion of the left hand by the right hand and the severity of the condition. In a number of the affected areas it was possible to cause minor bleeding by simply making a fist, which stretched the skin and aggravated the condition.

The first session was devoted to determining the nature of the stress. The client's problem seemed to arise from a stringent need to be competent. For example, he reported feeling most uncomfortable when he was not competent in whatever he was doing. This unrelenting need to be competent was designated as the excessive self-standard.

At the second meeting a week later, the idea of relaxing his thoughts of having to be competent was approached around the client's need to return a new automobile battery that he regretted having to do. He said that he usually became embroiled in vehement arguments around such issues and was upset because he usually hurt his own case. The issue of having to be competent in returning the battery was discussed from the viewpoint of excessive standards often proving debilitating.

The third session occurred the following week and the patient reported that by keeping in mind that he did not have to obtain a new battery he was able to control his hostility and, as he explained, this allowed the salesperson to correct the situation without becoming defensive.

At this point the groundwork had been laid for introduction to the countersensitization procedures. The person was introduced to the relationship between stress resulting from excessive self-expectations and physical disorders. It was pointed out that inattention and recklessness resulting from stress probably account for many automobile accidents and consequent injuries. It was further indicated that gastrointestinal ulcers and cardiovascular disorders were also related to stress; necessary surgical interventions such as colectomies were also mentioned. During this period the client was providing many illustrations of the types of disorders that can arise from stress; in his opinion "hay fever" was a particularly good example. It was also agreed that the dermatitis condition was the result of stress. The inevitable conclusion was that excessive standards need to be controlled in order to forestall not only inferior performance but possible physical disorders as well.

It was in this context that the procedure was introduced for use by the client. He was first asked to close his eyes and speak aloud, "I have to be competent." Immediately following this he was asked to imagine a physician sitting at his desk saying, "You have to have your fingers amputated." (This was with the clear understanding on the part of the client that medically this was unlikely, but of the order of possibilities that have resulted from stress, as in the colectomy.)

Having completed those two steps, the equivalent of the first half of a characteristic covert sensitization approach has been accomplished. The person has associated a very aversive condition with a particular response. There are two important differences, though: First, the response is not a behavior such as smoking but the verbal expression of the person's excessive self-standards; second, it occurs in a highly abbreviated form.

The next step corresponds to the recovery phase of the characteristic covert sensitization procedures in that the person responds in the desired manner and associates a reduction in anxiety with this. In the earlier illustration of overeating, relief occurred in connection with the cessation of eating; the person was relieved of nauseous feelings by the time he had placed the fork containing the piece of pie on the table again. The recovery phase in the present method involved the utilization of two more lines: "I *don't* have to be competent," and then picturing the physician saying, "You *don't* have to have your fingers amputated."

Thus, the entire countersensitization treatment was as follows:

The client says: "I have to be competent."

Next he imagines a physician saying the following, which the client states aloud: "You have to have your fingers amputated."

Then the client says: "I *don't* have to be competent."

Finally he imagines a physician saying the following, which he states aloud: "You *don't* have to have your fingers amputated."

The client was then instructed to use this approach and to repeat the four lines whenever he felt anxious. This procedure was practiced for a number of trials in the office to be certain the client could execute the procedure accurately.

The fourth and fifth sessions, again spaced at weekly intervals, simply reinforced use of the countersensitization statements and monitored the client's progress. The client maintained a high level of motivation in implementing the procedures and expressed satisfaction with the results as the neurodermatitis was improving.

By the sixth session, two weeks later, the client's condition was virtually nonexistent. The client ascribed the improvement to the statements he was using. His wife, who accompanied him on this visit, indicated the important difference to her was that he no longer felt the need to scratch the affected areas.

Following the sixth session there were two follow-up visits over the course of a year and the client reported he was continuing the countersensitization procedures. While he had experienced a mild recrudescence of the neurodermatitis, there was no evidence of the condition at the time of the follow-up visits. The patient stated that the condition had been controllable through the use of the countersensitization procedure.

During the therapy there were potentially confounding variables. For example, the client changed employment during treatment. However, the causal network is probably a complex one; for example, the client attributed the successful attainment of another employment position to the statements. He said that the use of countersensitization made the stress of seeking another position bearable. Thus, the use of countersensitization in this case probably directly and indirectly had some influence on the client's recovery.

DISCUSSION

Countersensitization procedures using physical disorders as the aversive component may be especially advantageous in psychosomatic cases. The client had real concerns regarding the welfare of his hands and this probably contributed to the motivation and presumed effectiveness of the treatment. Within limits it is feasible that the more advanced a particular condition the greater the impact of countersensitization statements. Therefore, in contrast to the usual situation, a person with an advanced condition may have a better prognosis using countersensitization.

Based on the widely held view that excessive self-standards give rise to stress, this chapter dealt with the application of covert sensitization to the inhibition of those standards. In a conditioning paradigm excessive standards were seen as originating to a significant degree from sensitization of more moderate standards. Hence, the sensitization of excessive standards to counter earlier similar conditioning of moderate standards was termed *countersensitization*. Such a procedure utilizing a physical disorder as the aversive component was illustrated in a case study. This method has both conceptual and practical implications. It offers especially significant advantages in both engendering considerable self-motivation and being self-administerable. In view of the benefits offered, further investigation in countersensitization needs to be undertaken.

REFERENCES

Barlow, D.H., Leitenberg, H., and Agras, W.S. Experimental control of sexual deviation through manipulation of the noxious scene in covert sensitization. *Journal of Abnormal Psychology*, 1969, 74, 596–601.
Cautela, J.R. Covert sensitization. *Psychological Reports*, 1967, 20, 459–468.
Mahoney, M.J. *Cognition and behavior modification.* Cambridge, Mass.: Ballinger, 1974.

8

Cognitive Behavioral Techniques in the Management of Pain

DENNIS C. TURK

The purpose of the present chapter is to examine the utility of a variety of cognitive behavioral treatments designed to enhance tolerance for painful stimuli. The chapter is organized into three main sections. First, before describing the specific coping strategies employed, a brief overview of the phenomenon of pain will be provided. Such an overview underscores the complexity and intractability of this universal experience, and reveals the bases for the traditional therapeutic modalities employed to ameliorate pain.

The second section reviews some of the cognitive behavioral treatments designed to modify anxiety-based dysfunctions with emphasis on the implications of such techniques for the management of pain.

The final section examines some of the specific cognitive behavioral coping skills that have been employed to enhance pain tolerance. In this section strategy-specific as well as multidimensional

DENNIS C. TURK • Department of Psychology, Yale University, New Haven, Connecticut 06520.

approaches with both laboratory-analog and clinical pain will be outlined. Special attention will be focused on *stress inoculation,* a particular cognitive behavioral coping-skills regimen developed by Meichenbaum and his colleagues (Meichenbaum, 1975; Meichenbaum and Cameron, 1973; Meichenbaum and Turk, 1976). The stress-inoculation treatment regimen has received the most extensive investigation (Horan, Hackett, Buchanan, Stone, and Demchik-Stone, 1977; Turk, 1975, 1977a). These initial results indicate the promisory value of this adjunctive treatment approach.

CONCEPTUALIZATIONS OF PAIN

The question, What is pain? has been debated by philosophers, physicians, and psychologists for centuries. From the time of Aristotle until the latter part of the 19th century, pain was conceived of as an emotion, the opposite of pleasantness, a quale, or quality of the soul. The development of sensory physiology and psychophysics during the late 1800s argued that an affective explanation of pain was inadequate and at best such affective experiences were of secondary importance. The relative contributions of sensory stimulation, emotions, and cognitions to the experience of pain remains, even today, unresolved and continues to be a center of controversy among theoreticians. Even while the debates have continued, thousands of nostra and procedures have been employed in the quest to relieve suffering. Some of the earliest attempts included the administration of emetics, enemas, blister-raising, bleeding, application of soothing potions, and the administration of a variety of palliatives. Modifications and refinements of these primitive techniques, no less esoteric, are currently utilized to facilitate the relief of pain. Among the most frequently employed are (1) pharmacological agents whose site of action might be at the receptor, the peripheral nerves, or at higher levels of the nervous system, such as the brain stem; (2) anesthetic nerve blocks that require injection of alcohol or local anesthetic (e.g., Novocain) into a nerve root; and (3) surgical procedures performed at nearly every possible site among the pathways from the peripheral receptors to the cortex, e.g., from the sectioning of peripheral nerve to thalamotomies and prefrontal lobotomies.

Most of the current views of pain may be characterized by their unidimensional focus. That is, pain is conceptualized as primarily a function of sensory input. The central assumption of these views is that it is the physical aspects of the noxious stimulus being transmitted along the nervous system that determine the sensations subsequently perceived as pain. Therapeutic modalities following from this assumption are designed to cut or block the "pain pathways." The inadequacy of the sensory-input assumption is most evident from clinical observations.

Physicians have frequently noted that similar wounds, which presumably produce similar "pain sensations," may give rise to strikingly different "reaction patterns" (Beecher, 1959; Bond, 1976). Clinical observations also reveal that treatments designed to inhibit sensory input for patients ostensibly manifesting the same pain syndromes have proven to be differentially effective. In addition, it has been acknowledged that ". . . treatments based on the sensory input model often result in untoward effects with a disheartening tendency for a recurrence of pain at some time following treatment" (Melzack, 1973). Thus, to date none of the more commonly employed therapeutic procedures designed to inhibit or modulate noxious sensory input have proven to be completely satisfactory for consistent, adequate, or permanent amelioration of pain.

Laboratory investigations of the contributions of psychological mediators have underscored the complexity of the pain phenomenon. For example, the literature on predictability and control of pain (e.g., Bandler, Madaras, and Bem, 1968; Bowers, 1971; Staub, Tursky, and Schwartz, 1971) indicates that the subject's perception of control results, in most instances, in higher pain thresholds and/or tolerance. Other investigators (e.g., Bobey and Davidson, 1970; Johnson, 1973; Neufeld and Davidson, 1971) have demonstrated the effect of preparatory communications and information that subjects receive prior to the onset of pain on various pain parameters. Still other investigators have related pain perception and tolerance to prior conditioning (e.g., Pavlov, 1927, 1928), early experiences (e.g., Melzack and Scott, 1957), sociocultural background (e.g., Wolff and Langley, 1968), the meaning of the situation (e.g., Beecher, 1959), attentional focus (e.g., Blitz and Dinnerstein, 1971), social modeling (e.g., Craig, Best, and Reith, 1974), suggestions and placebos (e.g., McGlashan, Evans, and Orne, 1969), various individual difference measures (e.g., Andrew, 1970; Petrie, 1967), as well as anxiety regarding the nature and cause of the noxious stimulation (e.g., Hill, Kornetsky, Flanary, and Wikler, 1952a, b) among others. The important influence and relative neglect of such mediators may explain some of the anomalies noted and the apparent inadequacy of the unidimensional sensory models of pain.

Recent reviews of the pain literature (e.g., Clark and Hunt, 1971; Liebeskind and Paul, 1977; Turk, 1975) have provided compelling arguments that pain is not simply a function of the amount of tissue damage nor can it be defined adequately by specifying parameters of physical stimuli as suggested by sensory–physiological theories. Rather, pain should be considered a subjective experience defined by an individual, with the amount and quality of the pain determined by various factors: previous experiences, how they are recalled, ability to understand the cause and the consequences of the pain, all in addition to the sensory input. Taken together, the clinical observations and laboratory data suggest that an adequate conceptualization of pain must be multidimensional in nature, incorporating cognitive and affective phenomena as well as the physical stimuli and sensory physiology.

A similar conclusion was reached by Melzack and Casey (1968):

> The surgical and pharmacological attacks on pain might well profit by redirecting thinking toward the neglected and almost forgotten contribution of motivational and cognitive processes. Pain can be treated not only by trying to cut down sensory input by anesthetic blocks, surgical intervention and the like, but also by influencing the motivational-affective and cognitive factors as well. (p. 435)

Melzack and Wall (1965) posited a conceptualization of pain that emphasizes such a multidimensional perspective. Their gate-control theory postulates that the perception of pain is a complex phenomenon resulting from the interaction of sensory-discriminative, motivational-affective, and cognitive-evaluative components. While the physiological and anatomical bases for the gate-control model are speculative and have been questioned (e.g., Nathan, 1976), the multidimensional view of pain has received considerable support (e.g., Tursky, 1976).

The renaissance of emphasis on the contribution of cognitive and affective factors to the experience of pain has led a number of investigators to question how best to manipulate psychological mediators to augment existing medical treatments. The goals of such multidimensional approaches include the elimination of reliance on some of the more drastic medical treatments (e.g., lobotomies and addictive narcotics), reduction in the incidence of recurring pain following treatment, making pain more bearable when it cannot be totally eliminated, and increasing tolerance for unavoidable noxious stimulation (e.g., unpleasant medical procedures, including debridement of burns and endoscopic examinations, cf. Fagerhaugh, 1974; Johnson and Leventhal, 1973).

COGNITIVE BEHAVIORAL TREATMENTS FOR ANXIETY-BASED DYSFUNCTIONS—COPING-SKILLS APPROACHES

The examination of cognitive behavioral techniques employed for anxiety-based dysfunctions is undertaken for three reasons. First, anxiety is perhaps the earliest and most consistently identified psychological mediator of the pain experience (e.g., Hill, *et al.*, 1952a, b). In fact, some investigators have suggested that reducing anxiety in and of itself would be sufficient to attenuate the experience of pain (Shor, 1962). Secondly, a number of the specific cognitive and behavioral techniques employed to reduce anxiety have been utilized to modify pain perception and tolerance. And, finally, many of these specific techniques have been incorporated into innovative multifactored cognitive behavioral regimens utilized in pain management.

One of the major treatment approaches for anxiety-based dysfunctions developed out of the work of Wolpe (1958), who employed a counterconditioning model and a procedure he labeled "systematic desensitization." Systematic densensitization involves the construction of a graduated hierarchy of anxiety-inducing stimuli, relaxation training, and the gradual pairing of items from the hierarchy with a relaxed state. As noted above, the conceptual model that gave rise to this approach is one in which situation-specific responses are treated in a counterconditioning manner. The pairing of the hierarchy items with the relaxed state is considered a counterconditioning process, "reciprocal inhibition" (Wolpe, 1958), in which prior (maladaptive) conditioning is countered through the physiological process of relaxation.

The adequacy of the counterconditioning model has been challenged by a number of investigators (Davison and Wilson, 1973; Mahoney, 1974; Meichenbaum, 1977). Partially as a function of these criticisms, there has been a shift to a more coping-skills model that takes into consideration cognitive, affective, as well as behavioral domains (Mahoney, 1974; Meichenbaum, 1977). Conceptualizing anxiety-based dysfunctions in this manner parallels the emphasis of Melzack and Wall (1965) on the importance of the interaction of cognitive, affective, and behavioral contributions to the total pain experience. A review of some of the skills-training approaches that have been employed will reveal a number of common features that may be incorporated into multidimensional, cognitive behavioral approaches designed to enhance tolerance for noxious stimulation.

The investigations of Goldfried and his colleagues (Goldfried, 1971, 1973; Goldfried, Decenteceo, and Weinberg, 1974; Goldfried and Trier, 1974) illustrate one approach to the training of coping skills. Goldfried (1971) has viewed systematic desensitization as a way of teaching his subjects a broad set of self-relaxation skills that can be employed while imagining a number of scenes from different target hierarchies. Emphasis is placed on four components, namely, describing the therapeutic rationale in terms of skills training, the use of relaxation as a generalized coping strategy, the use of multiple-theme hierarchies, and training in "relaxing away" scene-induced anxiety (in contrast with the traditional method of terminating a scene at the first indication of subjective distress, Wolpe, 1958). Self-instructional training (Meichenbaum, 1973, 1974) and stimulus labeling strategies have been incorporated in later refinements of this coping-skills package.

One by-product of the shift to coping-skills models has been a greater concern with the role of cognitive processes. The cognitive processes have been conceptualized in a number of different ways in order to train coping skills (Meichenbaum, 1977). One way has been the systematic rational restructuring approach of Goldfried

(Goldfried *et al.*, 1974). This approach is designed to place rational-emotive therapy (Ellis, 1962) into a behavioral framework. Rational-emotive therapy takes as its major premise that maladaptive feelings result from maladaptive thoughts; major emphasis is thus on the cognitive component. Ellis (1970) suggests that client's

> psychological problems arise from the misperception and mistaken cognitions about what they perceive; from their emotional underreactions or overreactions to normal and unusual stimuli; and from their habitually dysfunctional behavior patterns, which enables them to keep repeating nonadaptive responses even when they know that they are behaving poorly. (p. 8)

Basically, Goldfried contends that the way an individual labels or evaluates a situation (e.g., anxiety-provoking) can differentially determine his subsequent emotional reaction. Goldfried's assumption is that an individual can acquire a more effective coping repertoire with which to control his behavior by means of modifying the "cognitive set" that is employed when approaching potentially anxiety-provoking situations or events. To accomplish this modification in cognitive-set and enhanced coping repertoire, Goldfried has outlined a five-step procedure in which the individual is (1) exposed (through imaginary scenes or role-playing) to an anxiety-provoking situation; (2) asked to evaluate just how anxious he is; (3) called on to use this anxiety as a signal to notice any self-defeating, anxiety-provoking cognitions he has about the situation; (4) encouraged to rationally re-evaluate these cognitions, or self-statements; and (5) to take note of the level of anxiety following this "rational re-evaluation."

Another approach to coping-skills training has been developed by Suinn and Richardson (Richardson and Suinn, 1973; Suinn, 1972; Suinn and Richardson, 1971) and labeled "anxiety-management training." As in the Goldfried approach, anxiety-management training emphasizes relaxation as an active coping skill. This approach is theoretically and procedurally linked to systematic desensitization. The training involves arousing anxiety in the subject through the use of imaginal scenes. Subsequently, the subject is encouraged to use anxiety responses themselves, rather than anxiety-arousing scenes, as the discriminative stimuli in the emission of relaxation responses. The anxiety-management training may be viewed as a self-control procedure that is relatively non-situation specific and that involves the subject in the exercise of coping skills during laboratory stress conditions.

Yet another coping-skills package is described by Meichenbaum and Cameron (Meichenbaum, 1975; Meichenbaum and Cameron, 1973) and labeled "stress inoculation." Briefly, it involves (1) a discussion of stress reactions (with emphasis on labeling, attribution, and arousal-inducing self-statements and images); (2) relaxation training (presented as an active coping skill); (3) guided practice in the use of coping self-statements at various points during exposure to anxiety-provoking or stress situations; and (4) practice in the utilization of the coping skills in a novel, laboratory stress situation. The stress-inoculation package calls for a detailed review for it has been suggested as a potentially useful package in the modulation of pain (Meichenbaum, 1975; Meichenbaum and Turk, 1976).

Stress Inoculation for Anxiety-Based Dysfunctions. Meichenbaum and his colleagues (Meichenbaum and Cameron, 1973b; Meichenbaum, Turk, and Burstein, 1975) reviewed the stress literature and concluded that a successful program aimed at training adaptive coping skills should (1) be flexible enough to incorporate a variety of strategies that can be differentially employed in potential stress situations; (2) encourage cognitive plans that would reduce anxiety and lead to more adaptive coping responses; (3) encourage utilization of available information that stimulates mental rehearsal (i.e., the "work of worrying," Janis, 1958); (4) be sensitive to individual and situational differences; and (5) provide trial exposure to less threatening stress events during which coping skills can be consolidated and "tried on," i.e., inoculation.

A similar approach has been advocated by Orne (1965):

> One way of enabling an individual to become resistant to stress is to allow him to have appropriate prior experience with the stimulus involved. The biological notion of immunization provides such a model. If an individual is given the opportunity to deal with a stimulus that is mildly stressful and he is able to do so successfully (mastering it in a psychological sense) he will tend to be able to tolerate a similar stimulus of somewhat greater intensity in the future. . . . It would seem that one

can markedly affect an individual's performance in the situation . . .
and his feeling that he can control his own behavior. (pp. 315–316)

In light of these concerns, Meichenbaum and Cameron (1973)
developed the stress-inoculation procedure outlined above. Specifically, the procedure consists of three phases: (1) an educational
phase, (2) a rehearsal phase, and (3) application training.

The first phase of the stress-inoculation training is designed to
provide the subject with an explanatory scheme for understanding
the nature of his response to stressful events. The most important
aspect of this phase is that the conceptual framework should be
plausible to the subject and its acceptance should lead naturally to
the practice of specific, cognitive, and behavioral coping techniques.

In treating multiphobic clients, Meichenbaum and Cameron
(1973), consistent with Schachter's (1966) theory, suggest that the
client's fear reaction involves two major elements, namely, (1)
heightened arousal (e.g., increased heart rate, rapid breathing, and
bodily tension) and (2) a set of anxiety-engendering avoidant
thoughts, images, and self-statements (e.g., disgust evoked by the
phobic object, a sense of helplessness, catastrophizing thoughts,
etc.). They then indicate that the treatment is directed toward (a)
helping the subject control his physiological arousal; and (b) substituting positive coping self-statements for the anxiety-engendering
self-statements that habitually occupied him when under conditions of stress.

The educational phase concludes with a discussion designed to
modify the subject's view of his phobic or stress reaction from one of
an overwhelming panic reaction to a series of phases. Four phases
are suggested: preparing for a stressor, possibly being overwhelmed by a stressor, confronting or handling a stressor, and finally, reinforcement for adaptive coping.

This initial educational phase of the stress-inoculation training
is designed to provide the phobic subject with a cognitive framework
to better understand his reaction to stress. It provides for the transi-
tion into the second, rehearsal phase of training.

The rehearsal phase of the training is designed to provide the
subject with a variety of coping techniques to employ at each of the

various phases of coping process. The coping techniques employed by Meichenbaum and Cameron (1973) were both direct-action and cognitive coping modes (cf. Lazarus, Averill, and Opton, 1974). Direct-action modes include collecting information about the phobic object, arranging for escape routes, and learning about physical relaxation. The cognitive coping modes are treated by viewing such processes as sets of self-statements that the subject thinks (or images) to himself. The modification of the subject's internal monologue is accomplished by having him become aware of and monitoring the negative, anxiety-engendering, self-defeating self-statements emitted in phobic situations. Meichenbaum and Cameron emphasize that treatment generalization is built into the training package by encouraging the subjects to use their maladaptive behaviors, thoughts, and feelings as signals (i.e., discriminative stimuli) to engage in the coping techniques that had been taught.

Once their subjects had become proficient in the use of such behavioral and cognitive coping skills, Meichenbaum and Cameron suggest that they test out or practice these coping skills by actually employing them under stressful conditions other than the phobic situation (i.e., novel stress situation). At this point the subjects were exposed to unavoidable electric shock. Meichenbaum and Cameron reported substantial improvement in the subject's ability to cope with the phobic situation and a second phobic situation that was not included within the training, demonstrating generalization of the affect of the training.

Recently, Novaco (1977) successfully adapted the stress-inoculation paradigm for use with individuals with problems of chronic anger (cf. chap. 5). The coping skills consisted of (1) differential awareness of personal anger problems (subjects became observers of their own behavior); (2) attunement to anger arousal and its cognitive components (monitoring their internal monologues); (3) the ability to alternatively construe provocation and to control arousal by means of relaxation; (4) covert self-regulation to guide structuring of events and nonantagonistic encounter; and (5) the ability to remain task-oriented rather than ego-oriented when provoked. Novaco (1976) has continued to adapt the stress-inoculation procedure and has recently conducted a study in which he employed the stress inoculation with law-enforcement officers on a preventive basis.

In summary, the stress-inoculation training employed by Meichenbaum and Cameron (1973) and Novaco (1976, 1977) involved discussion of the nature of the stress reaction, provocation reaction and emotions, rehearsing cognitive and behavioral coping skills, and testing these skills under a "novel" stress or provocation condition.

A growing number of variations of the cognitive behavioral coping-skills treatment packages have been developed and successfully utilized with a number of different target populations. These include public-speaking anxiety (Meichenbaum, 1972), social anxiety (Kazdin, 1973, 1974), test anxiety (Sarason, 1973), alcoholism (Sanchez-Craig, 1974), social incompetence (Glass, Gottman, and Shmurak, 1976), and *pain* (Horan *et al.*, 1977; Turk, 1975, 1977a). Common elements underlying many of these coping skills-training approaches include: (1) the provision of accurate and authoritative information, (2) adaptive modeling, (3) self-monitoring and self-control, (4) attention-focusing, (5) relaxation training, and (6) guided practice (mental or behavioral rehearsal). From this list, it can be noted that the coping-skills approaches address cognitive, affective, as well as behavioral contributions to individual's responses in anxiety-eliciting situations. Within this approach, human behavior is viewed as complex and multiply determined.

Interestingly, each of the elements underlying the coping-skills approach for anxiety-based dysfunction has received similar attention by investigators attempting to attenuate pain. As indicated previously, investigators have noted the impact of a number of psychological variables and coping skills on the modification of pain tolerance: provision of accurate and authoritative information (Johnson, 1973; Johnson and Leventhal, 1974), adaptive modeling (Bobey and Davidson, 1970; Chaves and Barber, 1974), self-monitoring and self-control (Kanfer and Goldfoot, 1966; Kanfer and Seidner, 1973), attentional focus (Blitz and Dinnerstein, 1971; Turk, 1975, 1977a), relaxation (Bobey and Davidson, 1970; Johnson, 1974) and guided practice (Neufeld and Davidson, 1971; Turk, 1975, 1977a). However, it is important to note that only rudimentary efforts have been devoted to combining these elements into an integrated, multidimensional treatment approach.

Before examining the multidimensional treatment regimens designed to enhance tolerance for pain, a review of some specific coping strategies will be undertaken. This review will lead to a better understanding of the variety of cognitive and behavioral coping skills that have been employed.

COGNITIVE AND BEHAVIORAL COPING STRATEGIES

A number of investigators (Chaves and Barber, 1974; Horan and Dellinger, 1973; Kanfer and Goldfoot, 1966; Kanfer and Seidner, 1972; Knox, 1972) attempted to provide subjects with behavioral and/or cognitive coping strategies designed to enhance coping repertoires. Though the utilization of cognitive strategies for the reduction of pain has recently become a research interest, individuals have engaged in the utilization of cognitive strategies for as long as man has experienced pain. The Stoic philosophers believed that man could get the better of pain by force of reason, by the "rational repudiation" of pain. Descartes and Spinoza recommended that pain should be overcome through "permeation" of reason.

Perhaps the oldest cognitive technique employed has been distraction or attention-diversion. Kant (as cited by Fulop-Miller, 1938) provides the following example of his utilization of attention-diversion:

> For a year I have been troubled by morbid inclination and very painful stimuli which from others' descriptions of such symptoms I believe to be gout, so that I had to call a doctor. One night, however, impatient at being kept awake by pain, I availed myself to the stoical means of concentration upon some different object of thought such for instance as the name of "Cicero" with its multifarious associations, in this way I found it possible to divert my attention, so that pain was soon dulled. . . . Whenever the attacks recur and disturb my sleep, I find this remedy most useful. (p. 28)

A number of other cognitive and behavioral methods have been employed to enhance pain tolerance, including (1) *somatization* (e.g., Bobey and Davidson, 1970; Evans and Paul, 1970)—focusing on the existence, production, or inhibition of bodily processes or sensations, including the experimentally induced pain (Knox, 1972, pp. 23–24), e.g., comparing pain sensations to an arm that has fallen asleep; (2) *imaginative transformation of pain* (e.g., Blitz and Dinnerstein, 1968, 1971; Knox, 1972)—"acknowledgement of the experimentally induced sensation, but transforming or interpreting these sensations as something other than pain, or minimizing the sensation as trivial or unreal" (Knox, 1972, p. 24), e.g., imagining the limb as numb, injected with Novocain; (3) *imaginative transformation of context* (e.g., Blitz and Dinnerstein, 1968; Knox, 1972)—"acknowledgement of the experimentally induced pain but transformation of the context in which the pain occurs" (Knox, 1972, p. 24), e.g., imagining oneself as a spy, shot in the arm; and (4) *relaxation and deep breathing* (e.g., Bobey and Davidson, 1970; Mulcahy and Janz, 1973; Neufeld and Davidson, 1971).

The typical experimental design of studies that have employed the strategies detailed above has been to instruct an experimental group to employ *one* of these strategies while a second group either employs a different strategy or functions as a control group given no instructions concerning a specific strategy. The results have been disappointing in their inconsistency. The ambiguity of findings is understandable, since most subjects would come to an experimental situation with some well-learned strategies that they have employed in the past. If they are required to tolerate a noxious stimulus without being given instructions regarding the use of a specific strategy, then subjects will no doubt resort to the use of the particular techniques that have proved to be helpful previously (Chaves and Barber, 1974; Kanfer and Goldfoot, 1966; Kanfer and Seidner, 1973). Turk (1977a) has recently reported that subjects varied substantially in their preferences for different categories of coping strategies. Thus, the data obtained in these studies represent only the relative effects of experimental strategies compared to the uncontrolled effects of previously learned strategies. In fact, the provision of instructions to employ a specific strategy may prove to have a negative effect on the subject if it is a strategy that is not congruent with his already well-learned coping repertoire.

The research detailed above, while giving tacit acknowledgment to the significance of a variety of psychological factors, has tended toward isolation and manipulation of specific cognitive and behavioral coping strategies. Thus, it is not surprising that the results have proved to be equivocal.

The data reviewed indicate that, in certain instances and with certain qualifications, pain can be attenuated by minimizing the subject's anxiety, by enhancing the subject's expectancy that he can decrease the pain he experiences (a sense of control), by asking the subject to imagine situations that are incompatible with the experience of pain, by distracting the subject, and by giving the explicit suggestion of pain reduction. Several authors (e.g., Meichenbaum and Cameron, 1973; Melzack and Casey, 1970) have suggested that although a wide variety of procedures are capable of reducing pain, a more effective means of modifying an individual's perception of a stressful situation would be to "tailor" a procedure to meet the needs of the specific individual in the specific situation. That is, one could use a multifactor approach that enables the subject to employ those features of the "treatment package" that are most salient for him in the given situation.

Multidimensional, Cognitive Behavioral Approaches for Pain Management—Clinical

Several early studies (Chappell and Stevenson, 1936; Draspa, 1959; Egbert, Batit, Welch, and Bartlett, 1964) reported the use of cognitive behavioral approaches to control pain associated with organic syndromes. Chappel and Stevenson employed a treatment with 32 peptic-ulcer patients that included: (1) the provision of information in the form of a conceptualization of the relationship between emotions and gastric physiology; (2) suggestion; and (3) "directive therapy" (consisting largely of instructions on how to change habitual patterns of thinking). This treatment was combined with the standard medication and dietary regimen typically employed with ulcer patients. The patients receiving the multidimensional treatment were compared to a group of patients who were treated exclusively with medication and a controlled diet. At the end of a two-month period, only one of the patients receiving the multidimensional treatment reported any recurrence of painful symptoms while 19 of the 20 control patients had serious recurrences. On a three-year follow-up, 10 of the patients who had received the multidimensional treatment were symptom-free while none of the control subjects were free of recurrences.

The Chappell and Stevenson study nicely demonstrates how cognitive and affective techniques can be combined with more traditional medical treatments. This study underscores the importance of providing the patient with a conceptualization of how thoughts and feelings contribute to physical symptoms and the provision of cognitive-coping skills to help modify maladaptive cognitions.

Draspa (1959) employed a multidimensional approach with patients manifesting muscular pain of various etiologies. The approach consisted of supportive therapy (reassurances as to the innocuous nature of the pain), "insight psychotherapy" (information related to the causes of excessive muscle contraction, promotion of changes of internal or environmental situations), and relaxation of the affected muscles. One hundred and twelve patients receiving the multidimensional treatment were compared to a matched control group that received standard physical treatments and a third group that received a combined treatment, including the physical treatment and the cognitive behavioral training. Draspa reported the combined treatment was the most effective approach resulting in a significant reduction in reported pain.

The study conducted by Draspa illustrates again the value of combining cognitive behavioral techniques with the more traditional medical procedures. This study also demonstrates the efficacy of self-controlled, coping skills that a patient can employ when needed. The procedures employed by Draspa built in generalization as the patients were encouraged to attend to internal and external environmental cues of muscle tension and to utilize the relaxation skills when indicated by their self-monitoring.

Egbert et al. (1964) reported that surgical patients who were taught relaxation, deep-breathing techniques, and bodily maneuvers designed to make movement more comfortable during the postoperative period, and who were provided reassurances by their anesthesiologist, required smaller amounts of narcotics following surgery and were discharged earlier than a control group of uninstructed patients. The Egbert et al. study attests to the utility of a multidimensional, skills-training regimen in a more acute situation than the Chappell-Stevenson and the Draspa studies.

Although these studies demonstrate the efficacy of multidimensional approaches, the Chappell and Stevenson and the Draspa studies have received little attention in the medical-therapeutic literature. The Egbert *et al.* study, on the other hand, is frequently cited, but usually as just another study demonstrating the value of preparatory information prior to surgery. Little attention has been given to the contribution and value of the self-controlled relaxation and breathing exercises or the training in bodily procedures to increase comfort.

We can readily note similarities between the cognitive behavioral strategies employed with anxiety-based dysfunctions discussed above and the pain-treatment studies of Chappell and Stevenson, Draspa, and Egbert *et al.* Similarities include the role of relaxation, self-monitoring, self-instructional training, reassurances concerning the innocuousness of the particular target problem, and emphasis on the individual's self-control of his thoughts and emotions. However, it should be noted that the pain treatments described above did not employ specific cognitive or behavioral rehearsal of the various coping skills as did the anxiety-based treatments. In addition, in the pain studies the conceptualizations and particular information were presented in a didactic fashion with little opportunity for the patients to discuss effective utilization or implementation of the information. Part of the efficacy of the cognitive behavioral, coping-skills approaches employed for anxiety-based dysfunctions has been attributed to the client's opportunity to discuss any difficulties and to rehearse and practice the utilization of the learned skills (Meichenbaum and Turk, 1976).

These preliminary attempts at the development of multidimensional treatments for the amelioration of pain are confined to the medical literature. More recently, interest in the development of such approaches for pain management has arisen among psychologists. A number of investigators (e.g., Gottlieb, Hockersmith, Koller, and Strite, 1975; Langer, Janis, and Wolfer, 1975; Levendusky and Pankratz, 1975; Reeves, 1976; Sachs, Feuerstein, and Vitale, 1976) have effectively employed cognitive behavioral coping-skills training to augment pain tolerance in clinical settings.

Langer *et al.* (1975) reported that they were able to train surgery patients to use coping devices such as reappraisal of the anxiety-provoking events, calming self-talk, and a cognitive coping (instructions to direct attention to the more favorable aspects of the situation) to alleviate postoperative pain. Patients were encouraged to engage in these cognitive coping strategies whenever they began to feel upset about unpleasant events, or aspects of the surgical experience and/or experienced any pain. Patients receiving the coping-skills training demonstrated marked reductions in requests for postoperative analgesics and sedatives and were rated by nurses as manifesting less stress immediately prior to surgery and postoperatively, compared with subjects who received either no training or only preparatory presurgery information.

A comprehensive treatment program has been reported by Gottlieb *et al.* (1975) at the Casa Colina Hospital for Rehabilitative Medicine. Gottlieb and his colleagues have noted the important role of such cognitive and social factors as anger, depression, anxiety, feelings of helplessness, and social reinforcement in the etiology and maintenance of chronic low-back pain. The treatment program of the Casa Colina group is comprised of a variety of interventions, including traditional medical and psychotherapeutic techniques as well as cognitive and behavioral coping strategies: biofeedback (EMG, GSR) and autogenic training, psychotherapeutic techniques (individual, group, and family therapy), assertion training, behavioral treatment of depression (Lewinsohn, 1968), a self-medication reduction program, a physical-restoration program (individualized exercise program), educational lectures (information about the back and how psychophysiological factors play a role in back pain), a systematic social reinforcement program for target nondisability behavior, and a therapeutic milieu designed around relaxation. This innovative treatment approach has only recently been developed and little data supporting its efficacy has been provided. The program does appear to hold much promise and makes a significant contribution by including the patient's family in the total treatment of the pain problem and illness behavior (Pilowksy, 1975).

Recently, Sachs *et al.* (1976) reported the successful utilization of a multidimensional, cognitive behavioral treatment with eight chronic pain patients (pain duration 8 months to 23 years). The treatment developed included the following components: (1) relaxation; (2) hypnotic training designed to increase duration of focused attention; (3) self-monitoring to provide clear and precise phenomenological descriptions of pain sensation and to identify particular thoughts, feelings, and images associated with deeper levels of relaxation; and (4) cognitive-skills training designed to increase the production of thoughts, feelings, and images incompatible with features of the pain. Generalization was built into the training by encouraging the use of self-controlled pain-incompatible strategies in progressively more real-life situations.

Sachs *et al.* reported that on a four-month follow-up their patients indicated significant reductions in daily pain intensity, the degree to which pain interfered with major life areas (e.g., sleep, social activities), life dissatisfaction and suffering, and the percentage of self-administered pain medications. This study is limited by the omission of control groups but the lack of effective prior medical intervention and the magnitude of the changes observed support the utility of this treatment. Note the use of a cognitive behavioral approach as a primary treatment for pain management rather than as an adjunct to conventional medical interventions.

In a case study of a sixty-five-year-old male with symptoms of chronic abdominal pain, Levendusky and Pankratz (1975) employed a cognitive behavioral, coping-skills treatment approach. The patient was taught to control pain through a program of relaxation, a cognitive coping strategy, and cognitive relabeling. With these strategies, the authors report the patient was able to greatly reduce his extensive intake of analgesic medications. One particularly interesting point to note in this study is the use of the patient as a collaborator in the development of personally relevant cognitive-coping strategies. This approach can be contrasted to the more usual procedure of imposing a particular strategy on the patient. Such individualized tailoring of the training might be a useful addition to each of the cognitive behavioral treatments reviewed above (cf. Meichenbaum and Turk, 1976).

In another case study, Reeves (1976) combined self-instructional training (Meichenbaum, 1973, 1975) with EMG biofeedback for a patient with tension headaches. In this study, Reeves had his patient, a twenty-year-old female, collect baseline data on EMG and daily headache activity (emphasizing specification of environmental stressors), focus on identifying negative self-statements (thoughts and images), trained the patient to replace negative self-statements with coping self-instructions (Meichenbaum and Turk, 1976; Turk, 1975, 1977a), provided the patient with an opportunity to rehearse with the coping self-statements, and finally provided biofeedback training. Reeves noted that the combined, cognitive behavioral treatment reduced headache activity by 66% with no resumption of symptoms on a six-month follow-up. The value of combining the behavioral technique of biofeedback with cognitive coping strategies is illustrated by this study.

One common factor present in each of the cognitive behavioral, coping-skills treatment approaches for the management of pain reviewed is that the patient is provided with training in the use of a number of different coping skills that are self-controlled. This underlying feature can be compared with the traditional medical interventions, which require the patient to be a passive, "helpless" recipient. In chronic conditions where conventional treatments are unsuccessful in controlling pain (e.g., low-back pain, rheumatoid arthritis) or likely to lead to iatrogenic complications (e.g., analgesic nephritis, narcotic addiction) as well as in instances of less intense pain (e.g., dental procedures, endoscopic examinations), the active participation of the patient, employing self-controlled coping skills, seems appropriate.

While clinical and clinical-case studies such as those reviewed here are encouraging, controlled, empirical laboratory investigations and replications are needed to support the therapeutic value of specific interventions. Some beginning in this direction has been initiated by several investigators (Horan *et al.*, 1977; Turk, 1975, 1977a) who have conducted laboratory investigations of cognitive behavioral, coping-skills treatments for the enhancement of tolerance for laboratory-produced pain.

MULTIDIMENSIONAL COPING-SKILLS FOR PAIN MANAGEMENT—
LABORATORY-ANALOGUE STUDIES

The most extensively examined cognitive behavioral, skills-training approach for management of laboratory-produced pain is stress inoculation (Horan *et al.*, 1977; Turk, 1975, 1977a). This treatment regimen has consistently demonstrated attenuation of pain and thus a detailed elaboration seems appropriate.

Stress Inoculation—A Coping-Skills Treatment for Pain Management. Although stress inoculation was originally designed to modify the behavior of neurotic clients, the procedure poses an important analogue for research on stress in general, and specifically for research regarding the cognitive behavioral management of pain. The stress-inoculation procedure explicitly teaches the subject to cognitively cope, by such diverse means as using distractions, self-instructions, relaxation, altering attributions and self-labels, imagery rehearsal, and shifting attention. Thus, when confronting a stressful situation, each subject can employ one or more of a number of strategies, whichever are most helpful for him. Here, one can note that the subject is provided with a number of skills, along with elaboration and extension of the strategies that he brings to the situation. No strategy is imposed upon the subject, but he is made aware that a number are available and is encouraged to "try them on." Armed with a variety of strategies and an understanding of why he responds in a specific manner, the subject is prepared to employ the techniques that he feels are most applicable in the situation.

The stress-inoculation procedure is a coping-skills approach that trains subjects in a variety of techniques, which can be employed differentially across situations and across individuals. Such an approach has been lacking in the studies attempting to enhance pain tolerance by a specific strategy.

The first attempt to employ the stress-inoculation procedure to enhance tolerance for pain was conducted by Turk (1975). In that study, aversive stimulation was produced by the submaximum effort tourniquet technique (Smith, Egbert, Markowitz, Mosteller, and Beecher, 1966). This procedure involves the inflation of a blood-pressure cuff at a high level (240 mm Hg) followed by a moderate amount of exercise by that arm (squeezing a hand dynamometer). The intense pressure produced by the inflation of the cuff serves to block the brachial artery and consequently the flow of blood to the lower arm and hand. The exercise serves to deplete the available oxygen producing muscle ischemia and subsequently a steadily intensifying, aching pain.

The format of the skills training developed by Turk (1975) and Turk and Meichenbaum (1976) was analagous to that of the stress-inoculation paradigm of Meichenbaum and Cameron (1973) described above. As in the Meichenbaum and Cameron study, the training began with an educational phase. Recall that in the Meichenbaum and Cameron study, with phobic clients, a Schachterian explanation of emotion was provided for the subjects to conceptualize their stress reactions and to provide the logic for the treatment procedures employed. In the Turk (1975) study, the gate-control theory of Melzack and Wall (1965, pain experience composed of three components: sensory-discriminative, motivational-affective, and cognitive-evaluative) served a similar function. Following this educational phase, Turk proceeded to describe the various coping techniques that the subject could employ to handle each of the components of the pain experience (skills-acquisition phase).

First, the subjects were informed that they could control the sensory input or sensory-discriminative component of pain by such means as physical and mental relaxation and by attending to slow, deep breathing. The work on "natural childbirth" (Dick-Read, 1959) was offered as an illustration of how expectations concerning pain increased anxiety, in turn fostering muscle tension, leading to more pain and consequently more anxiety in a vicious cycle. The suggestion was offered that this cycle could magnify the perception of any noxious sensation but the cycle could be interrupted by the implementation of relaxation exercises and controlled breathing (e.g., Paul, 1966; Meichenbaum, 1973).

Next, subjects were informed that the motivational-affective component of pain included the feelings of helplessness and absence of control that frequently accompanied experience of an aversive stimulus. The suggestion was made that these feelings could be "short-circuited" by the individual engaging in a number of cognitive coping strategies. The strategies included:

1. Attention diversion—focusing attention on things other than the experimentally induced pain. For example, doing mental arithmetic or

attending to cues in the environment such as the ceiling tiles, cloth-
ing, etc.

2. Somatization—focusing attention on bodily processes or bodily sensations including the experimentally induced pain. For example,
watching and analyzing the changes in the part of the body receiving
the intense stimulation.

3. Imagery manipulations—changing or transforming the experience of
pain by means of fantasy:

   a. Imaginative inattention in which the individual ignores the ex-
   perimentally-induced pain by engaging in "goal-directed fantasy," which, if real, would be incompatible with the experience
   of pain. For example, lying on a beach on a pleasant day.

   b. Imaginative transformation of pain in which the individual includes the experience of pain in the fantasy, but transforms or interprets these sensations as something other than pain or mini-
   mizes the sensations as trivial or unreal. For example, imagining
   that the part of the body receiving the sensations is numb as if it
   had been injected with Novocain, or imagining that only one of
   the many sensations was actually being received while ignoring
   the others.

   c. Imaginative transformation of context in which the subject includes the pain in the fantasy, but now transforms the context or
   setting in which the pain occurs. For example, imagining that one
   is a spy who has been shot in the arm and who is being chased by
   enemy agents in a car down a winding mountain road. (Knox,
   1972)

Turk presented the subjects with each of the cognitive coping
strategies that was mentioned in the strategy-specific studies discussed previously, allowing for individual preferences. The subjects
were encouraged to select from these strategies in a "cafeteria
style." Subjects were also encouraged to develop a "plan" to deal
with the pain and especially to employ such coping techniques at
"critical moments" when the pain seemed most unbearable.

Control of the cognitive-evaluative component of the pain experience was addressed by conceptualizing the aversive situation as
consisting of several phases: preparing for the noxious stimulation,
confronting and handling the unpleasant sensations, coping with
feelings at critical moments, and self-reflection. The importance of
the subjects' thoughts, feelings, self-statements, and images at each
of these stages was underscored. In collaboration with the trainer,
the subjects generated lists of self-statements or self-instructions
that could be emitted at each of the phases of the stress situation.

The stress-inoculation training, where subjects are exposed to a

variety of cognitive and behavioral coping strategies, can be contrasted with most studies designed to enhance tolerance for pain.
As was noted, the pain literature is replete with examples of studies
in which the investigator chooses one specific coping strategy and
then compares its effectiveness with a no-treatment control group
(e.g., Chaves and Barber, 1974; Horan and Dellinger, 1973, Kanfer
and Goldfoot, 1966). In the skills-training procedure employed by
Turk, the subject became a collaborator, helping to generate from
his own experience and with the advice and support of the trainer,
an individually tailored coping package. The subject could pick and
choose from the array of cognitive and behavioral techniques a
sequence of coping strategies to be employed in a posttraining noxious situation.

Whereas in the stress-inoculation training employed by Meichenbaum and Cameron (1973) the application included exposure to
a real stressor (viz., electric shock), in the Turk (1975) study the
application phase was conducted by means of mental rehearsal and
role-playing, two widely used behavioral techniques. In order to
review and consolidate the training procedure, subjects were asked
to imagine themselves in stressful situations, including the ischemic pain situation they had experienced during the pretraining
trial. The subjects were asked to imagine how they would use the
variety of coping techniques (e.g., stages of stress experience, self-
statements, imagery, attention-diversion, relaxation). Such mental
rehearsal can be viewed as the subject providing himself with a
model of how he should behave in a stressful situation, what Sarbin
(1972) called muted role-taking. Prior research (Kazdin, 1973, 1974;
Meichenbaum, 1971, 1972) has indicated that one can enhance the
therapeutic value of such covert modeling procedures by having the
subject imagine himself faltering, experiencing anxiety, and then
coping with these feelings of inadequacy. In this way the trainer
anticipated the thoughts and feelings his subject was likely to experience in the real-life situation, and by including them in the mental rehearsal process they later assume a déjà vu quality. The subject's anxiety, tenseness, negative self-statements, self-doubts, etc.,
become something he was prepared for: they were the cues, the
reminders, to use the coping procedures. Thus in the mental rehearsal procedure, the skills-training subjects were encouraged to

include any failings, self-doubts, or anxiety and to then see themselves coping with these.

In order to further consolidate the coping strategies, subjects were asked to role-play giving advice to a novice subject on how to cope with stress, specifically with the experience of pain. The trainer assumed the role of the novice subject, while the subjects played the role of trainers. Turk (1975) states that the role-playing was designed to have the subjects improvise for, according to research on attitude change (Hovland, Janis, and Kelley, 1953), in such situations the subject will ". . . think up exactly the kinds of arguments, illustrations and motivating appeals he regards as most convincing. In this way, the subject 'hand tailors' the content of his role in such a manner as to account for the unique motives and predispositions of one particular person, namely, himself" (Turk, 1975, p. 193).

Thus prepared with one hour of skills training, male college students underwent a posttraining trial on the ischemic task. Turk (1975) reports that on the pretraining trial the subjects in the skills-training groups were able to tolerate the intense stimulation for a mean of 17 minutes; while on the posttraining trial they tolerated the ischemic pain for a mean of 32 minutes, a significant increase ($p < .002$). An attention placebo group increased tolerance from 18 minutes on the pretraining trial to 19 minutes on the posttraining trial. The 15-minute improvement in tolerance demonstrated by the stress-inoculation training group is particularly impressive when one learns that Smith, Chiang, and Regina (1974) found that subjects' tolerance for ischemic pain was enhanced by only 5 to 10 minutes following the administration of 5 mg of morphine.

In a more recent study, Turk (1977a) extended and replicated the earlier results substantiating the relative efficacy of the stress-inoculation training. In this latter study, the training was increased to 3½ hours with the addition of expanded training in the use of relaxation, imagery rehearsal, and attentional focusing, as well as exposure to a novel stressor (the cold pressor task). Table I contains an outline of the expanded-stress-inoculation training.[1] In this study (Turk, 1977a), not only was the relative efficacy of the stress-

---

[1] A detailed training manual is available from the author (Turk, 1977b).

TABLE I. SUMMARY OF TRAINING [a]

1. Conceptualization of the "pain experience" with two components: the sensory input and the reactions of the individual to that sensory input. Each of these two components can be brought under the individual's control.

2. Relaxation can be employed to reduce the sensory input. Focus on:
   A. Tensing and relaxing the various muscles that receive the intense stimulation
   B. Slow, deep breathing, with 3–5 seconds holding, and 5 seconds exhaling
   C. Thinking of pleasant or relaxing words or pictures while exhaling, for example, the word "calm," or a picture of a feather gently floating

3. Attention-diverting coping strategies. Note:
   A. One cannot focus on more than one thing fully at any one time.
   B. A person can select what he will focus his attention upon and what to exclude from his attention.
   C. A variety of different coping strategies are available for a person to employ at various times in a stressful situation. One can switch from one strategy to another as often as he wishes.
   D. Types of coping strategies:
      (1) Focusing attention on physical characteristics of the environment. For example, counting the ceiling tiles, studying the construction of something in the room, studying articles of clothing.
      (2) Focusing attention on various thoughts. For example, doing mental arithmetic, making a list of all the things you have to do over the weekend, thinking of and singing the words of various songs you recall.
      (3) Focusing attention on the part of the body receiving intense stimulation. For example, analyzing the sensations in one part of the body and comparing them to another part, analyzing the intense stimulation as if preparing to write a biology report regarding the sensations experienced, studying the sensations and physical changes and comparing them to the feelings and changes noted at other times when you have experienced intense stimulation.
      (4) Imaginative inattention. Ignoring the intense stimulation by engaging in a mental image, which if real, would be incompatible with the experience of pain. For example, imagining yourself enjoying a pleasant day on the beach, at a party you recently attended during which you had a lot of fun, or spending an enjoyable afternoon with your girl friend.
      (5) Imaginative transformation of pain. Interpreting the sensations you are receiving as something other than pain, or minimizing those sensations as trivial or unreal. For example, visualizing and thinking about the part of the body receiving the intense stimulation as having been filled with Novocain and feeling the numbness produced, seeing or picturing yourself as the "6 million dollar man," whose limbs are mechanical and capable of great feats of strength but incapable of experiencing pain, imagining the part of the body receiving the intense stimulation as being made of rubber and thus unable to feel pain, and considering all the implications of what it would be like to have a rubber limb.

(continued)

TABLE I. SUMMARY OF TRAINING (*continued*)

(6) Imaginative transformation of context. Picturing an image or mental scene in which the intense stimulation received is different from the actual situation. That is, you are aware of the sensations but you picture them arising in a different context. For example, picturing yourself as James Bond having been shot in a limb, driving a stick-shift car while being chased by enemy agents, picturing yourself receiving an injury in a hockey or football game but continuing to play despite the injury, visualizing yourself receiving an injury while on a date and not wanting to let your girl friend know that you are hurt.

E. Coping strategies that employ visual images are like mental pictures that can be related to a wide variety of situations. The greater the degree of involvement, absorption, and vividness of the image, the more effective such strategies are in coping with a stress.

4. Self-instructional training. Self-instructional training involves breaking a stressful situation down into three phases with self-reflection throughout the situation. The phases are:

A. Preparing for the intense stimulation before it becomes too strong. Self-instructions and statements that can be made at this phase include:

(1) What is it I have to do? (viewing the situation as a problem that you can do something about).

(2) I can develop a plan to deal with it (preparing oneself by making a plan or mental outline of how you will deal with the sensations when they arise).

(3) Just think about what I have to do (focusing on what the situation requires).

(4) Think of the things that I can use to help cope (review all the strategies that you know and that may be helpful).

(5) Don't worry; worrying won't help anything (use any anxiety or worry as a cue to remind you to focus on what you have to do).

(6) Remember, I can shift my attention to anything I want to (reassure yourself about your ability to employ various coping strategies).

(7) When I use mental imagery, I'll see how vivid I can make the scene (review various aspects of the different images and strategies that can be used).

B. Confronting and handling the intense stimulation (self-instructions and statements that can be made at this phase include):

(1) I can meet this challenge (view the situation as a challenge that you deal with).

(2) One step at a time, I can handle the situation (don't do everything at once and don't be overwhelmed; rather, use each of the skills you have learned).

(3) Just relax, breathe deeply, and use one of the strategies (review and use any of the strategies that you have outlined in your plan for coping).

(4) I won't think about any pain, just about what I have to do (focus your attention on the task at hand and what you can do right now to help you cope).

(5) I'm feeling tense; that can be an ally, a cue to switch strategies and to

take some slow deep breaths (expect to feel tense at times; that's not unusual, but use your tenseness as a cue to relax and to review which strategy to employ next).

(6) Remember, I can switch back to some strategies that I used before but switched from (there is no reason why you can't return to some strategies already used).

C. Coping with thoughts and feelings that arise at critical moments (when you notice that the intensity of the sensations seems to be increasing or you think you can't go on anymore). Self-instructions or statements that can be made at this phase include:

(1) When I feel any pain, just pause, keep focusing on what I have to do (keep in mind the task at hand and what you have to do).

(2) Don't try to eliminate the pain totally, just keep it manageable (remember, you expected to detect some intense stimulation, but don't overreact and make things worse).

(3) I knew the sensations would rise; just keep them under control (don't magnify the intensity of the sensations you experience).

(4) Remember, there are a lot of things I can do; I can keep things under control (you have been taught a number of different strategies that will help you keep the intense stimulation under control).

(5) Things are going pretty bad; I can't take any more—just pause; don't make things worse. I'll review my plan of strategies to see what I can switch to (sometimes you may have unpleasant thoughts or feelings; use those as cues to review the strategies available for you to use).

(6) My arm looks terrible; things are falling apart; I better stop—relax. I can focus my attention on something else; keep things under control (if you find yourself focusing on unpleasant sensations or thoughts, remember you can choose what you will focus your attention upon).

D. Self-reflection and positive self-statements. Throughout the three phases outlined above you might evaluate your performance. For example, how am I doing, that worked pretty well, etc. Remember, people frequently criticize themselves but rarely praise their behavior. Throughout a stressful situation evaluate how you are doing. If you think you should be doing better you can use that as a cue to try different strategies. If you are doing well you should give yourself a "pat on the back." Self-reflective statements that might be used throughout a stressful situation:

(1) That's it. I've outlined what I have to do, what strategies I can use and which ones I will switch to.

(2) I'm doing pretty well; it's not as hard as I thought.

(3) I'm doing better at this all the time.

(4) I won't let negative thoughts interfere with using my plan.

(5) Wait until I tell the trainer which things worked best.

(6) I knew I could handle it; I'm doing pretty well.

(7) I'm doing better than I expected; wait until I tell my mother.

5. The attention-diverting coping strategies and the self-instructional training can help you deal with the reactive component of the "pain experience." Thus, by also using relaxation to deal with the sensory input, along with the coping strategies and self-instructional training, you will be able to enhance your pain tolerance and alter your perception of intense stimulation.

---

[a] From Turk (1977a).

inoculation training confirmed, but generalization of the training to the novel, cold pressor stress was also demonstrated.

Horan *et al.* (1977) have provided an additional replication of the efficacy of the stress-inoculation procedure. In their study, Horan, *et al.* extended the Turk results by employing both male and female subjects as well as male and female trainers. This study was designed to examine the contribution of several components of the training (i.e., the initial conceptualization, exposure to multiple stressors, and the coping-skills training). The results of the Horan *et al.* study indicate that neither the initial conceptualization, or repeated exposures to a stressor were sufficient to increase tolerance times, while the combined stress inoculation significantly enhanced tolerance and also reduced the amount of discomfort reported by the subjects.

These authors did note that the stress-inoculation training did not generalize to a novel stress situation. The generalization task used in this study, however, was the pressure algometer test. Since maximum tolerance time on this particular task is quite brief (usually 1 to 2 minutes) as compared with 5 minutes on the cold pressor task and 55 minutes on the ischemic task, a possible explanation for the failure to demonstrate generalization may be that this brief exposure did not afford the subjects sufficient opportunity to employ the various cognitive and behavioral coping skills. The question of generalization requires further investigation before any firm conclusion can be made in this regard. The inconsistent results regarding generalization of the training suggest that, at least at the present time, training should be directed toward coping with the type of pain that patients are most likely to experience.

A major issue in any laboratory analogue study concerns the external validity of the procedure; that is, the degree to which results generalize to other populations, behaviors, and settings. The laboratory procedures employed in the stress-inoculation studies reviewed above (Horan *et al.*, 1977; Turk, 1975, 1977a) attempted to simulate clinical pain as well as can be achieved in the laboratory. Beecher and his colleagues (Beecher, 1966; Smith *et al.*, 1966) demonstrated that the submaximum effort tourniquet technique employed in the two Turk studies (1975, 1977a) produces a dull, aching, slowly mounting pain that most closely approximates pathological pain. Sternbach (1974) reports that this technique mimics the duration and severity of somatogenic pain producing the marked autonomic changes that frequently accompany pain of pathological origin, and Clark and Hunt (1971) have suggested that ischemic and cold pressor stress [utilized in the Horan et al. (1977) and Turk (1977a) studies] are the best laboratory analogues to the pain encountered in clinical settings. The questions of external validity can only be resolved by further research with clinical-pain populations.

Conclusion

When compared with single-treatment strategies, whether medical or psychological, multidimensional approaches appear to offer a promising and pragmatic approach to teach the control of pain. The use of training regimens that employ the various cognitive and behavioral strategies and coping-skills training described above should prove to be a valuable adjunct to traditional pain treatments. In particular, the comprehensive stress-inoculation procedure is viewed as a promising tool to be added to the clinician's armamentarium.

References

Andrew, J.M. Recovery from surgery with and without preparatory instruction for three coping styles. *Journal of Personality and Social Psychology*, 1970, *15*, 223–226.

Bandler, R., Jr., Madaras, G., and Bem, D. Self-observation as a source of pain perception. *Journal of Personality and Social Psychology*, 1968, *9*, 205–209.

Barber, T.X., Spanos, N., and Chaves, J. Implications for human capabilities and potentialities. In T.X. Barber, N. Spanos, and J. Chaves (Eds.), *Hypnosis, imagination and human potentialities*. New York: Pergamon Press, 1974.

Beecher, H. *Measurement of subjective responses: Quantitative effects of drugs*. New York: Oxford, 1959.

Beecher, H. Pain: One mystery solved. *Science*, 1966, *151*, 840–841.

Blitz, B., and Dinnerstein, A. Effects of different types of instructions on pain parameters. *Journal of Abnormal Psychology*, 1968, *73*, 276–280.

Blitz, B., and Dinnerstein, A. Role of attentional focus in pain perception: Manipulation of responses to noxious stimulation by instructions. *Journal of Abnormal Psychology*, 1971, *77*, 42–45.

Bobey, M., and Davidson, P. Psychological factors affecting pain tolerance. *Journal of Psychosomatic Research*, 1970, *14*, 371–376.

Bond, M. Pain and personality in cancer patients. In J. J. Bonica and D. Albe-Fessard

(Eds.), *Advances in pain research and therapy* (Vol. 1). New York: Raven Press, 1976.

Bowers, K.S. The effects of USC temporal uncertainty on heart rate and pain. *Psychophysiology*, 1971, 8, 382–389.

Chappell, M.N., and Stevenson, T.I. Group psychological training in some organic conditions. *Mental Hygiene*, 1936, 20, 588–597.

Chaves, J., and Barber, T.X. Cognitive strategies, experimenter modeling, and expectation in the attenuation of pain. *Journal of Abnormal Psychology*, 1974, 83, 356–363.

Clark, W.C., and Hunt, H.F. Pain. In J.A. Downey and R.C. Darling (Eds.), *Physiological basis of rehabilitation medicine*. Philadelphia: W.B. Saunders Company, 1971.

Craig, K., Best, H., and Reith, G. Social determinants of reports of pain in the absence of painful stimulation. *Canadian Journal of Behavioral Science*, 1974, 6, 109–177.

Davison, G.C., and Wilson, G. T. Processes of fear reduction in systematic desensitization: Cognitive and social reinforcement factors in humans. *Behavior Therapy*, 1973, 4, 1–21.

Dick-Read, G. *Childbirth without fear*. New York: Harper & Row, 1959.

Draspa, L.J. Psychological factors in muscular pain. *British Journal of Medical Psychology*, 1959, 32, 106–116.

Egbert, L., Batit, G., Welch, C., and Bartlett, M. Reduction of post-operative pain by encouragement and instruction. *New England Journal of Medicine*, 1964, 270, 825–827.

Ellis, A. *Reason and emotion in psychotherapy*. New York: Lyle Stuart Press, 1962.

Ellis, A. *The essence of rational psychotherapy: A Comprehensive approach to treatment*. New York: Institute for Rational Living, 1970.

Evans, M., and Paul, G. Effects of hypnotically suggested analgesia on physiological and subjective response to cold stress. *Journal of Consulting and Clinical Psychology*, 1970, 35, 362–371.

Fagerhaugh, S. Pain expression and control on a burn care unit. *Nursing Outlook*, 1974, 22, 645–650.

Fulop-Miller, R. *Triumph over pain*. New York: The Literary Guild of America, 1938.

Glass, C.R., Gottman, J.M., and Shmurak, S.H. Response acquisition and cognitive self-statement modification approaches to dating skills. *Journal of Counseling Psychology*, 1976, 23, 520–526.

Goldfried, M. Systematic desensitization as training in self-control. *Journal of Consulting and Clinical Psychology*, 1971, 37, 228–234.

Goldfried, M. Reduction of generalized anxiety through a variant of systematic desensitization. In M. Goldfried and M. Merbaum (Eds.), *Behavior change through self-control*. New York: Holt, Rinehart and Winston, 1973.

Goldfried, M., Decenteceo, E., and Weinberg, L. Systematic rational restructuring as a self-control technique. *Behavior Therapy*, 1974, 5, 247–254.

Goldfried, M., and Trier, C. Effectiveness of relaxation as an active coping skill. *Journal of Abnormal Psychology*, 1974, 83, 348–355.

Gottlieb, H., Hockersmith, V., Koller, R., and Strite, L. *A successful treatment program for chronic back pain patients*. Symposium presented at the annual meeting of the American Psychological Association, Chicago, Ill., 1975.

Hill, H., Kornetsky, C., Flanary, H., and Wikler, A. Effects of anxiety and morphine on discrimination of painful stimuli. *Journal of Clinical Investigation*, 1952a, *31*, 473.

Hill, H., Kornetsky, C., Flanary, H., and Wikler, A. Studies on anxiety associated with anticipation of pain, I. Effects of morphine. *Archives of Neurology and Psychiatry*, 1952b, *67*, 612–619.

Horan, J.J., and Dellinger, J.K. "In vivo" emotive imagery: A preliminary test. *Perceptual and Motor Skills*, 1974, *39*, 359–362.

Horan, J.J., Hackett, G., Buchanan, J.D., Stone, C.I., and Demchik-Stone, D. Coping with pain: A component analysis of stress-inoculation. *Cognitive Therapy and Research*, 1977, *1*, 211–221.

Hovland, C., Janis, I., and Kelley, H. *Communication and persuasion: Psychological studies of opinion change*. New Haven: Yale University Press, 1953.

Janis, I. *Psychological stress*. New York: John Wiley and Sons, 1958.

Johnson, J. Effects of accurate expectation about sensations on the sensory and distress components of pain. *Journal of Personality and Social Psychology*, 1973, *27*, 261–275.

Johnson, J., and Leventhal, H. The effects of accurate expectations and behavioral instructions on reactions during a noxious medical examination.*Journal of Personality and Social Psychology*, 1974, *29*, 710–718.

Johnson, R.F.Q. Suggestions for pain reduction and response to cold-induced pain. *The Psychological Record*, 1974, *24*, 161–169.

Kanfer, F.H., and Goldfoot, D. Self-control and tolerance of noxious stimulation *Psychological Reports*, 1966, *18*, 79–85.

Kanfer, F.H., and Seidner, M. Self-control factors enhancing tolerance of noxious stimulation. *Journal of Personality and Social Psychology*, 1973, *25*, 381–389.

Kazdin, A.E. Covert modeling and the reduction of avoidance behavior. *Journal of Abnormal Psychology*, 1973, *81*, 87–95.

Kazdin, A.E. Covert modeling, model similarity, and reduction of avoidance behavior. *Behavior Therapy*, 1974, *5*, 325–340.

Knox, V.J. Cognitive strategies for coping with pain: Ignoring vs. acknowledging. Unpublished doctoral dissertation, University of Waterloo, 1972.

Langer, E., Janis, I., and Wolfer, J. Reduction of psychological stress in surgical patients. *Journal of Experimental Social Psychology*, 1975, *1*, 155–166.

Lazarus, R.S. *Psychological stress and the coping process*. New York: McGraw-Hill, 1966.

Lazarus, R.S., Averill, J.N., and Opton, E.M., Jr. The psychology of coping: Issues of research and assessment. In G. Coelho, D. Hamburg, and J. Adams (Eds.), *Coping and adaptation*. New York: Basic Books, Inc., Publishers, 1974.

Levendusky, P., and Pankratz, L. Self-control techniques as an alternative to pain medication. *Journal of Abnormal Psychology*, 1975, *84*, 165–168.

Lewinsohn, P. Depression: A clinical-research approach. Paper presented at the Washington-Oregon Psychological Association joint meeting. Crystal Mountain, Washington, 1968.

Liebeskind, J.C., and Paul, L.A. Psychological and physiological mechanisms of pain. *Annual Review of Psychology*, 1977, *28*, 41–60.

Mahoney, M.J. *Cognition and behavior modification*. Cambridge, Mass.: Ballinger Publishing Company, 1974.

McGlashan, R., Evans, F., and Orne, M. The nature of hypnotic analgesia and placebo response to experimental pain. *Psychosomatic Medicine*, 1969, *31*, 227—246.

Meichenbaum, D. Examination of model characteristics in reducing avoidance behavior. *Journal of Personality and Social Psychology*, 1971, *17*, 298–307.

Meichenbaum, D. Cognitive modification of test anxious college students. *Journal of Consulting and Clinical Psychology*, 1972, *39*, 370–380.

Meichenbaum, D. Cognitive factors in behavior modification: Modifying what clients say to themselves. In C. Franks and T. Wilson (Eds.), *Annual review of behavior therapy: Theory and practice*. New York: Brunner/Mazel, 1973.

Meichenbaum, D. Self-instruction and the therapeutic modification of self-statements or cognitive-behavior therapy. Paper presented at the eighth annual convention of the Association for the Advancement of Behavior Therapy, Chicago, Ill., 1974.

Meichenbaum, D. A self-instructional approach to stress management: A proposal for stress inoculation. In C. D. Spielberger and I.G. Sarason (Eds.), *Stress and Anxiety* (Vol. 1). Washington, D.C.: Hemisphere Publishing Corporation, 1975.

Meichenbaum, D. *Cognitive-behavior modification: An integrative approach*. New York: Plenum Publishing Company, 1977.

Meichenbaum, D., and Cameron, R. Stress inoculation: A skills training approach to anxiety management. Unpublished manuscript, University of Waterloo, 1973.

Meichenbaum, D., and Turk, D. The cognitive-behavioral management of anxiety, anger, and pain. In P. Davidson (Ed.), *The behavioral management of anxiety, depression, and pain*. New York: Brunner/Mazel, 1976.

Meichenbaum, D., Turk, D., and Burstein, S. The nature of coping with stress. In I. G. Sarason and C.D. Spielberg (Eds.), *Stress and anxiety* (Vol. 2). New York: Hemisphere Publishing Corporation, 1975.

Melzack, R. *The puzzle of pain*. Harmondsworth, England: Penguin, 1973.

Melzack, R., and Casey, K. Sensory, motivational and central control determinants of pain: A new conceptual model. In D. Kenshalo (Ed.), *The skin senses*. Springfield, Illinois: Charles C Thomas, 1968.

Melzack, R., and Casey, K. The affective dimension of pain. In M. Arnold (Ed.), *Feelings and emotions*. New York: Academic Press, 1970.

Melzack, R., and Scott, T. The effects of early experience on the response to pain. *Journal of Comparative and Physiological Psychology*, 1957, *50*, 155.

Melzack, R., and Wall, P. Pain mechanisms: A new theory. *Science*, 1965, *150*, 971.

Mulcahy, R., and Janz, N. Effectiveness of raising pain perception threshold in males and females using a psychoprophylactic childbirth technique during induced pain. *Nursing Research*, 1973, *22*, 423–427.

Nathan, P.W. The gate-control theory of pain: A critical review. *Brain*, 1976, *99*, 123–158.

Neufeld, R., and Davison, P. The effects of vicarious and cognitive rehearsal in pain tolerance. *Journal of Psychosomatic Research*, 1971, *15*, 329–335.

Novaco, R.W. The treatment of chronic anger through cognitive and relaxation controls. *Journal of Consulting and Clinical Psychology*, 1976, *44*, 681.

Novaco, R.W. A stress inoculation approach to anger management in the training of law enforcement officers. *American Journal of Community Psychology*, 1977, *5*, 327–346.

Orne, M.T. Psychological factors maximizing resistance to stress with special reference to hypnosis. In S. Klausner (Ed.), *The quest for self-control*. New York: Free Press, 1965.

Paul, G.L. *Insight vs. desensitization in psychotherapy: An experiment in anxiety reduction.* Stanford: Stanford University Press, 1966.

Pavlov, I.P. *Conditioned reflexes.* Milford, 1927.

Pavlov, I.P. *Lectures on conditioned reflexes.* International Publishers, 1928.

Petrie, A. *Individuality in pain and suffering.* Chicago: University of Chicago Press, 1967.

Pilowsky, I. Dimensions of abnormal illness behavior. *Australian and New Zealand Journal of Psychiatry*, 1975, *9*, 141–147.

Reeves, J.L. EMG-biofeedback reduction of tension headaches: A cognitive skills-training approach. *Biofeedback and self-regulation*, 1976, *1*, 217–227.

Richardson, F.C., and Suinn, R.M. A comparison of traditional systematic desensitization, accelerated massed desensitization, and anxiety management training in the treatment of mathematics anxiety. *Behavior Therapy*, 1973, *4*, 212—218.

Sachs, L.B., Feuerstein, M., and Vitale, J.H. Hypnotic self-regulation of chronic pain. Paper presented at American Psychological Association annual convention, Washington, D.C., 1976.

Sanchez-Craig, B.M. A self-control strategy for drinking tendencies. *Ontario Psychologist*, 1975, *7*, 25–29.

Sarason, I.G. Test anxiety and cognitive modeling. *Journal of Personality and Social Psychology*, 1973, *28*, 58–61.

Sarbin, T. Imagining as muted role-taking: A historical-linguistic analysis. In P. Sheehan (Ed.), *The function and nature of imagery.* New York: Academic Press, 1972.

Schachter, S. The interaction of cognitive and physiological determinants of emotional state. In C.D. Spielberger (Ed.), *Anxiety and behavior.* New York: Academic Press, 1966.

Shor, R. Physiological effects of painful stimulation during hypnotic analgesia under conditions designed to minimize anxiety. *International Journal of Clinical and Experimental Hypnosis*, 1962, *10*, 183–202.

Smith, G., Chiang, H., and Regina, E. Acupuncture and experimental psychology. Paper presented at symposium, Pain and Acupuncture, Philadelphia, 1974.

Smith, G., Egbert, L., Markowitz, R., Mosteller, F., and Beecher, H. An experimental pain method sensitive to morphine in man: The submaximum effort tourniquet technique. *Journal of Pharmacology and Experimental Therapeutics*, 1966, *154*, 324–332.

Staub, E., Tursky, B., and Schwartz, G. Self-control and predictability: Their effects on reactions of aversive stimulation. *Journal of Personality and Social Psychology*, 1971, *18*, 157–162.

Sternbach, R. *Pain patients: Traits and treatments.* New York: Academic Press, 1974.

Suinn, R.M. Removing emotional obstacles to learning and performance by visuo-motor rehearsal. *Behavior Therapy*, 1972, *3*, 308–310.

Suinn, R.M., and Richardson, F. Anxiety management training: A nonspecific behavior therapy program for anxiety control. *Behavior Therapy*, 1971, *2*, 498–510.

Turk, D.C. Cognitive control of pain: A skills-training approach. Unpublished master's thesis, University of Waterloo, 1975.

Turk, D.C. A coping skills-training approach for the control of experimentally-produced pain. Unpublished doctoral dissertation, University of Waterloo, 1977a.

Turk, D.C. A coping skills-training approach for control of experimentally-produced pain—training manual. Unpublished manuscript. Yale University, 1977b.

Turk, D.C. Application of coping-skills training to the treatment of pain. In C.D. Spielberger and I.G. Sarason (Eds.), *Stress and anxiety* (Vol. 5). New York: Brunner/Mazel, 1978.

Turk, D.C., and Meichenbaum, D. Cognitive behavior modification of pain. Paper presented at tenth annual convention of the Association for the Advancement of Behavior Therapy, New York, 1976.

Tursky, B. Laboratory approaches to the study of pain. In D.I. Mostofsky (Ed.), *Behavioral control and modification of physiological activity*. Englewood Cliffs, N.J.: Prentice-Hall, Inc., 1976.

Wolff, B., and Langley, S. Cultural factors and the response to pain: A review. *American Anthropologist*. 1968, *70*, 494–501.

Wolpe, J. *Psychotherapy by reciprocal inhibition*. Stanford: Stanford University Press, 1958.

Zimbardo, P. *The cognitive control of motivation: The consequences of choice and dissonance*. Glenview, Illinois: Scott, Foresman, and Co., 1969.

9

The Clinical Implementation of Behavior Change Techniques

A COGNITIVELY ORIENTED CONCEPTUALIZATION OF THERAPEUTIC "COMPLIANCE" AND "RESISTANCE"

ROY CAMERON

Consider the following situation: Two clients present what appear to be highly similar problems related to interpersonal anxiety. The assessment suggests that each of the two clients is experiencing anxiety in a wide variety of situations, and it seems appropriate to train anxiety-management skills. To accomplish this, stress-inoculation training (Meichenbaum, 1975a; Meichenbaum and Cameron, 1973) is initiated with both clients. We have, then, two clients who present with highly similar problems, both of whom receive the same sort of therapy. One of the clients quickly masters the anxiety-management skills. He gradually begins to report enthusiastically that he is no longer experiencing debilitating anxiety and, in due course, terminates treatment with his problem resolved. You have, no doubt, already anticipated what happens with the second client.

ROY CAMERON • Department of Psychology, University of Saskatchewan, Saskatoon, Saskatchewan, Canada S7N 0W0.

Although the specific intervention that was employed has worked successfully with other similar clients in the past, in this instance it fails miserably. The client does not do homework assignments, begins to miss appointments, and eventually disappears altogether (frequently to the great relief of the therapist).

Although many cognitive behavioral "techniques" have been developed for treating a broad spectrum of clinical problems, anyone actively engaged in clinical work recognizes that there is an "art" to successfully implementing such techniques in clinical situations. It is generally recognized that "nonspecific" or "technique-independent" factors influence the course and outcome of therapy. The practical problem is to identify these "technique-independent" factors so that we can systematically attend to them, avoiding potential pitfalls and capitalizing on "nonspecific" factors that may promote therapeutic change.

There is, of course, an extensive literature dealing with the role of nonspecific factors in therapeutic endeavors of all sorts. Jerome Frank's *Persuasion and Healing* (1961) and Arthur Shapiro's (1960, 1971) fascinating reviews of the literature on placebo effects, for instance, are classic contributions to the psychotherapy literature. Behaviorally oriented therapists are becoming increasingly concerned with the "art" of their clinical work and with the technique-independent factors that influence therapeutic processes (e.g., Davidson, 1976; Davison, 1973; Goldfried and Davison, 1976; Goldstein, 1962, 1975; Goldstein, Heller, and Sechrest, 1966; Gottman and Leiblum, 1974; Lazarus, 1971, 1976; Meichenbaum, 1975b, 1976, 1977). Nonetheless, Wachtel has suggested recently that behavior therapists might find it profitable to devote even more attention to factors that affect therapeutic compliance and resistance:

> The issue of resistance . . . is an important topic and one that has been insufficiently addressed in the behavior therapy literature. Whether the term "resistance" is accepted or not, most practicing behavior therapists will acknowledge the not infrequent occurrence of behaviors that run counter to the desirable course of therapy. Much of the clinical skill of the behavior therapist involves figuring out how to enlist the patient's cooperation in carrying out the therapeutic assignments they have agreed upon. (Wachtel, 1977, pp. 187–188)

The present chapter presents an attempt to view the issue of therapeutic compliance and resistance to behavioral interventions from a cognitive point of view. It is not a detailed review of the literature, nor a report of empirical findings. Rather, it is an outgrowth of clinical experience based on *post hoc* analyses of successful cases and "postmortems" of clinical failures. Most of my own clinical work is with adults (especially psychosomatic patients) and the content of the present chapter will reflect this. Readers who work primarily with children are encouraged to read the third chapter of Meichenbaum's (1977) recent book.

The following analysis of therapeutic compliance and resistance is concerned primarily with the cognitions the client has regarding the therapeutic process *per se*. There is an underlying assumption that "one thing psychologists can count on is that their clients will talk, if only to themselves; and not infrequently, whether relevant or irrelevant, the things people say to themselves determine the rest of the things they do" (Farber, 1963, p. 196). Cognitively oriented behavior therapists have committed themselves to this notion that the cognitive processes of their clients contribute to their presenting problems, and as the present volume attests, have been quite inventive about developing intervention strategies designed to facilitate therapeutic change by changing those maladaptive cognitions. However, the thesis of the present paper is that it may be productive to focus not only on our client's cognitions vis-à-vis his presenting problem, but also on his cognitions about the therapeutic process *per se*. Meichenbaum has recently called upon therapists to "be concerned not only with the client's self-statements and attributions concerning his presenting problems, but also with those concerning the therapy process . . ." (Meichenbaum, 1977, p. 222). The following is an attempt to construe the important issues of therapeutic compliance and resistance in terms of the client's cognitions as they relate to the therapeutic process. Simply stated, the suggestion is that "negative" cognitions regarding the therapeutic process result in "resistance," while "positive" cognitions about the therapeutic process promote therapeutic compliance. Thus, the general notion is that to the extent that the therapist arranges things in a way that increases "positive" cognitions, and reduces "negative" cognitions about the therapeutic process, he increases the likelihood that his intervention, whatever it is, will be successful.

From this point of view, the important issues of therapeutic compliance and resistance reduce to two key questions. What sorts of cognitions regarding the therapeutic process would facilitate therapeutic change (and, conversely, what sorts of cognitions would impede or preclude change)? If we can answer this first question, we are immediately faced with a second: What can we do to ensure that our clients' cognitions about the therapeutic process are positive rather than negative? These are the basic questions to be addressed in the present chapter. Although these questions are undoubtedly important, the suggestions provided below are offered tentatively, with a recognition that they are far from complete and unsubstantiated by sound empirical data.

After a client is referred to us and therapy is initiated, the therapeutic process evolves through a series of stages (e.g., Gottman and Leiblum, 1974; Meichenbaum, 1975b, 1976, 1977). For present purposes, therapy will be construed as moving through three phases. We must quickly begin to establish a "therapeutic alliance," or cooperative working relationship, with the client. We go through a problem-formulation phase, during which therapist and client develop a shared conceptualization of the problem. We then move into an intervention phase. This division of the therapeutic process is done for heuristic purposes with the recognition that it is quite artificial and arbitrary; in reality, the various therapeutic activities described tend to blend into one another. There appear to be specific cognitions related to therapeutic compliance and resistance associated with each stage of therapy. Therapeutic movement may be facilitated or impeded by the client's cognitions about the process at any stage: at the referral stage, the stage of developing a therapeutic alliance, the problem-formulation stage, or the intervention stage. The remainder of the chapter will be devoted to a discussion of factors that may affect compliance and resistance at each stage of the therapeutic process.

THE REFERRAL STAGE

We are more likely to be successful with a client who comes to us with belief that he will improve than we are with a client who is more pessimistic (Frank, 1961; Lefcourt, 1976; Seligman, 1975). Goldstein's (1962) work suggests that positive expectations facilitate therapy, although the relationship between expectancy and improvement may be curvilinear. In short, it will be advantageous if we can arrange things so that clients come to us with positive but realistic expectations for improvement.

Frequently the clients who come to us are referred by members of other professions. The nature of the referral process may have a marked effect on the expectancies of the client, and thus on the course and outcome of therapy. The first key factor in shaping the client's expectations is the perception that the referring agent has regarding the psychologist and his treatment approach. Related to this is the referring agent's motivation for making the referral. Both the referring agent's perceptions of psychological treatment and his motivation for making the referral may well be transmitted to the client. If his perceptions of the psychologist are positive and realistic, and he is making a referral because he genuinely believes that the psychologist can help his patient, the latter is likely to come to the psychologist in an optimistic, nondefensive, cooperative frame of mind. Unfortunately, this is often not the case. All too often when another professional makes a referral to a psychologist, he does so as an act of desperation. He doesn't really expect the psychologist to help—he may even think the case hopeless and psychologists quacks—but he doesn't know how else to dispose of the person. The psychologist is likely to have much more difficulty with a client referred in this context. The person tends to be unenthusiastic, pessimistic, defensive, and very difficult to "hook." Psychologists may realize substantial clinical dividends if they invest the time and effort required to cultivate relationships with referring agents by providing information about the nature of the therapy, the rationale underlying it, its limitations, data pertaining to its effectiveness, and prompt feedback on all cases referred. The goal is to have the referring agent making appropriate referrals for positive reasons; he anticipates his patient will be treated competently by someone who can help. These are the attitudes we want transmitted to clients being referred to us.

Perhaps an (admittedly extreme) example will illustrate the potential importance of these issues. Several years ago, when I was working in another setting, a chronic low-back pain patient was referred for assessment and possible treatment. The referral slip tersely indicated "probable hypochondriasis, hysteria, or malingering." The woman was extremely defensive when she came for her interview. Eventually, she reported that she had been hospitalized for a couple of weeks, during which she went through an extensive series of tests. All results were negative. The morning the referral was made, she allegedly overheard her physician say to his assistant, "What a crock! Get one of the spooks to have a look at her." She felt that her physician thought she was crazy, that her pain wasn't real. Who would not be defensive and unenthusiastic under such circumstances? To acknowledge any psychological distress in her life or to show any improvement in response to psychological intervention would, in her mind, confirm that her physician was correct and cost the patient her dignity.

This same case illustrates a second factor that warrants attention in some instances. When a person goes to a physician with a medical problem (or a problem that the patient, at least, construes as a medical problem), the physician's timing of the referral to the psychologist can play an important role in determining how the patient will interpret the psychologist's involvement. Imagine yourself coming into the hospital for a diagnostic workup for, say, chronic low-back pain. Like the woman in the example cited above, you go through a frustrating two weeks of extensive, uncomfortable tests, all of which prove negative. You then hear that your physician has ordered a psychological consultation for you. What thoughts would you have about this referral? By its very context, the referral that comes after all medical tests have been completed and proven negative implies to the patient that his physician has ruled out a physical basis for the presenting complaints and now believes that the person has a psychiatric problem. It is far easier to work with clients referred for psychological consultation concurrently with other consultations. Hackett (1967) and Gentry and Cameron (1975) have previously commented on the importance of timing in making such referrals.

Finally, the client's attitude toward therapy may be affected adversely if he interprets the referral process as coercive. It is not uncommon for referring agents to "order" clients or patients to see a psychologist. If the client values his relationship with the referring agent, he may feel obliged to comply, even though he is resentful and defensive. Brehm's reactance theory (J.W. Brehm, 1966; S.S. Brehm, 1976) and Bem's self-perception theory (Bem, 1972; Brehm, 1976) would both suggest that a client who perceives himself as being coerced into therapy is likely to be more "resistant" and less committed to therapy. When clients are referred by third parties, it may be useful to see the client once in order to create realistic expectancies about therapy, including an explicit message that therapy can only be successful if the client is fully committed, since effective treatment requires active cooperation on the part of the client. The psychologist can add that since the person was referred, he is not sure whether the person genuinely wants treatment himself, or whether he has felt pressured to seek psychological therapy. The person can be asked to think about it, and to call back if he is interested in treatment; if he doesn't call, it will be assumed that he has decided against treatment at this time. There is still a social pressure on the person to enter treatment (although some will, of course, opt out). However, the pressure is less salient and the client regards therapy as something he has chosen rather than something forced upon him.

To summarize, among clients referred by third parties the nature of the referral process may affect the client's initial expectancies and attitudes toward therapy, and these expectancies and attitudes in turn may influence the extent to which the client is initially compliant or resistant. It is quite likely that we can facilitate therapeutic compliance by attending to the subtleties of the referral process and arranging things so as to promote positive cognitions about treatment. Specifically, it may be helpful to "educate" referral agents about psychological treatment so that they view psychological therapy in positive terms and transmit positive expectancies to potential clients. It can be very profitable to discuss the referral process *per se* with referring agents to ensure that important details (such as the timing of referrals) are finessed in a way that enhances the client's perception of the referral. And, finally, ensuring that the client has an opportunity to "choose" to enter treatment, rather than perceiving himself to be coerced into it by the referral process, may foster a more positive attitude and increase compliance.

Establishing a Therapeutic Alliance

Once he has direct contact with the client, the therapist's first objective is to begin to establish a therapeutic alliance. That is, he wants to ensure that the client perceives him as an ally who can help him resolve his problem. From the present point of view, then, the therapist should consider what sorts of cognitions would facilitate or impede the development of a cooperative working relationship.

There are several sorts of cognitions that interfere with establishing a therapeutic alliance. At the most fundamental level, a belief that one's problem is not psychological in nature virtually precludes the possibility that the client will regard a psychologist as a potential source of help. Psychosomatic patients who are referred by their physicians, for instance, almost never regard their problems as psychological. Before he does anything else, the psychologist who is confronted with such a client needs to deal with the client's belief that he is irrelevant. If he does not do so, "resistance" is both understandable and inevitable. The issue may be broached by asking the client whether the referring agent had explained why he was asking the client to see a psychologist. The psychologist may then provide a clear and reassuring explanation that incorporates the explanation of the referring agent. For instance, when I first meet chronic pain patients, I generally say something like, "Did Dr. X. explain to you why he was asking me to see you? (Often the answer is no!) Frequently the pain patients I see are initially a little uneasy about seeing a psychologist. Let me assure you that no one thinks you are crazy or that your pain isn't real. On the contrary, Dr. X. realizes that the pain you are experiencing is severe and that it is likely seriously interfering with your life. In order to make sure that everything possible is done for pain patients, Dr. X. routinely includes a psychological assessment as part of a comprehensive workup. What we want to do is find out how your pain is affecting your life, since we can often find ways of relieving problems caused by the pain. How does your pain affect your life?" This sort of introduction enables the client to understand the relevance of a psychological consultation, reduces defensiveness and elicits cooperation.

The belief that the psychologist is an adversary, or the agent of an adversary, also precludes the development of a therapeutic alliance. This is frequently a source of resistance when individuals are referred by courts or seen in other institutional settings. It is also common when children and especially adolescents see a psychologist at the insistence of their parents. Psychosomatic patients may be wary of the psychologist, believing that he is trying to prove that their problem is "all in my head." In many cases, this sort of resistance is obvious—the person is overtly negativistic—and the psychologist is forced to recognize and deal with the issue. In other cases, however, the resistance is much more subtle: The person goes through the motions of being cooperative, but nonetheless remains extremely guarded. Psychosomatic patients, for instance, are not usually overtly resistant; they are often invested in projecting a healthy, well-adjusted image and ostensibly cooperate with the psychologist in order to maintain this image. However, their reluctance to speak candidly about psychological and interpersonal matters frequently reflects an underlying belief that anything they say will be used against them; they are perceiving the psychologist as an adversary rather than an ally. The best strategy for reducing such resistance seems to be to clearly acknowledge the legitimacy of the physical complaint, to note that it must create difficulties in living, and to suggest that it might be possible to work together to alleviate any such difficulties.

A third negative set that often interferes with establishing a working alliance is the belief that psychological interventions are not effective. A large number of people frankly doubt that mental-health professionals are helpful. Such doubts may result in rather perfunctory involvement in the therapeutic process. Unless the client raises this concern, it is probably best for the psychologist to avoid raising it directly; we don't want to plant misgivings where none exist. However, spontaneous comments from the therapist indicating that he is optimistic, that he has had good success in treating similar problems in the past, etc., may alleviate some of the doubts. In making such statements, it may be useful to allude to some of the details the client presents as being particularly good prognostic signs when this is reasonable. For instance, it is quite common for chronic pain patients to report that their "nerves are bad" and that they find it helpful to get off by themselves to lie down or have a hot bath. In introducing relaxation training, the psychologist can allude to the fact that the client has felt better after relaxing this way as a good prognostic sign. The belief that psychological interventions are not effective is potentially a very serious source of resistance if the client has received ineffective therapy in the past. In commenting on clients who have experienced unsuccessful therapy, Goldfried and Davison (1976) suggest that the therapist should emphasize the differences between his approach and that of the previous therapist or self-help program in a way that gives the client reason to believe that the current approach will be more effective.

Problem Formulation

The therapist and client usually must evolve a shared conceptualization of the problem prior to intervention (Meichenbaum, 1975b, 1976, 1977). This process includes two components, namely, (a) eliciting information from the client about his problem, and (b) "educating" the client so that he comes to view his problem in terms that render it amenable to solution. Any client cognitions that interfere with candid provision of information or receptivity to an appropriate conceptualization of the problem will lead to "resistance" to the process of problem formulation.

A major belief that leads to conscious withholding of information is the belief that the therapist will disapprove of the client or discount his problem if he divulges certain embarrassing information about himself. The therapist who demonstrates basic interpersonal skills (Truax and Carkhuff, 1967; Egan, 1975) will behave in a way that gradually reduces the client's fears in this regard. It is often useful to consider what sorts of disclosures would be most threatening for specific clients, to have in the back of one's mind the question, What sort of information is likely to be withheld by this particular client because it is embarrassing? It is then possible to offer "permission-giving" statements to make the material less threatening to the client. For example, back pain frequently interferes with a person's sex life, and it is not uncommon for such patients to feel uncomfortable discussing this. If the person does not spontaneously broach the subject, the simple statement that it is common for back-pain patients to find that the pain interferes with their sex lives is often enough to overcome inhibition.

The belief that the information-gathering process is random and aimless will also reduce the level of client cooperation. The client who understands how the information that is being solicited is relevant to the solution of his problem is likely to provide more complete and more pertinent information. If the psychologist communicates his observations, the rationale for his questions, and the hypotheses he is entertaining, the client is better able to comprehend the process and to respond appropriately.

The objective of developing a shared conceptualization of the problem is also facilitated if the therapist shares his own reasoning processes with the client in this way. The client is able to follow the therapist's formulation of his problem and to contribute to the conceptual process by confirming, elaborating, clarifying, or correcting as necessary. When he has contributed in this way to the conceptualization of his problem, the client is almost certain to "buy into" the conceptualization, so there is a firm shared understanding of the problem and a solid basis for moving into the intervention phase.

On the other hand, the client is likely to be resistant to attempts to educate him if he believes that the therapist is mechanically imposing a prefabricated conceptualization upon his problem, in a "hard sell" fashion. One of the major hazards of using a "hard sell" approach is that the client may easily come to believe that he is unable to challenge the therapist's conceptualization. The therapist appears to him to be so invested in his point of view that any questioning of the conceptualization would be futile. As a consequence, the client may be overtly compliant, but harbor serious reservations or misunderstandings that are never dealt with. In order to please the hard-sell therapist, the client may engage in much head-nodding even though he doesn't comprehend, may turn in bogus homework assignments, and even report counterfeit improvement. While it is undoubtedly advantageous for a therapist to be enthusiastic with clients, clients need to believe that they can honestly report lack of understanding, misgivings, or lack of progress.

In helping the client conceptualize, it may be useful to use metaphors, aphorisms, and simple demonstrations that capture the conceptualization in a concise and vivid manner. For instance, I sometimes want to communicate to a pain patient that distraction can be an effective strategy for coping with pain. This can be tricky since it can imply to the patient that I really do not think there is a physical basis for his pain, that it is all in his head and if he keeps himself busy it will go away. If he interprets me this way, he is likely to resist construing distraction as a viable coping mechanism. In order to facilitate communication, I often use a demonstration and a metaphor. First, I ask the patient to be aware of the sensations in his thighs as he sits in his chair.[1] I note that those sensations are real, and they have a physical basis, but they are not normally experienced because other things occupy his attention. Then I suggest that he think of a TV set: he could block out the channel 9 signal by tuning in channel 11; the channel 9 signal is still there, but not being tuned in. I suggest that while his pain signals are real, he can learn to "tune them out." Tying the conceptualization to an image not only facilitates communication of the conceptualization, but often serves a "bell ringer" function as well. A number of pain patients have reported that they frequently think of the TV metaphor when experiencing pain and take appropriate action to "tune out."

INTERVENTION

Once therapist and client have arrived at a common understanding of the problem, they naturally progress to the intervention phase. The client's cooperation with intervention strategies will be facilitated if his private monologue regarding his change attempts is dominated by two inter-related themes, namely, "This is working" and "I can change." If he becomes caught up in thinking, "This is not working" or "I cannot change," his negative self-statements may trigger a negative "self-fulfilling prophecy." His negative thoughts about the effectiveness of therapy or about his capacity to change lead to perfunctory compliance with the therapeutic regi-

---

[1] I am grateful to Ronald Melzack, from whom I learned this simple but often effective demonstration.

men, overinterpretation of slow progress and setbacks, and discounting of successes, all of which in turn reduce his success and thus exacerbate the negative self-monologue.

The practical problem, then, is to figure out what we can do to facilitate positive self-statements and discourage negative self-statements about the change process. The beliefs, "This is working, I can do it," are triggered only if the client perceives evidence of therapeutic movement. The beliefs, "This is not working, I can't change," occur when the client perceives lack of movement or setbacks. The key, then, is to structure therapeutic interventions in a way that maximizes the likelihood of success at each stage. This is certainly not a novel suggestion. Indeed, the practice of organizing therapeutic objectives so that problems are treated in ascending order of difficulty seems to be a standard rule of thumb among most behavior therapists. Graduating the change process into the smallest possible steps and using scales with a broad range to monitor change can enhance success experiences and a perception, "This is working, I'm on my way." For instance, if we are doing relaxation training with anxiety or pain patients, we indicate that the first treatment goal is to learn how to relax, to reduce general emotional arousal. When relaxation is begun, clients are asked to record their tension level on a 10-point scale before and after relaxing. The range of the scale is such that some success is virtually certain from the outset, and increased skill is reflected in the increasing magnitude of pre-post changes as the person becomes more proficient.

The client's belief that the intervention will work is in jeopardy from the beginning if he believes that the intervention proposed is not proportional to his problem. For instance, a back-pain patient may find it incredible that a simple intervention such as progressive relaxation could provide any pain relief when he has had six back operations, very major interventions, which were not helpful. If there is such a lack of credibility, it is unlikely he will cooperate with any conviction or enthusiasm. However, if EMG biofeedback is introduced as a vehicle for training muscular relaxation, the status of the intervention is boosted; the level of technology being brought to bear on the problem may appear more commensurate with the problem. Therapeutic compliance may increase if the therapist chooses and presents interventions in a way that allows the client to view them as being sufficiently potent to deal with his problem.

Almost every client experiences periods of slow progress and setbacks even though the intervention strategies may have been well conceived. As indicated earlier, slow progress and setbacks typically result in the client engaging in a negative self-monologue about the effectiveness of therapy and his own ability to change, and thus lead to "giving up." There are a number of things that can be done to prevent over-reaction to slow progress and setbacks. First, the therapist can discuss the time-frame for change with the client at the time interventions are begun. Many clients have unrealistic expectations about how quickly they can change. A person who thinks he is going to change in a month well-ingrained patterns of interaction acquired over a lifetime is almost certainly going to be disheartened by the pace of therapy. Second, structuring therapy so that there are a progressive series of specific intermediate goals rather than a few vague, long-range goals increases the sense of progress. Third, anticipating failures and setbacks may short-circuit over-reaction to them. The therapist can indicate that while these things are normal, people tend to become discouraged in response to them, to have doubts about whether therapy will work for them or whether they can ever change. In anticipating this negative self-monologue, the therapist can note that it is important for the client to expect this so that when the negative thoughts begin he recognizes them as a normal part of the therapy process and doesn't take them too seriously. The therapist can wrap up his statement with a suggestion that he has found that simply anticipating these negative thoughts tended to short-circuit them; the client will likely find that when he has such thoughts he will recall this conversation and this will make it possible for him to dismiss the negative self-talk as normal. It might be noted parenthetically that several clients have commented spontaneously that whenever they began to think negatively about their ability to change, they recalled this discussion and broke out of the negative set. This preparation may be followed up by enquiring about negative self-talk in sessions when the client reports setbacks. Occasionally, the negative thoughts about the therapeutic process must become the focus of therapy before movement toward other therapeutic goals can proceed.

The therapist is not only concerned with bringing about change during the intervention phase, he wants to promote changes that will endure after therapy terminates. There are at least two sorts of client cognitions that might be expected to contribute to maintenance of treatment effects. The first is the belief, "What I have learned is a coping skill," versus "I have overcome my problem and never expect to experience it again." The second is the belief, "I am responsible for the changes I have experienced," versus "My improvement resulted from external factors."

In our society, therapeutic agents are epitomized by the physician, and medical treatment is the paradigm of the therapeutic process. The optimal goal of medical treatment is to completely eradicate physical pathology and associated symptoms. It is not uncommon for the clients who come to us to have therapeutic expectancies that are based on this model. Specifically, they may expect that if therapy is successful, they will be freed completely from anxiety, depression, marital conflict, poor eating habits, or whatever problem is being treated. In most instances, this is an unreasonable expectation. Most of the problems with which clients present will in fact be experienced again after treatment, even if treatment is successful: anxiety, depression, marital conflict, etc., occur in the normal course of almost everyone's life. Maintenance of therapeutic gains may be facilitated if the client anticipates that his problem will recur after treatment, and that the goal of therapy is to provide him with skills to cope with the problem as it recurs, rather than to eradicate the problem *per se* (Meichenbaum and Cameron, 1973). For instance, in a weight-reduction program we are conducting, we emphasize that what we are training is a *method of changing* eating and exercise habits. We note that while we expect habits to change for the better over the term the group is meeting, habits frequently shift, and we anticipate that after the group ends, some of the new habits may fade and old habits return. This will be reflected in weight gain. When the person notes such a relapse, he is to use this as a signal that his habit patterns have shifted, and to respond by actively monitoring and changing his behaviors using the methods he learned in the group. The idea is to anticipate a relapse, and to arrange things so that the relapse triggers active coping. If the client does not anticipate relapse, when it occurs he is likely to interpret it as a sign that treatment was not really effective after all, and to give up.

Treatment gains are more likely to be enduring if the client attributes positive changes to himself as opposed to external factors (Davison, Tsujimoto, and Glaros, 1973; Davison and Valins, 1969; Frank, 1976). Conceptualizing therapy as a skill-training process encourages self-attribution. Detailed *post hoc* analyses of the client's success experiences, during which the client is prompted to articulate precisely how he facilitated the change, can be valuable for consolidating self-attributions.

Concluding Statement

The issues of therapeutic compliance and resistance are as complex as they are important. The objective of this chapter was not to make a definitive statement on these issues, but simply to make a preliminary attempt to cast them into the same conceptual framework many cognitively oriented behavior therapists are using in their clinical practice. This attempt was prompted by a conviction that our therapeutic work will progress more smoothly if we attend to our client's cognitions regarding the therapeutic process, and do what we can to ensure these cognitions are facilitative. The author recognizes that the ideas presented in this chapter are, in the main, not well supported by empirical evidence. Systematic study of technique-independent process variables that may affect the course and outcome of cognitive-behavioral treatment would appear to be a fruitful direction for research at present.

References

Bem, D.J. Self-perception theory. In L. Berkowitz (Ed.), *Advances in experimental social psychology* (Vol. 6). New York: Academic Press, 1972.

Brehm, J.W. *A theory of psychological reactance*. New York: Academic Press, 1966.

Brehm, S.S. *The application of social psychology to clinical practice*. New York: Wiley, 1976.

Davidson, P.O. Therapeutic compliance. *Canadian Psychological Review*, 1976, *17*, 247–259.

Davison, G.C. Counter-control in behavior modification. In L.A. Hamerlynck, L.C. Handy, and E.J. Mash (Eds.), *Behavior change: Methodology concepts and practice.* Champaign, Ill.: Research Press, 1973.

Davison, G.C., Tsujimoto, R.N., and Glaros, A.G. Attribution and the maintenance of behavior change in falling asleep. *Journal of Abnormal Psychology,* 1973, *82,* 124–133.

Davison, G.C., and Valins, S. Maintenance of self-attributed and drug-attributed behavior change. *Journal of Personality and Social Psychology,* 1969, *11,* 25–33.

Egan, G. *The skilled helper.* Monterey, Calif.: Brooks/Cole, 1975.

Farber, I. The things people say to themselves. *American Psychologist,* 1963, *18,* 185–197.

Frank, J.D. *Persuasion and healing.* Baltimore: Johns Hopkins University Press, 1961.

Frank, J.D. Psychotherapy and the sense of mastery. In R.L. Spitzer and D.F. Klein (Eds.), *Evaluation of psychological therapies.* Baltimore: Johns Hopkins University Press, 1976.

Gentry, W.D., and Cameron, R. Psychodiagnostic evaluation of pain and disability. In J.C. Davis and J.P. Foreyt (Eds.), *Mental examiner's source book.* Springfield, Ill.: Charles C Thomas, 1975.

Goldfried, M.R., and Davison, G.C. *Clinical behavior therapy.* New York: Holt, Rinehart and Winston, 1976.

Goldstein, A.P. *Therapist-patient expectancies in psychotherapy.* New York: Pergamon, 1962.

Goldstein, A.P. Relationship-enhancement methods. In F.H. Kanfer and A.P. Goldstein (Eds.), *Helping people change: A textbook of methods.* New York: Pergamon, 1975.

Goldstein, A.P., Heller, K., and Sechrest, L.B. *Psychotherapy and the psychology of behavior change.* New York: Wiley, 1966.

Gottman, J.M., and Leiblum, S.R. *How to do psychotherapy and how to evaluate it: A manual for beginners.* New York: Holt, Rinehart and Winston, 1974.

Hackett, T.P. The surgeon and the difficult pain problem. In H.S. Abram (Ed.), *Psychological aspects of surgery.* Boston: Little, Brown and Co., 1967.

Lazarus, A.A. *Behavior therapy and beyond.* New York: McGraw-Hill, 1971.

Lazarus, A.A. *Multi-modal behavior therapy.* New York: Springer, 1976.

Lefcourt, H.M *Locus of control: Current trends in theory and research.* Hillsdale, N.J.: Erlbaum, 1976.

Meichenbaum, D. A self-instructional approach to stress management: A proposal for stress inoculation training. In C. Speilberger and I. Sarason (Eds.), *Stress and anxiety in modern life.* New York: Winston, 1975a.

Meichenbaum, D. Self-instructional methods. In F.H. Kanfer and A.P. Goldstein (Eds.), *Helping people change: A textbook of methods.* New York: Pergamon, 1975b.

Meichenbaum, D. Toward a cognitive theory of self-control. In G.E. Schwartz and D. Shapiro (Eds.), *Consciousness and self-regulation: Advances in research* (Vol 1). New York: Plenum, 1976.

Meichenbaum, D. *Cognitive-behavior modification: An integrative approach.* New York: Plenum, 1977.

Meichenbaum, D., and Cameron, R. Stress inoculation: A skills training approach to anxiety management. Unpublished manuscript, University of Waterloo, 1973.

Seligman, M.E.P. *Helplessness.* San Francisco: Freeman, 1975.

Shapiro, A.K. A contribution to the history of the placebo effect. *Behavioral Science,* 1960, *5,* 109–135.

Shapiro. A.K. Placebo effects in medicine, psychotherapy, and psychoanalysis. In A.E. Bergin and S.L. Garfield (Eds.), *Handbook of psychotherapy and behavior change.* New York: Wiley, 1971.

Truax, C.B., and Carkhuff, R.R. *Toward effective counseling and psychotherapy: Training and practice.* Chicago: Aldine, 1967.

Wachtel, P.L. *Psychoanalysis and behavior therapy.* New York: Basic Books, 1977.

Author Index

Italic numbers refer to references at the end of the chapters.

Subject Index